Lancaster Bale Out

To Mike Stevens with best wishes

Clive Smith

CLIVE SMITH

"GREATER LOVE HATH NO MAN THAN THIS, THAT HE LAY DOWN HIS LIFE FOR HIS FRIENDS"

John 15:13

Copyright © Clive Smith - August 2013
All rights reserved

ISBN 978-1-907516-26-9

Design © TUCANN*design&print*

No part of this publication may be reproduced or transmitted in any way or by any means, including electronic storage and retrieval, without prior permission of the publisher.

Produced by: TUCANN*Limited*,
19 High Street, Heighington Lincoln LN4 1RG
Tel & Fax: 01522 790009
www.tucann.co.uk

CONTENTS

1. THE SEARCH FOR ANSWERS 8
2. ACKNOWLEDGEMENTS 13
3. INTRODUCTION 16
4. BOMBER COMMAND - MINIONS OF THE MOON 17
5. COAL MINING - RAF VOLUNTEER RESERVE 20
6. NAVIGATION - SENT TO CANADA 26
7. OPERATIONAL TRAINING - FORMING A CREW 34
8. CONVERSION TO LANCS - EXPANDING THE CREW 54
9. 106 SQUADRON - SYERSTON 61
10. 1ST OP - TARGET FRANCE 69
11. ONSLAUGHT - THE AIR BATTLE OF THE RUHR 75
12. OP 20 - RETURN TO COLOGNE 96
13. HOME FRONT - KENT 105
14. DOWN IN FRANCE - EVASION 107
15. 9 SQUADRON - BARDNEY 123
16. FRIENDLY FACES - RAF COMPANY 130
17. SEPARATION - AND THEN THERE WERE TWO 141
18. SOLITUDE - DESPAIR 150
19. ANOTHER JOURNEY BY TRAIN - FREEDOM 157
20. BACK TO PARIS - CAPTURE 161
21. BACK TO FRANKFURT - DULAG LUFT 178
22. PRISONER OF WAR - STALAG IVB 186
23. A NEW IDENTITY - ESCAPE 209
24. VICTORY IN EUROPE - LIBERATION 232
25. BACK IN ENGLAND - WELCOME HOME 241
26. DEMOB - POST WAR 251
27. EPITAPH - HERE ARE THE YOUNG MEN 254
28. CRASH SITE - QUIÉVY WHEATFIELD 255
29. EPHEMERA - WILL AND LETTER 258
30. POST WAR - THE MISSING 265
31. THE ULTIMATE SACRIFICE - FRENCH HELPERS 271
32. SOURCES 272

Lancaster Bale Out

- APPENDIX A - BATTLE OF THE RUHR OPS 275
- APPENDIX B - AIRCRAFT/AIRCREW LOSSES 277
- APPENDIX C – FRED SMOOKER ESCAPE AND EVASION DIARY 285
- APPENDIX D – BOMBER LOSS CARD 290
- APPENDIX E – GENDARME REPORTS 291
- APPENDIX F - LUFTWAFFE NIGHT FIGHTERS 292
- APPENDIX G - GESTAPO WARNING TO FRENCH HELPERS 293
- Appendix H - Abbreviations and Terms 294
- INDEX OF PEOPLE, AIRCRAFT AND PLACES 296
- FOOTNOTES 297

LIST OF ILLUSTRATIONS

Photo 1	The Houghams (C. Smith)	8
Photo 2	Gunner G. G. Smith, Royal Artillery (C. Smith)	9
Photo 3	Lancaster by Moonlight (D.D. Winston)	17
Photo 4	Aircraftman Fred Smooker, Aberystwyth 1941 (F. Smooker)	24
Photo 5	LAC Fred Smooker, Niagara Falls, 1942 (F. Smooker)	31
Photo 6	Gene Rosner, Training in Alabama, 1940 (R. Schwartz)	36
Photo 7	Sgt. Gene Rosner, RCAF (R. Schwartz)	37
Photo 8	Bill Bailey at home (D. Bailey)	39
Photo 9	Bill Bailey (Left), during Training (D. Bailey)	39
Photo 10	Aircraftman Jack Hougham, No. 10 RC Blackpool, 1941 (C. Smith)	41
Photo 11	Sgt. Jack Hougham, No.8 AGS, Evanton (C. Smith)	43
Photo 12	Sgt. Arnie Turner (LAC Canada)	44
Photo 13	Sgt. Arnie Turner (M. Turner)	50
Photo 14	Aircraftsman Ted Amor (J. Fricker)	54
Photo 15	Jim Calder, No.6 BGS, Canada (R. Calder)	55
Photo 15	Sgt Jim Calder (LAC Canada)	59
Photo 16	F/O Walter Thompson (W. R. Thompson)	61
Photo 17	Flt. Sgt. Jim Calder, Syerston (F. Smooker)	63
Photo 18	F/O Les Brodrick (L. Brodrick)	67
Photo 19	Briefing room (J.N.M. Haffer)	68
Photo 20	Out to the Dispersal (Mrs M. Claridge Collection)	69
Photo 21	Into the Aircraft (Radio Times Hulton Picture Library)	70
Photo 22	Bomb Aimer position (Portsmouth and Sunderland Newspapers)	71
Photo 23	Lancaster wireless operator position (Paul Popper)	72
Photo 24	Into the Trent (E. Dickinson)	73
Photo 25	Lancaster Rear Gunner position (K. Delve)	74
Photo 26	Crews waiting for take-off, Syerston 1942 (J.F. Wickins)	75
Photo 27	Lancaster Pilot position (Radio Times Hulton Picture Library)	79
Photo 28	Lancaster Navigator position (Radio Times Hulton Picture Library)	81
Photo 29	Sgt. Jack Hougham, home on leave (C. Smith)	85
Photo 30	Lanc Flight Engineer position (Radio Times Hulton Picture Library)	94
Photo 32	Sgt. Eugene Rosner (LAC Canada)	95
Photo 31	F/O Gene Rosner, on leave in London (R. Schwartz)	96

Lancaster Bale Out

Photo 32	Cologne Battle Order (C. Smith)	98
Photo 33	P/O Geoff Disbury (M. Disbury)	99
Photo 34	Over the Target (Imperial War Museum)	100
Photo 35	Lancaster Mid Upper Gunner position (Imperial War Museum)	102
Photo 36	Lancaster loss (P.B. Browning)	104
Photo 37	Missing (C. Smith)	105
Photo 38	Standard Casualty Letter (C. Smith)	106
Photo 38	Lancaster Wreckage (J. Alwyn Philips)	107
Photo 39	Lancaster ED720 Crash Site (Ordnance Survey)	109
Photo 40	Monsieur Bauduin and Family (S. Besin)	112
Photo 41	Juste Caullery, alias 'Chamberlain' (S. Besin)	113
Photo 42	Map of Béthencourt and Caudry (Ordnance Survey)	114
Photo 43	Lucien Janssoone (S. Besin)	116
Photo 44	Gilbert Janssoone and fiancée (F. Smooker)	116
Photo 45	Fred and Janssoone (F. Smooker)	117
Photo 46	Dr Lesage (S. Besin)	118
Photo 47	Gilbert and Fred (F. Smooker)	119
Photo 48	Sqn. Ldr. Bufton, Janssoone and Sgt. Crampton (S. Besin)	120
Photo 49	Edouard Richez (S. Besin)	121
Photo 50	Maurice Thuru (S. Besin)	122
Photo 51	Lanc ED480 'U' Uncle (N. R. McCorkindale)	123
Photo 52	Flt. Sgt. David 'Mac' McMillan (J. McMillan)	125
Photo 53	Map of Troisvilles and Le Cateau (Ordnance Survey)	125
Photo 54	Madame and Monsieur Bates (S. Besin)	126
Photo 55	Map of Le Cateau and Pommereuil area (Ordnance Survey)	128
Photo 56	Mac's Identity card in the name 'David Marc' (J. McMillan)	129
Photo 57	Harry Brown (1st left), Mac (2nd left) and crew (J. McMillan)	130
Photo 58	Mrs Mouse (S. Besin)	133
Photo 59	AVIS, warning to French helpers (C. Smith)	145
Photo 60	Geoffrey Ball next to Typhoon, 2nd from right (RAF Museum)	154
Photo 62	Fresnes Prison, Cell House (J. Edgley)	167
Photo 63	Warning to airman about Dulag Luft (L.F. Lampitt)	180
Photo 64	Lanc R5573 ZN 'B', October 1942 (Imperial War Museum)	182
Photo 65	Entrance to Stalag IVB (T. Hunt)	186
Photo 66	Inside the huts (T. Hunt)	188
Photo 67	Appell (T. Hunt)	189
Photo 68	Sketch of Stalag 4B Camp (F. Smooker)	190
Photo 69	Red Cross Parcel (C. Smith)	192

Lancaster Bale Out

Photo 70	Football Newspaper (V. Stothard)	195
Photo 71	Sketch of Hut 34B (F. Smooker)	198
Photo 72	The Funeral of Taffy Jones (T. Hunt)	201
Photo 73	F/E Kelvern 'Lofty' Snell (V. Stothard)	214
Photo 74	German Ausweis forged by Lofty (V. Stothard)	216
Photo 75	Map of Eastern Germany (Ordnance Survey)	219
Photo 76	Map of POW Camps (Red Cross)	235
Photo 77	Cologne Cathedral - defiant amid the destruction (Popperfoto)	240
Photo 78	POW Airlift (F.D. Wolfson)	241
Photo 79	Fred Smooker, 1946 (F. Smooker)	251
Photo 80	Lancaster ED720 wreckage (A. Verriez)	257
Photo 81	Jack Hougham article	258
Photo 82	Jack Hougham Will (C. Smith)	259
Photo 83	Cambrai Cemetery, Joint Grave Disbury / Hougham (C. Smith)	265
Photo 84	MRES Officers Exhuming a Grave (A. Archer)	266
Photo 85	Cambrai Cemetery, 1946 (C. Smith)	268
Photo 86	Cambrai Cemetery, 1996 (J.C. Lamant)	268
Photo 87	Permanent Headstone Information (C. Smith)	269
Photo 88	American Military Cemetery, Normandy (ABMC)	270
Photo 89	Grave of Lucien Janssoone (S. Besin)	271
Photo 90	ED720 Bomber Loss Card (RAF Museum)	290

1.
The Search for Answers

On my 4th birthday in 1967, John Hougham died aged 81. Three weeks later his wife Ada Hougham died too, aged 82. Their only son, Jack, had been killed in the war - they had never got over his loss. Their house, 'Bank Cottage' in Guilton, Ash, in Kent, then stood empty, and the job of clearing it fell to Ada's sister Minnie, my grandmother, who lived nearby in Deal and other family members. Her husband, 'Vic', who was an ex-Royal Marine, had been called upon to carry out similar tasks in the past and was not a great one for hoarding family mementoes. A logbook belonging to Jack Hougham though, detailing his service in the RAF, was amazingly spared from the bonfire. Years later, after my grandparents had died, it then came into the possession of my own family.

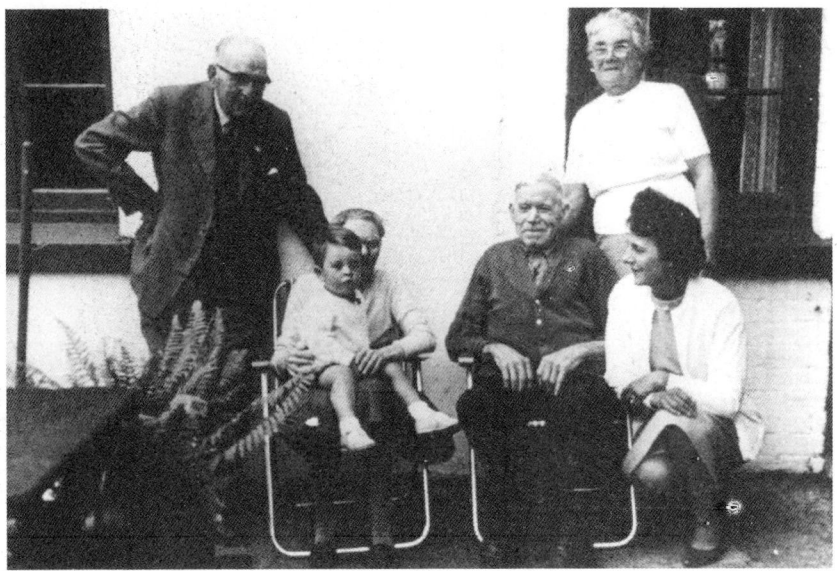

The Houghams (C. Smith)

[1.] *L to R, Victor Adams, Clive Smith, Ada Hougham, John Hougham, Minnie Adams, Doris Smith*

My dad had been an Officer in the Army during the war, and I had grown up with an interest in WWII. He had been in France in 1940 as a Bofors Gunner in the Royal Artillery, but managed to escape the German advance, via La Rochelle. I used to ask him about his experiences, but he never seemed willing to talk about it. As an inquisitive, young child I would often look through family papers and would be drawn to an old blue book, bulging with letters and photographs. The cover read 'Form 1767 - Observer's and Air Gunner's Flying Log Book', Sgt Jack Hougham, 1271588. I would sit down and digest its contents, reading the hand-written ink-pen entries and stare in awe at the photographs and letters from the Air Ministry.

Gunner G. G. Smith, Royal Artillery (C. Smith)

Lancaster Bale Out

There were official letters, and I tried to imagine what it must have been like to receive them. The letters were optimistic at first; 'your son set out to bomb Cologne but was not heard from again', 'This does not necessarily mean that he is killed or wounded, and if he is a prisoner of war then he should be able to communicate with you in due course'. However as time went by the tone changed to, 'In view of the time which has elapsed since he was reported missing, there can be practically no hope of his survival' and then finally confirming his parents' worst fear. There were a number of entries in red ink, mainly of German cities - Essen, Frankfurt, Wuppertal, Cologne but it was always the last entry, 'Failed to Return - Death Presumed' that grabbed my attention. How did he die? What had happened that night? There were a couple of photos of a cemetery, showing a cross, bearing the name of another airman as well. Who was he? There was also a hand-written will and a receipt for an engagement ring. To a young child here was a mystery to which no one seemed to know the answers.

When occasionally travelling through France on holiday, I wished that we could go and find the cemetery that I had seen in the photographs, but we never did. It was not until 1988 that I realised my childhood ambition, and my journey began. Driving back through France my wife and I drove off the Autoroute and arrived in Cambrai. We drove around looking for road numbers and soon headed out towards Solesmes - we were close. And then we stumbled upon it - Cambrai Communal Cemetery. It was late afternoon on a very grey, overcast day. The entrance to the cemetery was dwarfed by imposing trees, that made it look even gloomier. I walked in anticipation through the gate, passing rows of WWI German headstones before the line of conifers appeared, much larger now, but unmistakable as those in the old sepia photo. The gratifying sight of white, RAF headstones appeared in immaculate rows, some with flowers; all with a story locked below the ground. I moved slowly along, until I found the inscription I had waited to see all these years - 'Sgt. Jack Hougham - wireless operator / air gunner', this was him - my second cousin. To my knowledge no one else in my family had ever made this trip. Looking at the neighbouring headstones they too had '106 Squadron' engraved upon them, and the dates were the same. I counted six graves in total - Calder, Disbury, Hougham, Amor, Bailey and Turner - "these must have been all the crew members," I presumed, not knowing then that a Lancaster had a crew of seven. It all seemed to add up. Satisfied, I returned to the car and a few weeks later received a copy of the cemetery register from the Commonwealth War Graves Commission (CWGC). Something was not quite right though - If a P/O Disbury was the pilot, why was he not listed in Jack's logbook? Instead there was a F/O Rosner. Why had I not found a headstone for him? There was also no mention of him in the cemetery register. The CWGC could find no record of a 'Rosner' in their charge and suggested the American Battle Monuments Commission (ABMC). A letter to them returned with the information that they did have a 1st Lt. Eugene L. Rosner, who had died on the 8th July 1943, buried at the American Military Cemetery in Normandy. The picture was unfolding.

I wrote to the MoD Air Historical Branch and a reply returned with startling information. The letter revealed that there had actually been eight airmen on board the Lancaster that fateful night. P/O Disbury was not the pilot, but a trainee gaining experience. 1st Lt. Rosner had indeed been the pilot, but because he was American had been buried in a different cemetery. Then a further revelation. A Sgt. Frederick Henry Smooker[2], the bomb aimer, had survived and became a POW. All these years I believed that my second cousin had died along with his whole crew. What had happened to Sgt. Smooker? Could he still be alive? Now there was a glimmer of hope that there maybe someone who knew first hand what had happened.

At about the same time I got hold of a copy of 'The Lancaster at War' and on reading through I fell upon a story, 'The Cathedral and I survived' by Fred Smooker. I could not believe it, this must be the same person; the names in the story matched those in the cemetery. I read it and re-read it. My cousin was not mentioned but the events over Cambrai on 9th July 1943 stood out in black and white, and the story confirmed something else Fred Smooker had been alive in the early seventies.

The process of tracking someone down in the early 1990's, without the advances in computer technology (or the resources), required a

---

[2] *Frederick Henry Smooker was born on 29 January 1916 during the Great War into a mining family in County Durham. He was the second eldest of six having a brother and four sisters*

Lancaster Bale Out

manual search through the phone directories for the whole of the UK. 'Luckily' I thought, Smooker was such an unusual surname there couldn't be many, could there? After many hours of searching, only six entries were found, and only one F. Smooker - in County Durham. I sent a tentative enquiry off and waited, had I got the right person? Would he even be willing to discuss this tragic event with me if I had? A few days later a hand-written reply arrived - "Your search for Frederick Henry Smooker is ended. I am he. I am the only survivor out of all of the above mentioned young men and for more than fifty years I have lived with the question, Why me? The memories will live with me forever. I am now 78 and in a constant state of anxiety".

Not only had I found the one person that could hopefully answer my questions, but as I was soon to find out, he was pleased to be able to do so.

Fred had told the story of what had happened to him on numerous occasions, and had written down parts of it, but not all. After many letters were exchanged, he offered to write down the complete account, from start to finish. Over the next couple of years, his story arrived in instalments and began to unfold. I would get it typed, or do it myself, while researching the background and detail. There were many queries and loose ends, but piece by piece it came together, resulting in this work. The majority of the narrative is Fred's own words so is written in the first person from his viewpoint. I have merely collated it, added supporting information and clarified points that I was unsure of when I first read it. Detailed appendices have been included that list the crew ops, the circumstances of other crews losses and a diary of events.

Post Script
Since I began writing this account, Fred Smooker sadly passed away on 6th January 2008, at the age of 91. He had outlived the rest of his crew by more than 64 years.

Clive.Smith@Ghost428.co.uk
Fen Corner - Chapel Lane - Forest Row - East Sussex - RH18 5BS - England

2.
Acknowledgements

Writing/collating a book featuring a subject that had happened over seventy years previously, inevitably necessitates a lot of research, from a multitude of sources. During the past twenty years I have been fortunate to come into contact with a lot of very helpful people along the way, without whom the final picture would not have been so rich or complete.

First and foremost it is down to Fred, for without him the story would have remained a mystery to me, just like many other people who unfortunately lost relatives in similar circumstances. Discovering that Fred had survived, his story and then tracking him down and receiving his first letter was an outcome that I could never have imagined when I started. I still continue to be amazed by the power of the internet and how it has made contacting people so much easier. I have now managed to contact relatives of all the members of the crew, half of which have been initially through contacts and leads via the internet and e-mail.

In England I would like to thank Stewart and Dorothy Campbell (nee Bailey) and Marjorie Butler (nee Bailey) for providing information and personal memories of their brother Wilfrid Bailey. I would also like to thank Celia and Jeff Fricker, nephew of Eddy Amor, for the photograph that they provided that filled the gap of the last crew member. Thanks also to Margaret Disbury for providing information about her brother in law Geoffrey, whom she never got the chance to meet. The assistance of the Air Historical Branch at Great Scotland Yard must be acknowledged for help with providing information. Similarly, the Commonwealth War Graves Commission in Marlow have also been very helpful in answering queries. I would also like to thank my mum, Doris Smith, who carried out the extensive search of the phone directories whilst searching for Fred and also provided personal memories of Jack. Many thanks also to Audrey Gwynne, for doing the majority of the typing up of Fred's

Lancaster Bale Out

manuscript and to Jeremy Joseph and Geoff Leach for many hours spent proof-reading and suggesting improvements.

In America I have been fortunate to contact David Rosner, the nephew of Eugene, via his niece Debra Rosner and Ruth Schwartz, Eugene's sister and friend Pam Logan. Thanks to them for the information and photographs that they have provided me with. The American Archives in Virginia provided me with a complete dossier of information regarding Eugene Rosner's service records and the American Battle Monuments Commission and the Department of Veteran's Affairs were also very helpful.

In Canada I would like to thank Jean McMillan, wife of F/Sgt David McMillan. She has very kindly sent me all the information she knows about her husband's service in the Royal Canadian Air Force. Unfortunately he had Alzheimer's disease when I first contacted her, and so was unable to contribute directly to the story, and sadly has now passed away. Jean however, also put me in touch with Ralph Calder, who has kindly provided me with personal memories and photographs of his brother Jim. Thanks to him and his nephew Dan and his wife Sherry, who have provided a wealth of information and transcriptions of letters Jim sent home to his parents. They also helped me contact Marjorie Turner, widow of Gordon Turner, Arnie's youngest brother. Thanks to her for providing a photo of Arnie. The National archives of Canada, Ottawa, also provided information about the service records of the two Canadian Gunners (and Eugene Rosner who initially served in the RCAF) and further information was provided by Dave Champion.

In France I am indebted to Mme Suzanne Besin, a local historian, who took it upon herself to leave no stone unturned in the search for information regarding the courageous civilian helpers, known as 'Les Passeurs'[3], around the Cambrai area. She provided me with a wealth of information and photographs and put me in contact directly with people involved in harbouring not just Fred, but many Allied

---

3. *The term 'Passeurs' was applied to all the members of the civilian population that helped Allied airmen in their escape and evasion. Although often referred to as members of the 'Resistance', this term is more correctly used to describe the armed partisan groups of French fighters - FFI de l'intérieur.*

Airmen over the course of the war. All are acknowledged within the pages of this book. I would also like to thank Gilbert Janssoone, who as a teenager was directly involved with Fred's escape, and the members of the Cambrai Town Hall (Le Sous - Préfet de Cambrai) - Madame Denise Lorriaux (Marie Adjoint), for her own personal memory of the incident, Monsieur Jean Félix Labussiere, for putting me in touch with local historians and the Archives at Lille, and Jean-Pierre Laflaquiere at Lille Prefecture du Nord for putting me in touch with Nicolas Dhennin, another local historian.

In Germany, Herr Horst Diener, from Dortmund, provided most of the information regarding Luftwaffe personnel, for which I am grateful.

In Switzerland I would like to thank my sister, Rosalind Ehrensperger, who provided corrections to the German text and information from the crash site in Cambrai. I would also like to mention my brother in law, Peter Ehrensperger, who was born when Bomber Command was growing in strength in August 1941, on a day when four young airmen from 102 Squadron lost their lives when their Whitley crashed in training. He provided much encouragement to me over the years, especially after my dad died, and it's him that made this publication possible. (Carl Peter Ehrensperger - 21/8/1941 - 10/2/2012)

Finally I would like to thank my wife Jane for her help and encouragement over the years, as I've been through this journey, and also my children Isabelle, Lucia and Harry.

'The way is long, and difficult the road.'
Dante, The Inferno, Canto XXXIV

3.
Introduction

There was a terrific, sickening crash and the Perspex dome in the nose of the Lancaster disintegrated and a blast of ice-cold air gushed in swirling target maps and other sundry items about the place.
"There's a fighter!" yelled Jim Calder, our Canadian mid-upper gunner. I scrambled up into the front gun-turret but the controls were dead. I was helpless.
"The starboard inner's on fire," yelled Jim.
"OK, Ted," said the skipper, "get back up here."
"Turn to port," yelled Jim again.

They feathered the starboard inner as well now but suddenly the two port engines started to speed up in an increasing crescendo until they were almost screaming.
"Hey, you guys, we've got to bale out."
"Somebody get me my chute."
"Bale out, bale out, bale out…"

4.
Bomber Command - Minions of the Moon

Winter 1942/1943

Over the eastern counties of Lincolnshire, Yorkshire and East Anglia the night air is cold, dark and foreboding. Hundreds of piston engines twist propellers on heavy, laden, matt aircraft as they wind their way from scattered dispersals, around peri-tracks and onto huge concrete runways that disappear into the blackness. One by one they line up, apply full power and then slowly begin trundling down the long, straight path, that wishes rid of them into the rime-filled air. This is the Bomber Command machine in its fourth year of war. Night after moonless night, men and machinery deliver their explosive load into the German industrial heartlands, in an effort to degrade the ability of the enemy to fight, and bring about an end to the War in Europe. Night after night the number of men and machines returning home diminishes, as they succumb to flak, cannon shells and the reaper.

Lancaster by Moonlight (D.D. Winston)

Lancaster Bale Out

The war of production ensures that there are always more to fill their place. All the aircrew hope that the sky is dark enough to ensure anonymity and obscurity so the NachtJagder (night fighters) don't find them. The darkness is not enough though. Invisible radar beams scythe through the air and bounce silently off the metal machines, back to their scanners. The information is relayed to the hunters, guiding them to their prey. Others probe the zenith with pale fingers of vast beams of light, hoping to catch metallic lumps glinting like startled ants. If illuminated they dive for cover as they burrow into the crevices of the night and temporary safety. On clear, moon filled nights the bombers stand down, the darkness lit up and their cover exposed. The NachtJagders return to their airfields empty handed and the brushes of the symbol artists remain dry.[3a]

3rd September 1939

At the outbreak of war, RAF Bomber Command was immediately tasked to begin flying sorties against German targets. The aircraft available to it, and the number of personnel that they could call on then were really only able to harass the enemy with limited effectiveness, and the German Luftwaffe raids on England during this period had a much more devastating effect, in part because they had a shorter distance to fly and also because they could use the River Thames for navigation to London. By the cessation of hostilities, over five years later, Bomber Command had flown over 150,000 sorties and had grown into a formidable force - a very different machine to the one that it had been at the start. It was quickly forced to adapt and learn techniques to fly deep into Germany, attack industrial targets, and then have a chance of returning to England.

The initial concept of the self-defending bomber soon proved woefully unsustainable in the face of Luftwaffe opposition, and by the end of 1939 Bomber Command aircraft were forced to seek the cover of darkness to increase their chances of survival, as many appalling daylight losses began mounting. Navigation was a major problem in the moonless sky and electronic aids began to be developed to assist in this capacity. The endurance, reliability

---

[3a]. *It was common practice to paint symbols on the side of aircraft indicating operations or kills.*

and the bomb-carrying capacity of the early two engined aircraft was seriously lacking and much larger four engined aircraft were required, and eventually came. New bomber stations appeared as a matter of urgency, aircraft production expanded rapidly and the number of aircrew required to support this growth increased correspondingly, until, by the summer of 1942 the RAF was able to mount a 1,000 bomber raid - target Cologne.

As fast as Bomber Command grew and learnt the German defences and Night Fighters adapted and improved. Radar became the eyes of the defenders probing the darkness and relaying the information to the 'Wilde Sau' - the wild boar - fighters hovering, waiting, pouncing on their prey on route to or over the target. The Luftwaffe pilots were committed; after all they were defending their homeland and families. The Allied bomber stream relied on saturation, to get as many aircraft over the target in a short a space of time as possible. The ground defenders used vast arrays of searchlight beams illuminating the blackness and launching swathes of flak into the air, punching, exploding, tearing into anything in its path. In this inferno, aluminium-skinned aircraft seemed woefully thin and vulnerable.

The scene was set. The bombers were sent out night after night to destroy the Fuhrer's ability to wage war, the Luftwaffe and flak batteries were there to protect and defend the 'Fatherland'. Losses on both sides were appallingly high.

This is one account; of one bomber crew, in one squadron, in one group of Bomber Command. All aircrew risked their lives again and again, and often paid the ultimate price. This story pays tribute to them, and many others, in the knowledge that their sacrifice contributed to keeping Europe at peace for the last sixty odd years.

5.
Coal Mining - RAF Volunteer Reserve

I left school at fourteen and followed my father into coal mining. After three years I decided to study for a senior mining qualification, which lasted for eight years - from the ages of seventeen to twenty-five - by attending evening classes at local schools. For a while, I even went to a Saturday afternoon class, at the old Durham Johnson school, situated directly opposite Durham Cathedral, on the opposite side of the River Wear. There were no day-release courses then. If you wanted to improve your education, you had to do it in your spare time; which in my case was after working an eight-hour shift down the coal mine. You also received very little encouragement from the mine owners.

In 1941 the war was going very badly for the Allies. The British had been forced to retreat from Dunkirk, France was occupied, and the Germans were preparing to invade across the channel. At that time I was employed as a coal hewer[4], in a 2'6" coal seam, which consisted of digging coal with a hand pick and then shovelling it into wooden tubs. This was a boring, soul-destroying job, so I approached the mine manager and requested a different job, where I could improve my prospects for future promotion. His words to me were,
"Don't you know there's a war on? We need every shovelful of coal that we can produce."
It was however at this time that notices were displayed in prominent places declaring that 'Men in reserved occupations[5] could volunteer for aircrew'. Coal mining was, of course, one of these reserved

---

[4.] *Someone who heaved or hacked coal from the face using a hand or pneumatic pick.*
[5.] *Those occupations deemed by the government to be essential to the war effort. People in such industries were exempt from becoming servicemen, unless by choice. Ironically in December 1943, having lost some 36,000 miners to the services or better paid work, the government realised that it needed 40,000 miners to maintain output for the war effort and so began to compulsorily direct a percentage of conscripts into coal mining. These so called 'Bevin Boys', named after the Minister of Labour, numbered approximately 48,000 by the end of the war.*

occupations. If it hadn't been so, I think that women would had to have been recruited for the mines because there were numerous men being sent back from the army to continue working in the mines. Some miners did slip through the net though. Indeed I knew two middle-aged men, who had wives and families to keep and who had served in the First World War, who had again joined the army. Once their occupations were discovered, they were returned to work in the mines, much to their disappointment.

To say that I volunteered to join the RAF to escape from the mines or out of sheer bravado would be to do myself an injustice. Like every one else in those dark, early days of the war, I was worried about my country being over-run by the Germans. As aircrew seemed to be more important than coal-miners, I volunteered.

After being medically examined by six doctors at Durham City I was passed as A1. After a few weeks waiting, I, together with twenty other young men, boarded a train for Manchester and then on to No. 3 Reception Centre (RC), Padgate, near Warrington. At Padgate we had to state our preference for becoming either pilot, observer/wireless operator or air gunner. Although I'd never had any ideas about flying, let alone about being a pilot, like everyone else I stated my preference to be in that order. After medical tests from another four doctors I was passed fit for aircrew. We were then given an education test in maths and english, which again I passed with flying colours. An interview with three RAF Officers followed the next day and the first question I was asked was, inevitably,
"Why do you want to be a pilot?"
I gave the only answer that came to my mind. "I want to learn to fly a plane."
"If you left school at the age of 14, how come you have been able to get 100 per cent in your maths exam?" was the next question. I answered that I had never really left school at all, having spent over eight years studying at evening classes.
"We think you will make a good observer," said one of the Officers. "After all," he continued, "the pilot is only a bus driver. He steers the plane to wherever you tell him to go and when you get there, you have the job of dropping the bomb onto the target."
I had to agree with their summation and I was therefore passed to be

Lancaster Bale Out

an aircrew observer and returned home to await my 'call-up'. This period of waiting was called 'deferred service' and I found it to be very irksome. I continued working at the pit, coming home black with coal dust and bathing in a tin bath in front of the fire in the living room; there were no pit-head baths at our mine in 1941.

It was June 21st, 1941 when I received my call-up papers. I was now 1048639 Aircraftman Smooker, F.H. A railway travel warrant was enclosed, with orders for me to report to Torquay, Devon. Other than my journey to Padgate the furthest I had been from the County of Durham was an occasional weekend to see the Blackpool illuminations. "How did one get to Torquay though?" I thought. I headed to my nearest railway station at Crook and asked a guard there. He informed me
"Take the train to Darlington, Darlington to King's Cross then onto the Great Western Line from St. Pancras."
It was a long, lonely journey to Torquay and, despite the war and the London Blitz, the train was packed with holiday-makers. I spoke to no-one the whole journey, as I thought that they would not understand my broad Durham accent.

I disembarked at Torquay and was soon accosted on the station by an RAF corporal.
"Are you for the RAF?" he queried.
"Yes," I replied, pleased that at least someone was there to meet me, otherwise I'd have been lost.
"Climb aboard one of those lorries outside," he ordered.
I now found that I was not alone; there were two or three RAF lorries standing outside and many other young men were already aboard. When we had all been collected we were driven off, out of Torquay and eventually entered the beautiful seaside resort of Babbacombe, where we were billeted at the Sefton Hotel. We spent three weeks at Babbacombe where we were kitted out in our new uniforms. We had to parcel up our civilian clothes and send them home. We weren't allowed out on the town until we could, as was said, conduct ourselves in an airman-like manner, which meant shiny boots, creased trousers and caps tilted to one side; but not too much. I was terribly homesick for the first week, but soon

the beauty of the surroundings - the blue sea lapping at the red sandstone cliffs and beach - instead of the cold, grey North Sea and the grim environment of mining villages, made me realise what I'd been missing. In my mind it became paradise. A Scottish lad called Alistair Ross and I became friends. I thought that I had a strong accent and had travelled a long way from home, but Alistair was a broad Scot from Dundee. I think we became friends because we understood each other's vocabulary and besides we were much alike in our attitude to life. After three weeks at Babbacombe, where all we had learned was how to march in step, how to salute, who to salute, how to make up our beds and lay out our kit for inspection, about sixty of us were posted to Aberystwyth in West Wales.

Arriving at our destination we were met at the station by a Pilot Officer and one Sergeant Mansfield. Aberystwyth was the home to No.41 Initial Training Wing (ITW) and here our marching was increased to ninety steps per minute. We were billeted in the Lion Royal Hotel and from July to September we were pushed to the limit - square bashing, PT, lectures on navigation, aircraft recognition, Morse code, air force law and King's regulations. Personally I revelled in it.

I discovered that I was a good cross-country runner; I always came second out of a group of some two hundred. There was one man however, whom I could never beat, try as hard as I could. I don't know his name but he must have been a trained athlete. I had become quite strong doing the job that I did down the coal mine, but now I was becoming a lot fitter. I was enjoying ITW so much, that I had forgotten why we were there. Towards the end of our course, volunteers were called for, to train as Wireless/Telegraphy (W/T) observers. No one volunteered though. "We'll only be glorified wireless operators," was the cry. Actually the idea was for us to become navigators on twin-engined fighter-bombers. We were told that we would be given a Morse test, at eight words per minute, and those who passed would be trained as W/T observers with a month's extension at Aberystwyth. Some people failed the test deliberately, but I was never one for failing an exam on purpose. I passed the test, and therefore had another month there with my new Welsh girlfriend.

Lancaster Bale Out

Aircraftman Fred Smooker, Aberystwyth 1941 (F. Smooker)

Lancaster Bale Out

We were next posted to No.1 Signals School (SS) at Cranwell, Lincolnshire, the home of the RAF. It was here that I had my first flight - in an ancient Dominie. I was not greatly thrilled. I had visions of the floor of the plane falling out. On the ground we sat for hours on end, sending and receiving Morse code. We had lectures on the theory and workings of radio, sending and receiving with the Aldis lamp, and even doing semaphore with flags. We would be sent up into the air in Proctor aircraft and transmit and receive messages from the ground. This course lasted until January 1942 when I was assessed at nineteen words per minute, and was permitted to sew the 'sparks' badge onto the sleeve of my tunic, along with my Leading (LAC) propellers. We were then sent home on leave again.

After a couple of weeks at home, I received orders to report to Heaton Park in Manchester. This turned out to be an RAF transit camp (in reality just one building in the middle of the park which served as a reception and dining hall) where Airmen were assembled before being posted abroad. We were all billeted out with civilians in the town. I hated it - even though we were only there for a week. Luckily, we didn't have to stay any longer and we got on the train at Manchester and travelled to Gournock, on the Clyde in Scotland. We arrived at night and were immediately transported with all our kit, by lighters out into the Clyde where we boarded a troop ship called the *SS Orbita*[6], bound for Canada.

[6.] *The SS Orbita was built in 1914 by Harland and Wolff, Belfast, for the Pacific Steam Navigation Co of London. It was first used as an auxiliary cruiser before being refitted in 1940 as a troopship.*

6.
Navigation - Sent to Canada

The *SS Orbita* was described in a variety of derogatory terms. She was a hell ship, a convict ship, a rust bucket etc. When we climbed on board we were each issued with either a hammock or a mattress and told to go down below to the bunks. Going below really meant go down into the bowels of the ship. I had been issued with a hammock, which I tried to fasten onto the numerous pipes running overhead. Those with a mattress had to lie on the mess decks, three men on each, lying head to feet. The mess decks were actually long and narrow tables where one ate, and slept if possible. Having failed to secure my hammock successfully I asked a fellow if he would care to swap my hammock for his mattress, and he agreed. I kipped down the first night at the feet of another man. We had been told to sleep in our clothes, but to remove our boots, keeping them handy. We set sail during the night while I was asleep. When I woke up next morning, I sat up, but immediately lay down again. I felt queer. Reaching down to the floor I collected my boots, one at a time, and while still laying down, I raised each leg in turn and laced them. As soon as I had done this, I jumped over my makeshift bed and raced to the stairs, stumbling over recumbent bodies as I went. People were being sick all over the place. I managed to reach the deck before I deposited the contents of my stomach, over the side and into the Irish Sea. The ship was rolling and lurching awfully; I had never experienced anything like it before. Food was out of the question. All I wanted to do was lay down and die. I didn't return to my bed on the mess deck for about four days. With two or three other lads, I wandered about the ship searching for a place that was not moving. We tried sitting with our backs to the mast in the middle of the deck, not daring to look upwards to see the top of the mast doing cartwheels. How miserable I felt at the time. Eventually though, things began to settle down. I managed to get my 'sea-legs' and began to feel hungry. We heard of one poor lad though, who had been sea sick even before we set sail, and had spent the rest of the voyage in the ship's sick bay.

Because of the threat from German submarines - U-boats - we were not alone. There was another troop ship off to our port side and we were also surrounded by four Royal Navy escort vessels, for protection. We must have been a very important cargo, heading for Halifax, Nova Scotia. It took us almost two weeks to cross the stormy Atlantic. On moonlit nights it was a marvellous sight to stand in the bow of the ship and gaze at the mountainous waves; as far as the eye could see. We eventually landed safely at Halifax, to find a foot of snow lying on the ground.

We were taken by transport to a place called Moncton in New Brunswick, where we were billeted for a few days at the No. 31 RAF Personnel Depot, in centrally-heated barracks. I blamed the heating and extremes of temperature for the tonsillitis that I developed while there. This lad from the Durham coalfield was not used to indoor temperatures of some eighty degrees Fahrenheit. We did very little during our few days at Moncton and we were soon on our way further west. We travelled by train for nearly thirty-six hours to our next destination, which was a town called Goderich, on the shore of Lake Huron. Viewed from the train, Canada was a huge, lonely, empty country. Coming from England, of course, this was a natural impression.

After we arrived at Goderich, we boarded RAF lorries which transported us north, along a very rough, gravelled road for some ten miles before we came to our camp - No. 31 Air Navigation School (ANS). God, how homesick I was and I was not alone in my miserable state. The camp itself was good, but we seemed to be so isolated. Looking out the front of the camp gates, Goderich was ten miles to the left and another town called Kincardine was another twenty miles to the right. Straight ahead, across the road, was the tree-covered hillside, on the shore of the ice covered Lake Huron. We were here to do a course in navigation, which included classroom lessons and flying, alternatively as navigator or wireless operator. We would be sent up in Anson trainers together with the pilot to fly to certain destinations. We did this for some six weeks, but I soon found my interest waning, what with homesickness and the desolate, snow-covered outlook below. I knew I was going to fail, but somehow I didn't seem to care. The inevitable happened and I

Lancaster Bale Out

was 'washed out'. I was deemed to be too slow in the air even though I was OK in the classroom. I was not alone though - six of us were sent to a RCAF station at Trenton, a home for washed out pilots and W/T observers.

Trenton was in the province of Ontario, not far by Canadian distances from Toronto. It was not an aerodrome, merely a huge sprawling RCAF station, and as it was now spring time, it became very dry and dusty. There were hundreds of washed out pilots here, from Canada and the USA - all of us wondering what was going to happen to us next. I met two large lads here from North Shields called Bob Marriot and Alfie Railton. They had gone to school together, joined Newcastle City police force together and both joined the RAF as trainee pilots. They had been stationed way out in Alberta. Alfie had legitimately been washed out, but Bob, not wanting to be parted from his mate of long standing, had deliberately done something daft to fail. Alfie told me that Bob had been so homesick that he used to cry himself to sleep at night. It appeared that the mournful note of those Canadian trains passing over the Prairies had affected Bob very badly. I could hardly believe it, because they were both massive six footers.

We became friends, and used to go out at the weekends to Toronto together. I was still badly afflicted with home sickness, and one day while strolling down one main street in Toronto, something that I recognised in a shop window caught my eye. I went back to take another look and found that it was a huge, framed picture of Durham Cathedral. The sight of it reminded me of home even more. On one of these sojourns to Toronto I was greeted by a small man, who was standing on a street corner.

"What part of the old country do you come from?" he asked me.

"Durham County," I answered.

"I've been looking for someone from my home town ever since you boys came over," he said.

Very surprised, I asked, "Where's your home town then?"

"Glasgow!" he answered.

I assumed that he had failed to find any Scots, but was happy to settle for the closest thing - a Durham geordie. His name was Jim Bryce and he invited me to his home for lunch where I met his wife, who was Irish. This couple more or less adopted me because it seemed they had no family of their own. The next weekend Jim took me to Niagara Falls, at his expense, which I was very embarrassed about. We went on a motor boat, the *Maid of the Mist*, which took us as close to the Horseshoe Falls as it was possible to go - as we got near to the falls, the force of the water was so great that the boat could not get any closer.

During the bus journey to and from the falls, I began to realise that Canada was not just a frozen wasteland, as now in early summer it had become quite warm. There were peach orchards in abundance, and it had become so humid that we had to wear tropical kit, shirt and shorts. We were called for interview later on at Trenton, where we were informed that with the introduction of the huge, four engined bombers into the war, the observer's job had been split into navigator and a new trade of bomb aimer. The bomb aimers' role would be front gunner, second pilot and primarily be responsible for the aim and release of the bombs. He would also be a map-reading navigator. We weren't obliged to accept this new job, but most of my colleagues at the time did. I therefore found myself on the first course of bomb aimers in Canada, same rank, same pay etc, as if I had not failed the navigation course.

We were then sent to do a bombing and gunnery course at Picton, close to Lake Ontario, at No. 31 Bombing and Gunnery School (BGS). We did our flying there in single-engined bombers, called Fairey Battles. It was very exciting. During gunnery training I had to stand up in the rear cockpit, behind the pilot, and fire at a drogue being towed some distance away by another Battle. The gun we used was known as the Vickers Gas Operated Gun. The ammunition we fired was impregnated with a coloured dye, so that the number of bullets which had hit the drogue could be counted. I was actually beginning to enjoy myself now. In addition to the gunnery training, we used to drop practice bombs on a target out on Lake Ontario.

After our course in bombing and gunnery at Picton we were posted to No. 33 ANS in Hamilton, Ontario where we flew in Avro Ansons again. Our pilots took us on cross-country flights over a number of towns - Woodstock, London, Guelph, Kitchener, Sarnia - which we

Lancaster Bale Out

had to recognise from details on our maps. Sarnia was on the border with the USA, and our pilots had orders not to cross it because America was not as yet in the war. I also did some twelve hours on the Link trainer, because if the pilot was killed, I was supposed to take over the controls, until everyone else had baled out. I was then supposed to fly the plane to the nearest coast, bale out myself and let the plane crash into the sea. I occasionally flew at night and the view of the floodlit Niagara Falls was fantastic. I had a weekend at Niagara while stationed at Hamilton, together with one of the lads from our course. A society, which I believe was the RAOB[7], sent two free tickets for hotel accommodation and bus fares to our camp for anyone who wished to go. Rather strangely, no one else wished to avail themselves of this generosity, except an Irish lad named McGuire, and myself. The two of us went off together and while McGuire and I stood leaning on a fence, gazing at the mass of water tumbling over the cliffs, he turned to me and remarked,

"It's nothing really, only a lot of water falling over a cliff." He continued, "Now, if that water had been falling upwards it would have been something extraordinary." Niagara falls consisted of two vast columns of water flowing over the cliffs, one on the Canadian side and one on the American side. The Horseshoe falls, so-named because of the concave shape of the cliffs, were in Canada and were more spectacular than the American falls, although these were still a sight to behold. McGuire and I walked over the bridge below the falls, and crossed over into America. There was a customs post in the centre of this bridge, but we were allowed to cross; I can therefore say that I have been to the United States of America. On this side we actually walked under the American falls. A woodwork staging had been erected for viewers to do this and we paid a dollar or so, and got given some oilskin clothing, for protection from the spray. The noise from the vast amount of falling water was like continuous thunder. The two falls were separated by a place called 'Goat Island'. I was vividly reminded of the Frenchman, Blondin, who despite being blindfolded crossed these falls years ago on a tight-rope. I remember reading this in a book when I was a schoolboy.

---

[7] *The Royal Antediluvian Order of Buffaloes, a charitable organisation akin to the Masons and still active today.*

LAC Fred Smooker, Niagara Falls, 1942 (F. Smooker)

It was now mid-summer and the climate was so hot and humid that, although we were billeted in a huge, empty hangar, we could not sleep. Some of us used to get out of bed in the middle of the night and dive into an open-air swimming pool outside of our hangar barrack. Although I could swim a decent breaststroke, I was no match for my ex-policeman mate, Bob, who swam free-style. Relations though became strained between Bob and me because of his antics in the pool, as he used to push my head down under the water. He was at least five inches taller than me, and about two stones heavier than my twelve stone - I had gained at least a stone in weight while in Canada. Bob was never conscious of his huge bulk. Unlike his long time friend, Alfie, Bob could be very sarcastic. Actually as I got to know him better I would guess that he had been a school bully, constantly picking fights with the rest of his close colleagues. One time he and I had a mock fight and as we rolled about the ground I managed to get him in a head lock, and somehow got my legs around his waist in a scissors grip in which I had him helpless. Although it was all friendly, I was afraid to release him in case he actually turned really aggressive. The more he struggled the more I squeezed his ribs until he finally pleaded for me to let him go. He was turning blue in the face, so I apprehensively let him go. Bob was more subdued after this and remarked upon my steel-banded legs. Little did he know

Lancaster Bale Out

that my legs had been used for five or six years pushing coal tubs. Rather strangely, Bob was commissioned at the end of our course and after that we saw very little of him. When we did see him he always had something derogatory to say about us, even his long time friend Alfie. We never saluted him though! Except for Bob, all the rest of our course were made up to Sergeants and issued with three stripes. There were no bomb aimer brevets available at the time so we were issued with observers' brevets. Since we were the first course of bomb aimers to have passed out in Canada, at the end of the course volunteers were requested to continue on as instructors for future courses coming from the UK. Only one lad volunteered out of the course of thirty, and he only volunteered because he had a Canadian girlfriend. Everyone wanted to leave this huge, lonely country - even though it was flowing with milk and honey and bright lights - and return to blacked-out, ration starved, war-torn Great Britain.

We boarded our train at Hamilton weighed-down with our kit bags and haversacks full of tinned fruit, butter etc. I remember that I had a tin containing a 7lb ham joint in my kit bag, amongst other goodies for my family back home. At Halifax, Nova Scotia, we boarded our transport, the *SS Stirling Castle*[8]. What a contrast this was to our previous ship. We had cabins and bunks for sleeping, and a dining-room for eating. We were part of a huge convoy of troop-ships carrying cargo and thousands of Canadian soldiers and airmen, all bound for England. The journey across the Atlantic was uneventful, although we were rather apprehensive about threat from German U-Boats. We were escorted part of the way by Canadian naval vessels and our apprehension increased when they left the huge convey and returned to Halifax. West of Ireland the convoy separated, some turning north to Scotland, some south, but our troop-ship carried straight on around the north of Ireland and, after a journey of some ten days, we docked at Liverpool. We were disembarked at the docks and all RAF men were marched to the railway station. There we boarded a troop train and we journeyed south to Bournemouth,

---

[8] *The SS Stirling Castle was built in 1935 by Harland and Wolff, Belfast, for the Union Castle Line and from 1940 served as a troopship steaming over 500,000 miles and carrying 128,000 personnel.*

Lancaster Bale Out

where we were billeted in the numerous hotels in the town. Five of us, including my North Shields mate Alfie, were billeted in the Bathcourt Hotel. Every morning for five days we were paraded on the promenade, where we were bawled and shouted at by Canadian NCOs.

"Keep off the sidewalk," they bellowed.

Some of us resented being ordered about by Canadians, who seemed to have taken charge of us in our own country. The beach at Bournemouth was out of bounds for us, indeed, approaches to the beach were sealed off with barbed wire. One day we were there by the beach when two German fighters came hurling over the sea front and opened fire. We were really sitting ducks, but amazingly no one was injured.

After five days our documents were processed and we were sent on leave for two weeks, so once more I was on the train bound for Kings Cross station. Alfie and I travelled together; he bound for Newcastle on Tyne and I for Darlington. I don't know what happened to Bob, but since he was an officer now he would have travelled first class. In any event, after I left the train at Darlington, I saw neither of them ever again. I did hear from some source or other, now long forgotten, that they were posted to Coastal command, and one or the other had been killed[9]. Close friendships during the war years were difficult to keep because it was a case of here today, gone tomorrow. My sisters and parents were overjoyed to see me safely home again, and I was delighted to present my gifts of tinned ham, fruit and butter from Canada. I was a hero to some people, even though after some sixteen months in the RAF I had not yet fired a single shot in anger. Actually I became very bored after a week or so at home and was pleased when my posting orders arrived, with instructions for me to travel to Cottesmore, an Operational Training Unit (OTU) in Rutland.

[9.] *F/O Robert Marriot (129617) was killed on 10th March 1943. Sgt. Alfred Joseph Railton (1476472) was killed on 26th May 1943 whilst flying as a Rear Gunner with 166 Sqn on a raid to Dusseldorf (Wellington HE235).*

7.
Operational Training - Forming a Crew

Unlike Fighter Command, where the predominant requirement was for pilots and navigators, the aircrew who were to fly in Bomber Command required a diverse collection of 'trades' and skills. The size, and complexity, of bomber aircraft was such that to successfully fly operations into Europe, accurately deliver bombs and return to England required a multi-disciplined team. RAF recruits were subjected to various tests and exams, to ascertain their suitability for flying. If they got through that phase they would then be sent to one of the various training schools, specialising in each particular subject. During the period of training, aircraftmen were tested and had to achieve a particular pass rate at the end to become accepted. They would often be 'washed-out'[10] from a particular course, but if they showed aptitude in certain areas they could be sent elsewhere to re-train in another trade. Once this had been successfully completed the trainees would be posted to an OTU where they would form a crew and actually begin training together on bomber aircraft.

I arrived at No. 14 OTU, RAF Cottesmore, on 20th October, 1942. We were told to report to the Sergeants' mess there, which was nearly full to overflowing with pilots, navigators, bomb aimers, wireless operators and air gunners - all with their three stripes and badge of trade on the left breast of their tunics. I seemed to be the odd man out though, wearing my flying 'O' observer's badge. Most of the Airmen there were complete strangers, except for any that might have been at the same training schools together.

"Get crewed up in fives," we were ordered.
Immediately, everyone started to look for a good pilot. "How could one tell a good pilot from a bad one," I thought, just from

---

[10] *A term given to those who failed to meet the standards required for an aircrew discipline.*

appearances? First I approached a tall, gangly Canadian.

"Have you got a bomb aimer?" I asked.

He replied in the affirmative. Lady luck was on my side. This Canadian and his crew never left Cottesmore. On a training flight one of the engines on their Wellington cut out and it appears that this lad turned into his 'dud' engine[11], and they crashed. All were killed.

I next approached a pilot who was leaning on the bar. He had USA sewn onto his uniform sleeves.

"Have you got a bomb aimer?" I asked. He looked me up and down, all the while chewing his gum, looking very self-assured. He was about 5'10" tall, and had a swarthy olive look to his face.

"Do you want to be my bomb aimer?" he asked.

"Sure," I said.

"OK," he replied, "find a good navigator."

Again, how does one recognise a good navigator from a bad one? Everyone by now seemed to have organised themselves into a crew. I spotted a spare navigator and asked him,

"Are you a good navigator?"

"Of course," he said with a smile and laughed,

"I'm as good as any of these others."

In the meantime my American pilot, had found himself a wireless operator and a rear gunner, to complete the set.

Eugene 'Gene' Leon Rosner was born on 17th April 1920 into a Jewish family in Wilkes Barr, Pennsylvania. He was the eldest son of Isidore Harry Rosner (from Austro-Hungary - now Ukraine) and Esther Marcovici (from Romania), who emigrated to America before the first world war. He had an older sister and three younger brothers. Gene was raised in a mining town and after school went onto Ohio University in Athens, studying advertising from 1938-40. After the war had broken out in Europe Gene volunteered to become a Cadet in the United States Army Air Corps in mid 1940.

He trained at the Institute of Aeronautics in Tuscaloosa, Alabama, between August 1940 and January 1941, and passed his basic flying

---

[11] *The Wellington was a twin engined bomber, but did not fly well on only one engine. Inexperienced pilots could therefore easily get into trouble if an engine failed during flight. This pilot was F/Sgt. Douglas Farrell (See Appendix B)*

Gene Rosner, Training in Alabama, 1940 (R. Schwartz)

training. At this time however, the Air Corps was very selective, as America had not yet entered the war and did not have the need for vast numbers of pilots, and he was washed out before being commissioned. There is an alternative story within the Rosner family that Gene 'buzzed' a General's house, in order to impress his daughter, near the end of his pilot training and because of this incident was not given his commission, but it is not confirmed!

LAC Gene Rosner, RCAF (R. Schwartz)

Lancaster Bale Out

He therefore left the Air Corps in April 1941 but was still really desperate to fly, so he decided to cross the border and went and joined the RCAF in December 1941. He was accepted and a month later found himself aboard a ship bound for the UK, to continue his flying training at No. 15 (P) AFU (Advanced Flying Unit) in Leconfield, Lincolnshire. After only a week or so there he was deemed suitable for operational training.

Wilfrid 'Bill' Bailey (known to his family as 'Wilf') was the son of Thomas William and Ada Clarrie Bailey from Donisthorpe, Leicestershire. He was the eldest of five and had two brothers and two sisters. He was born on 8th December 1921 at Oakthorpe, Leicestershire. His father was a coal miner, and worked at a number of collieries in the area, including Swain's Park, Measham and Minorca, over the duration of his working life. Wilf was educated at Ashby Grammar school and was a gifted soprano singer as a teenager. He won prizes in a number of competitions and had the opportunity to join the Westminster choir school to further his singing ability, but the expense was prohibitive. His father was opposed to him becoming a miner, so after leaving school he became a cost accountant at the Charnwood Engineering Co. before joining the RAF.

After joining up he was sent to do an Air Observers Navigation course in Miami, Florida, between March and July 1942. On returning to the UK he did an advanced Navigation course at No. 3(O) AFU at Bobbington between August and October 1942. He passed the course as a fully qualified Navigator and was then sent to Cottesmore.

Jack Hougham was born on 9th June 1920, and was the only child of John 'Jack' Edmund and Ada Rose Hougham (nee Castle) of Guilton, Ash, Kent. Around the age of fourteen he went to work on the railway at Betteshanger Colliery, where his father already worked. He would have been working there for about four years when Britain went to War. Living in Kent he probably would have witnessed first hand the numerous dogfights between the RAF fighters and the Luftwaffe intruders, during the desperate summer of 1940. Perhaps seeing this strengthened his desire to 'do his bit',

Bill Bailey at home (D. Bailey)

Sgt. Bill Bailey (Left), during Training (D. Bailey)

Lancaster Bale Out

although like Fred he could have chosen to stay working at the mine as at that time joining the RAF was voluntary. His desire to contribute to the war effort was greater though and towards the end of 1940 Jack Hougham signed up and joined the RAF VR - Volunteer Reserve. He was passed fit on 12th November 1940, suitable for aircrew to train as a wireless operator/air gunner (WOp/AG).

Jack's call to arms finally came and he was requested to report to No. 10 Reception Unit, at Blackpool on 21st June, 1941. Here he was issued with his RAF uniform and after a period of general training, he returned to the mines on 'deferred service' to await the call to start training for real.

Around the middle of 1942, Jack's papers came through and he reported to No.4 Signals School, at Madley in Hertfordshire. Here he learnt the radio skills required to become an aircrew wireless operator. In the words of F/Sgt. Bruce Lewis, a 101 Squadron WOp,
"Combined with a liberal dose of ground tuition, we took to the air in what can only be described as 'flying classrooms'. The de Havilland Dominie was a 'joke' aircraft, originally designed as a biplane airliner. With a bored pilot flying round in circles, a harassed Corporal Instructor and four miserable pupils trying to tap out morse while on the point of throwing up, as the underpowered kite wallowed about the sky like a, one-winged duck, it was all stiflingly claustrophobic. Messages somehow got transmitted from the air to ground, and from ground to air in spite of it all. It was a pity that the transmitters/receivers were obsolete, and bore little relation to the much more sophisticated equipment we were to use in Bomber Command. The station appeared to be run by corporals who laboured manfully to turn us into WOp/AGs. They were supported by a few senior NCOs, but officers, if there were any, obviously had something better to do than take part in the training function."

Jack obviously survived this test and passed the W/Op course on 8th September 1942. Next came the second part of the training - to become an air gunner. He was posted to No. 8 Air Gunnery School (AGS) and F/Sgt Bruce Lewis continues,

Aircraftman Jack Hougham, No. 10 RC Blackpool, 1941 (C. Smith)

"No. 8 AGS was situated in glorious Scottish countryside, at Evanton, north of Inverness. The camp had a backdrop of magnificent mountains, while the runways stretched almost to the edge of the Moray Firth. Each morning at dawn we woke to the sound of pipes. The pipers, in a highland version of RAF uniform complete with kilt, would descend the mountainside or rise out of ditches and other mysterious hideaways and meet at the camp gate. During this period of coming together we cadets had to be

Lancaster Bale Out

up, washed, shaved and dressed ready to fall in behind them for a march down to the hangars. There, mounted on a rostrum, the padre offered a short prayer. The RAF flag was broken to the sound of a bugle as the parade was dismissed and the day's work began. It was unforgettable - the beautiful sunrises, the dark silhouettes of the aircraft, the skirl of the pipes. If the DH Dominie was a joke, the Blackburn Botha was beyond a joke. Originally developed as a torpedo bomber, this high-wing, twin-engine, underpowered aircraft proved to be useless for its intended purpose. It was relegated to the role of flying back and forth over the sea, while trainee air gunners took pot-shots at canvas drogues towed by single-engine Martinets. The pilots engaged in these exercises were not among the most enthusiastic I had met. They took care never to stray far from base as the 'Bloody Botha' was unable to maintain height on one engine should the other fail. It was a rule that the pupils had to wear full flying kit as if equipped for a night trip over Germany. This gear consisted of silk under-combinations, 'inner' and 'outer' flying suits, parachute harness, Mae West life-jackets, three pairs of gloves, flying helmet and oxygen masks.

In the sweltering heat of a brilliant summer, four sweating pupils stood in the forward cabin, beside a non-communicative shirt-sleeved pilot, waiting their turn to crawl down a narrow tunnel which led to the egg-shaped Fraser-Nash turret. In the classroom we had some inspirational guidance in Aircraft Recognition from a tour-expired Flying Officer air-gunner. Armed with a multitude of models he would zoom in and attack us from all angles, coming up from floor level, or standing on a desk and diving down unexpectedly. Using a projector, he would flash perhaps a head-on view of a Ju88 onto the screen for a split second. 'Come on, boys. What is it? Quick! Quick! Your life depends on it.' He went to infinite trouble to cut out endless jigsaw puzzles, the pieces made up of characteristic features of a variety of planes. He was a natural teacher, always happy to answer our questions, and we learned a great deal from him. He turned what some of us considered a dull subject into a topic of endless fascination."

Lancaster Bale Out

Sgt. Jack Hougham, No.8 AGS, Evanton (C. Smith)

Lancaster Bale Out

Jack completed the course on the 10th October 1942, passed out 'Average' on air-to-air firing, air-to-ground firing and night firing. He was awarded an AG brevet, promoted to Sergeant and posted to OTU Cottesmore.

Sgt. Arnie Turner (LAC Canada)

Dalton Arnold 'Arnie' Turner, son of John Stephen and Zephyr Victoria Turner (nee Weir) came from Ottawa, Ontario and was born on 13th November 1920 at Carleton Place. He was the eldest of three brothers, one of whom, Allan, also served in the RCAF. He became a welder when he left school before he joined the RCAF. He went to No.4 AGS in August 1942 and arrived in the UK at the beginning of September. He appears to have gone briefly to No. 23 OTU before moving on to Cottesmore. As can be seen from the height chart he was around 5' 8" tall.

We therefore became a crew of five to begin our operational training on Wellingtons - Gene Rosner (Pilot), from Pennsylvania, Bill Bailey (Navigator) from Leicester, Jack Hougham (Wireless Operator), an ex-coal miner from Kent, Arnie Turner (Rear Gunner), a short, stocky, Canadian[12] welder from Ottawa and myself Bomb Aimer, also an ex-coal miner from Durham.

Whilst at Cottesmore Arnie met a fellow Canadian gunner, Jim Calder, and they became good friends. Jim describes day to day life during training and flying through as series of letters[13] he wrote home to his parents:

Jim Calder's letter home (October 26, 1942):

"Rielly and I went into Oakham last night to a show and then spent the rest of the evening playing darts; that is the national game over here I think. No matter where you go there is a dart board up."

Jim Calder's letter home (November 23, 1942):

"I was down to Nottingham for a couple of days and after we left there we went to Leicester for a few days and then came back to Oakham for the last two days, so all in all I had a swell time. A lot of the boys head for London but I am not going there until I have lots of money. London doesn't hold any attraction for me. I can have just as good a time in the smaller cities and on less money, however I am going to London before long just to see what it is like. My pal and I got in a big fight in Nottingham. My pal was drinking and he got

---

[12] *The Commonwealth and Empire countries provided over a quarter of the airmen who flew with Bomber Command.*
[13] *Jim wrote a series of 30 letters to his parents and family over the course of his serving in the UK*

Lancaster Bale Out

in an argument with a British soldier, so he was pretty tight and the soldier was sober so I took the fight. I beat the soldier and then his pals started to get rough and it ended up with all the Canadians on one side of the hall and the English boys on the other. Boy what a time, and have I ever got a beauty of a shiner but it was fun, nothing like a little excitement I say. Boy we are sure driving Jerry (the Germans) now. We don't have much excitement but I think it will come before long. I don't expect to get into this war before spring, if it lasts that long. Canadians are big stuff over here. Every night we go to town we have to tame some Englishman down because a Canadian took his girl, but they generally get the worst of it when they start any arguments. Boy what fun.

The weather is holding us up quite a bit now. Boy when it gets foggy here it really gets foggy. You can't see a thing and sometimes it comes down so quick you are caught in it before you know it."

Jim Calder's letter home (November 29, 1942):

"We all went into a big formal dance at Oakham the other night, and at intermission the boys were feeling pretty good and they started shooting dice out in the middle of the floor. All the stiff collars and bow ties and tails standing around and all the Canadians in a circle on the floor shooting dice, it sure was funny. Some of the things the boys do over here are awful but we are all having a good time. The boys here do pretty much as they please and most of them get away with it. We sure are having a good time, I am glad I didn't stay in Canada now, but at times I wish I was back there, especially when somebody starts talking about steaks and apple pie."

Jim Calder's letter home (December 6, 1942):

"We went to town the other night and of course the boys got feeling pretty good and when I came out of the dance I met one of the fellows with a big white duck. He bought it at some affair for the Red Cross, paid a pound for it, so we have it tied outside the hut now and are fattening it up for Christmas. Boy we are sure going to have a feed."

Lancaster Bale Out

We did well as a crew at Cottesmore, and we were commended for one particular incident. One night we had to fly from our base in Rutland, westwards to the Menai Bridge in Wales where there was an infrared beam to be located by the bomb aimer with a camera instead of bombs. Soon after we left Cottesmore, we began to hear a deafening noise on our intercom. It reminds me now of hundreds of car alarms going off at once.

"Hey, Bailey, where are we?" yelled our skipper to our navigator.

"We must be over Leicester," he replied, "You had better start climbing."

The noise we were experiencing, apparently came from what were called 'Squeakers' from Barrage Balloons over Leicester. We started climbing but it took quite a while before we got rid of that infernal noise in our ears. In the meantime we were lost over blackened out England. Nothing could be seen. Bailey didn't know where we were either, but our skipper kept flying westwards. "Perhaps he is intending to fly home", I thought. After about an hour of this we were beginning to get worried, and then out of the blackness we spotted an airfield.

"Hey, you guys," called the skipper, "I'm going to use the Darkie Watch."

This was a navigational aid that lost crews could use, to find out where they were, but it had to be used correctly. So our skipper switched on his TR9[14], which was used to talk to the ground, and said in his Yankee voice,

"Hello, Darkie, Hello, Darkie, this is Bandwag 'D' Dog calling," and repeated it three times. After a few minutes, while the message was being authenticated I suppose, back came the answer,

"Hello Bandwag 'D' Dog, this is Jurby on the Isle of Man."

From there we set course for the Menai Bridge, but this was to no avail because we could not see it for cloud, so we returned to Cottesmore. The next day we received a commendation for initiative shown in using the Darkie Watch. It was the skipper's idea really, because I don't think any of the rest of the crew knew about it. We were treated to good-natured greetings for a while from our colleagues at Cottesmore. "Hello Darkie," became the greeting

---

[14] *The TR9 was a type of transmitter radio set used by the pilot.*

Lancaster Bale Out

of the day. Cottesmore was a good station, pre-war built, with comfortable centrally heated barracks. Our time was spent doing practice bombing at Wainfleet Sands in Lincolnshire. Sometimes bombing a moving target, being towed by a tug; It was said that one bomb aimer actually bombed the tug. Rosner practised landing on one engine, and flying on one engine. His instructor would tell him during the flight,
"Cut starboard engine," or "cut port engine," while we held our breath in apprehension, praying that he wouldn't cut them both.

Jim Calder's letter home (December 20, 1942):

"The weather is not very good and I am hoping that flying will be cancelled. We haven't been having very good weather lately, so we are a way behind on our course. I don't expect to finish training before March now and it may be even later. We are sure having a swell time now; we don't do anything when we aren't flying as we have now finished our ground school.

We are having a big Christmas party in the mess here tomorrow night they are just decorating it and from what I hear the Christmas dinner is going to be alright.

Well Mom I just walked all the way up to the hangers for nothing. Flying has been postponed until nine o'clock so I guess it will be cancelled, at least I hope so. We have a great time now, just about every time we go up now we have to land at some other station, and boy when we land at these other places do we ever have fun. We always get a real good meal as soon as we land, generally eggs; you know Mom eggs are quite scarce here now. We get a lot of these powdered eggs but it doesn't taste much like the real thing. We landed at a place last week and were there for three days. There was a big dance there in the Sergeants' mess so we took that in. Boy I was dressed to kill. I had my battle dress on, no shirt just a turtle necked sweater and my flying boots. Boy did we cut a dash there, but we had a great time, you know flying boots aren't the best thing in the world to dance in.

Well Mom from what I hear things are getting pretty well rationed over there now. Mom will you send me some cigarettes through the company, that is one thing I am really hard on now. I have been smoking my pal's for about three weeks now. It only costs $3 to send a thousand, so will you send some?

You know Mom it doesn't seem like Christmas at all this year. This is the first Christmas I have been away from home, and it's going to seem kind of funny but I guess I will have a good time. I hope you have a good Christmas. Well Mom I have met a lot of nice girls over here but they are not the same as the girls at home. I think I will wait until I get home until I get married (ha ha)."

We spent a snowy Christmas in 1942 there, in the Sergeants' mess dining-room. We were waited on by the officers and beer flowed like water. I'd never tasted beer before but I was poured a Dixie full. Jack Hougham, our big, hulking ex-coal worker wireless operator was also a non-drinker. I tasted my beer and exclaimed,
"Aargh, it tastes like vinegar!" Bill Bailey, our navigator, rather liked his beer and consumed ours as well as his own. Our leisure nights off were spent at the local dances or cinema in Oakham, the county town of Rutland. Bill Bailey would sometimes drink quite a lot on these occasions. Jack Hougham could not dance and just used to sit and watch, eyeing the girls. Arnie Turner, our little rear gunner with a toothbrush moustache, was awfully homesick for Canada, and spent most of his leisure time shooting crap with Jim and his fellow Canadians.

Rosner rarely seemed to leave the camp. I think he used to sit in the Sergeants' mess drinking whisky, smoking and playing poker, although I never saw him drunk.

Jim Calder's letter home (December 27, 1942):

"Well Mom, Christmas has gone and I sure hope you had a good Christmas. Boy I sure did. Let me know what you received and what you gave the boys for me also let me know if my cards got through. I received your airmail of December 30th today. I think

Lancaster Bale Out

Sgt. Arnie Turner (M. Turner)

you're a month ahead aren't you? I also received your birthday card along with a lot of Christmas cards.

I suppose I shouldn't tell you this but here goes anyway. I came home from the dance at Christmas and had exactly eight shillings in my pocket and they were shooting dice in the mess so I decided to take a chance on it. That's the first time I played dice, and when I left I had over eighty pounds and as you know that is over four hundred dollars, so I hope you didn't send me anymore. I have now fifty pounds in the bank so I won't need any money for a while now. Don't start worrying about me gambling because I won't be for a while. I have enough money to see me through for quite a while.

Now to tell you about the Christmas. We went into a dance in Oakham. We had a swell time and we had a real Christmas dinner here. Tomato soup, turkey and pork, roast potatoes, sage dressing, peas and sprouts, mince pie and all kinds of fruit, figs and dates. Boy, it was a real feast. Christmas night we had a big dance here on the station and had a swell time. I just had three days off and there were no trains so we couldn't go anywhere anyway but we had a swell time. It has been awful foggy since the day before Christmas so we haven't been doing anything.

Well we went into town to a show last night but came home early. We went in with a couple of girls from the stations here, and Oakham is pretty dead at the best of times but on Sunday it is terrible. There is a big New Years ball there tonight so I am hoping I am not flying, I've got a date with a dream."

Jim Calder's letter home (January 17, 1943):

"I expect to go on leave this week, I just have one more short trip and I will be finished here and will be going on two weeks leave. I haven't decided where to go yet, I think I will go down to see Gordon and then I may go to Leeds. There is a WAAF on the station here I have been going around with. She goes on leave Tuesday and she wants me to go up to her home for a few days, then I want to go to London and Bournemouth so I don't know what to do. I received your airmail of the 28th yesterday. Well Mom I lost four of my best pals the other day[15] I don't generally tell you of these things but I was really sorry to hear about these boys. They were all swell guys and I saw them go, we had just taken off and were circling the drome waiting for the other plane when I saw it. They just got off the deck when their motors cut out and they went right back in nose first, the only boy to get out was the gunner. They were boys we had been with a long time. Well Mom you think gunner is a dangerous job well it is just the safest place in today's Airplane. Since I came here of all the crashes we haven't lost a gunner yet, and in most cases he is the only one to come out, so don't worry about me.

Well Mom I will be glad when those shoes get here because the other ones are definitely unserviceable now (as we say here). If I wear them anymore I will be walking in my bare feet and you know boots aren't the best things in the world for dancing in. All our boys are on leave now and I will be, Tuesday I think, so it is quite likely we will all go to London together. Oh Boy it won't be a safe place to be if we do, and you can bet we all come back with a souvenir (a

---

[15] *The pilot was Sgt. William Rielly (See Appendix B)*

big shiner). We always do when we all go together, it seems some of these English boys think they are tougher than Canadians and of course they have to be shown that they aren't. I haven't done any boxing lately but they are talking about putting on a sports tournament here and if I am still here I think I will fight. I am in pretty good shape now and a lot heavier than when I left. I have met a lot of real nice English boys here but on the whole I don't think any more of them than I did in Canada. About those pictures, I will try to get some when I am on leave. They are quite hard to get here. My bomb aimer has a camera and some films so the first chance I get I will take some snaps of the boys and send them over to you. I have a good crew, a Scotch bomb aimer and is he ever fun. There are only two of us Canadians in the crew but the others are swell guys. I guess you heard about the big raid on Berlin last night eh, and we only lost one plane[15], not bad eh?"

After another couple of weeks of training we had now completed the eighty hours day and night flying required and finished at the OTU on 23rd January, 1943.

Jim Calder's letter home (February 23, 1943):

"Well here I am back in London again but only for a short time. We were supposed to get seven days but at the last minute they cut it down to three. I went back off leave the sixteenth and went on a commando course for a few days and boy I'm telling you it almost killed me. I was so stiff and sore I could hardly walk, so were all the rest of the boys. We were sent out to a station that was ten miles from the nearest town and there was no bus service, so we were stuck there for a week. The worst of all was that there was no mail service either, so I haven't had a letter for two weeks now but I expect there will be mail waiting for me at my new address when I get back. To tell you something about the station, it was a nice place and we had very good food, but what I didn't like was all the marching. We had to get up at seven every morning and we had pack drill, rifle drill, foot drill and everything that the army boys have to do; Route marches with full pack and cross country runs.

[15.] *61 Squadron Lancaster ED332, piloted by S/Ldr Parker. All were killed.*

Arnie and I walked all the way on the run, the rest of the boys were back before we got halfway, but we had a good time, we just took our time and stopped to talk to everybody and then got a ride back to camp. All in all we had fun while we were there, even if it was a bit hard on the constitution. I am in with a swell bunch of fellows now so it is O.K. We are really having a swell time, only Arnie and I keep running out of money. The only reason we were able to come to London this time was because they slipped up somewhere and paid us twice as much as they should have. I suppose they will catch up with us next payday but I would sooner have the money to go on leave than when I am in camp anyway so it won't be bad, we can get along without it when we are in camp. I had quite a bit of money for a while but twenty-five days leave cost us a lot of money. Arnie and I spent four hundred pounds between us but we really saw the country. We go on leave again in six weeks and Arnie says we are going to Edinburgh. We have only been up to Scotland once since we came over, but all the fellows tell us there is more fun there than in London so we are going up to find out for ourselves.

Well Mom it is dinner time and I have to get dressed yet. I've got a date with a dream this afternoon, she just called to let me know she got the afternoon off, so I guess I will have to close for now."

During their 3 months training at Cottesmore there had been 11 crashes which had killed 16 airmen and injured 20 more.

8.
Conversion to Lancasters - Expanding the Crew

After a period of leave, we were next instructed to report to Wigsley, home of No. 1654 Heavy Conversion Unit (HCU) in Nottinghamshire, where we were to be groomed for the mighty Lancaster. I arrived there on 1st March 1943 and what a contrast to Cottesmore this place was. We were billeted in Nissen huts, with no central heating and only a coal burning stove in the centre of the hut. This was a utility airfield, where I think the only bit of concrete was the single mile long runway. It was here that our original crew of five became seven.

Aircraftman Ted Amor (J. Fricker)

Jim Calder, No.6 BGS, Canada (R. Calder)

A flight engineer called Ted Amor turned up to join us. He had been in the RAF pre-war as an engineer, and for promotion purposes had volunteered for aircrew. He was a Londoner, quite small, very pleasant and easy to get along with. Edward 'Ted' William John Amor, (known to his family as 'Eddy') was the son of William and Frances Julia Amor from Palmers Green in Middlesex. He was the youngest of six, having five older sisters, and at 28 he was the oldest member of the crew. As there was only one training school for flight engineers, No. 4 School of Technical Training (SoTT), St. Athan,

Lancaster Bale Out

Ted would have gone there, probably around the middle of 1942. The Flight Engineer category was introduced with the advent of the larger 'heavy' four-engined bombers, which required a bigger crew to operate them. The use of two pilots was considered wasteful, given the heavy losses being suffered, and so the Flight Engineer became the pilot's assistant looking after the engines and monitoring the instruments, and was also expected to be able to fly the plane in an emergency. The course there was of about 6 weeks duration and additional training in Air Gunnery was also given so the F/E could also do this as well.

The seventh member was a tall (6' 2"), slim, Canadian called Jim Calder. James 'Jim' Reginald Calder (known to his family as 'Reg') was born on 25th January 1922 at Springhill, Nova Scotia and was the eldest son of George Neil and Nellie Odessa Calder (nee King). He had three younger brothers and, like his father, initially spent time as a coal miner before joining up. He was sent to No.6 BGS at Mountain View, Ontario, between June and July 1942, and qualified as an Air Gunner. He then left Canada for England and arrived in August 1942. After a short stay at No. 3 PRC, he was posted to Cottesmore on the 22nd September. Because he'd become best friends with Arnie at Cottesmore, they engineered somehow to swap crews so that he and Arnie could stay together, so although initially trained as a Rear Gunner Jim moved into the vacant Mid-Upper Gunner position.

Jim was a bundle of laughs. Unlike Arnie, he didn't seem to be homesick at all. Due to the muddy conditions at Wigsley in the middle of winter 1943, we used to wear Wellington boots all the time, in fact Jim never seemed to take his Wellies off. It was laughable to see him jitterbugging at the Navy, Army and Air Force Institutes (NAAFI) dances in them. That's the kind of guy he was, kind, cheerful and friendly.

Jim Calder's letter home (February 27, 1943):

"I just came back off leave and came out to this new station, so I haven't caught up with my mail yet. I am going to try to hold onto some money for my next leave which comes up in six weeks. It won't be hard because we are quite a way from town now so we won't be going out much. I am now flying with one of my best pals. We would have been split up here but I managed to trade places with the other gunner in their crew so now I am in their crew and we will be together now until we come back. He is a great boy, his name is Arnie Turner and his home is in Carleton Place, Ontario. We have been together for quite awhile now and I sure am glad we are staying together. He is the boy I mentioned in my letters. We were together on our leave and are very seldom apart now, he is a great boy, just like Gordon.

This place now is the final step in our training, we have gone onto a bigger plane but we are well satisfied now. When we finish here I will be all finished training and will I be glad."

Jim Calder's letter home (March 9, 1943):

"We were into Lincoln the other night and had a great time. It was the first time I had been to that town so we really had a good time. We went to the dance and gave the local girls a treat (ha ha). We had a big dance here in the Mess, Saturday night, so we really had a good time the last few nights. There is another big dance on the camp tomorrow night so this new station isn't too bad, although there is quite a bit of walking to do. We have to carry our own knives and forks to the Mess-by the way I have lost four sets already! I always get up and leave them.

I received two parcels and a package of cigs the other day also the chocolates from the church. I heard they were stopping the parcels being sent from Canada but I sure hope that isn't right, because I would sure hate to have to smoke these cigs I get here. We have had no snow here yet but I guess you have had plenty at home eh? Mom if you ever have the money I could use a cheap watch. I smashed the one I had and I can't get another one, and you can't buy them over here, so if you get around to it you could send me a cheap one. I wish you could have seen Arnie and I eating that corn, we just heated it over the fire in the hut and boy it really was good. I was sure glad to get those last parcels, we were both out of cigs but we both got them together so we have enough to do us for a little while now.

Lancaster Bale Out

There is something else I want you to send Mom, for my navigator, Bill Bailey. He's going to get married soon and he asked me to see if you could send some cosmetics and silk stockings. He will pay me for them, that is if you can get them. He is a great kid. He sends my laundry home with his and his mother does it, and she sends us cake and cookies all the time and has invited me to their home many times so if you could do it, please send them. He has a little sister[16] that has been in the hospital for ten months, so a lot of the candy you send me I send on to her. She is a cute kid and I feel sorry for her. Bill always sends his chocolate ration to her so I always give him part of my parcel for her, also Arnie gives him some candy out of his. So if there is anything you could send will you send it, his family is very nice and they are very good to Arnie and I. I mean anything in the line of sweets Mom, but of course I know you don't get very much yourself now so if you can't get it will be O.K."

Training at the HCU was initially for the pilot and the flight engineer to learn the characteristics of the new aircraft. They started the first week on Manchesters, the twin engined forerunner of the four engined Lancaster. We could not wait to get in the Lancasters, but since our skipper and engineer were moving from two engines to four, we were told we need not accompany them until they were proficient. After a week or so however, I took the plunge. We had to show Rosner that we had confidence in him, so we practised taking off and landing, flying and landing on three engines and then two engines. "Cut starboard outer," "cut port inner," "starboard inner," "port outer" ad infinitum, but never less than two engines. It was said that the Lancaster could climb on three engines, maintain height on two engines and even fly on one engine, but we never tried it.

Jim Calder's letter home (March 16, 1943):

"You were saying the weather was nice there, well we have had a great winter here, only had snow once and since I am gradually getting used to the climate it is alright here now. We have had beautiful sunny days here the last couple of weeks so we have been

---

[16.] *This was his younger sister Dot (Dorothy) who was 14 at the time and was in hospital for two years*

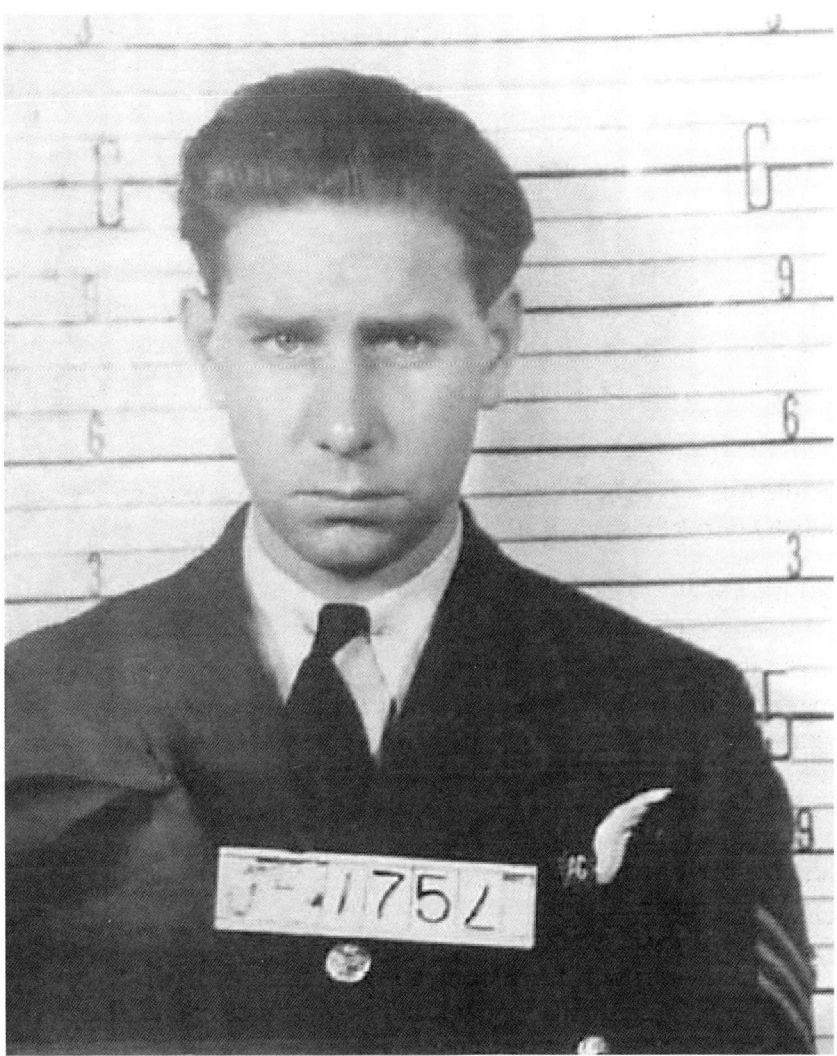

Sgt Jim Calder (LAC Canada)

getting lots of flying time. I was air sick today for the first time since I started flying. I was really sick all the while I was in the air but of course was O.K. as soon as we landed. It really was rough up there this morning. In your last letter you say you haven't heard from me since December 27th. Well Mom you should have because I write at least one letter a week but generally always write three a week, so I don't know why you haven't received them. Arnie's mother was

Lancaster Bale Out

saying in her last letter that she hadn't had a letter from him since December 28th and we both mailed all our letters together, so there must have been something wrong somewhere. I have received all the parcels O.K. so far. I had one from Lucie yesterday so I guess I will have to write to her tonight.

There is one thing I would like you to send Mom if possible and that is a couple of films 620. We have a camera here now and could get some snaps but we can't get films over here now. It seems that I write home for an awful lot of stuff Mom, but I just want you to send it if you can, if you can't make it, it will be alright, but I just make suggestions so that you will know what I like or need. But Mom as I said before cigarettes are the main thing. Arnie and I generally have them as we generally get them at different times but we are both running short now so we are hoping there are some in the next Canadian mail."

After only seventeen days of conversion to Lancasters, we were now ready for operational flying and posted as a crew to 106 squadron based at Syerston in Nottinghamshire.

9.
No. 106 Squadron - Syerston

RAF Syerston was a pre-war aerodrome, situated on the main road between Newark and Nottingham and was the home to 106 Squadron and 61 Squadron, in No.5 Group.

F/O Walter Thompson (W. R. Thompson)

In the words of F/O Walter Thompson, DFC and Bar, a 106 Squadron pilot who arrived on the 11th March 1943,
"Syerston was home to something over two and a half thousand people. Perhaps ten per cent of these were aircrew. The station, like all bomber stations, had its own living quarters, canteens, hospital, food stores, generating plant, playing field and combined dance hall and cinema. Certainly not lush, most of this was housed in austere Nissen huts or wartime buildings. The buildings were

heated by a round, coal-burning stove which never seemed to be lit. The officers' quarters were like all the rest, a Nissen hut with a coal stove. I slept in a bunk in a hut shared with half a dozen junior officers. In the bed next to me was a newly trained English pilot called Brodrick who arrived a couple of days after I did, a replacement for the crew lost on Stuttgart. The station had its own police, security staff and maintenance personnel. The aircraft stores had parts enough to make up a half dozen aircraft. The fuel dump had 2,500 gallon fuel trucks, called bowsers, just enough to deliver a full load of 2,154 gallons to a Lancaster with some to spare and there were small trailers with oil tanks. It took half a day to fuel the station's aircraft. In the bomb dump, crews brought out cases of incendiaries by hand to a section where these were packed into small bomb containers. Belts of ammunition were loaded and guns were sighted and cleaned. The larger bombs were taken out on trolleys and hauled to the aircraft. In the intelligence section, maps and escape kits were collected and sorted for an operation. The kitchen staff prepared and packaged sandwiches, tea, coffee, gum, barley sugar and chocolate for the aircrew. The meteorological staff made up the latest weather maps and wind data and the parachute section was forever airing parachutes in tall lofts and re-packing them for use. The place abounded with mud and consequently wooden paths laid on 2 X 4's led from one building to another. The maintenance crews at the aircraft dispersals built themselves crew huts out of any timber and corrugated tin that they could scrounge. Here again was a round stove and a writing bench for the aircraft records."

We arrived there on 25th March 1943, and were shown the crews' locker room where we stowed all our flying gear, and then were escorted to our barracks. Rosner had been commissioned at conversion unit, and was now a Pilot Officer, so he was escorted to the officers quarters. The rest of us, being Sergeants, were given a room containing twelve beds and lockers. We were however at present, the only occupants. Having settled in our barracks we all decided to go to the Sergeants' mess for a meal and on our way we noticed numerous black, brooding, Lancasters standing silently at their dispersals, at different parts of the airfield. When we reached the Sergeants' mess, coming down the steps from the main entrance, was a navigator, a young man of about twenty one. I didn't recognise

him until he said to me,

"Hello, Fred, have you just arrived?"

I looked again. "Why," I said, "Tom Jaye. We're just going to have a meal."

"Well, that's a pity," he said, "I'm just leaving," and with that I hurried on to catch up with my crew. Tom Jaye was on his way to Scampton to join 617 Squadron, The Dambusters.

Flt. Sgt. Jim Calder, Syerston (F. Smooker)

Lancaster Bale Out

Meeting Tom caused me to reminisce about Roddymoor, the village where we both came from, not far from Crook. His father Jimmy Jaye and my father Billy Smooker were coal miners at Roddymoor Colliery, where I would have been had I not volunteered for RAF aircrew. Tom Jaye had gone to grammar school and joined the RAF before me. I remember his mother telling me that he was based in Nottinghamshire while I was on leave, during training. Tom Jaye wouldn't have known what he was training for at Scampton, but his crew had been hand picked to fly on the Dams Raid[17a]. He and his crew never reached the target as they crashed in Holland on the way out and were all killed[17]. His name is inscribed on the war memorial in Crook.

We collected our meal in the dining room, feeling very conspicuous among quite a number of aircrew Sergeants, Flight Sergeants and Warrant Officers. We were what was known as a 'sprog' crew, as we hadn't done any ops yet. "How many ops have these fellows done?" I wondered. One could not tell. They all seemed quite normal.

If we thought our training was over we were wrong. Up to now we'd flown only in unladen aircraft. The next day we all clambered aboard a Lancaster loaded with about five tons of dummy bombs. The course was north, up to Scotland, east over the North Sea, south down to North Yorks, and west over to the Irish Sea. I always remember from a height of 20,000 feet, while I could see the Irish Sea at St. Bees in Cumbria, Arnie Turner in the rear turret still had the North Sea in view. We flew down the Irish Sea, where I had to locate an island off the Welsh coast and do a simulation bombing on it. We carried on south to the Bristol Channel, and then turned up the Severn Estuary to come home. It was here that I took over the controls of our Lancaster. Rosner called out,
"Hey, Smookie, come up here."
"God," I thought, "he wants me to take over."
Leaving my basic, comfortable position, lying on my stomach in the nose where I'd been watching the landscape pass by far below, I

[17a] *Not all the crews were hand picked for this raid but P/O Lewis Burpee was.*
[17] *Tom Jaye was the navigator of P/O Burpee's crew. As part of the third wave, they were tasked to attack the Sorpe dam, but were hit by flak on the way out and crashed near Gilze Rijen, Holland. They are buried in the Bergen-op-Zoom cemetery.*

went up the steps to find Rosner out of his seat.

"Take over," he said.

I gingerly got into his seat, grasped the control column and placed my feet on the rudders. I flew the plane for about fifteen minutes, but unfortunately I flew it as I'd been taught on the Link trainer, always gazing at the instruments. I tried to keep the artificial horizon level, but it kept moving either slightly above or below. Arnie Turner in the back was complaining about being on a roller coaster.

"Don't look at that," advised Rosner, "look at the natural horizon." This improved things, and I was quite thrilled actually. Although I knew in my own mind that I would have never made a pilot, I had enjoyed experiencing what it was like. We returned to base with Rosner back at the controls.

Jim Calder's letter home (March 26, 1943):

"I have been pretty busy changing stations again. I expect it to be the last change I will make for quite awhile. This place I am at now is very good. It is the best mess I have been in since I came over here and the food is very good. Our quarters are very good and there is lots of entertainment to keep you busy when you aren't flying. I am trying to catch up on my letters now, so Arnie and I are staying in tonight. Neither of us has written a letter for over a week so you can see we have dropped behind quite a bit. I haven't received any of the parcels that you mailed in February yet, so I guess I will drop a letter to Base Post Office tonight and see what is wrong. Some of February's parcels came through O.K. because I got one. I will sure be glad when the shirts and shorts get here as the ones I have now are pretty badly shot. If you can spare it after you get this letter, I could use a little money as I will be going on leave about the end of May and I could sure use all the money I can get.

Arnie and I went into Lincoln a week ago and had a pretty good time. We went to a show in the afternoon and then went to a dance that night, but we missed the last bus back to camp and it cost us a pound to get back in a taxi. It was lucky for us that it was after payday or we wouldn't have had the pound and we would have been stuck. We are in an awful fix right now. We have a big kit bag full of washing and we have to find a laundry. The result is now we are turning the shirts inside out, but they are all about worn on both sides now so I don't know what we are going to do until the rest comes back. This room we are in now there are just fourteen of us and we have all been together ever since we came over so you can imagine what it is like. There are pillows and blankets and everything flying down at the other end, I expect one to land here any minute now. It just reminds me of some of the battles at home when the kids get into it."

We were now very nearly ready for ops. On 27th March, Rosner was told that he was to fly that evening as a second pilot[18] - a 'second dickey' - with an experienced crew to see for himself what a real op was like. He nervously reported for briefing on his own, and the rest of us all assembled at the control tower to see him off, giving him 'V' signs and thumbs up as he and his temporary crew slowly trundled off down the runway in the early evening. We didn't know where they were going at that time. He returned safely in the early hours at about 3:30 am. We discovered the next day that he had been to Berlin with F/O Les Brodrick and crew.
"Hey you guys," he told us, "I know what to do now."
He had learned that to minimise the chance of being shot down it was necessary to keep applying a change of direction, and height, while all the time keeping the Lanc on the same track. By carrying out this sort of tactic, the German night fighters would have more difficulty keeping an enemy bomber in their sights than if they were simply flying straight and level. Of course this was not possible on the run up to the target.

A week later on 2nd April 1943 it finally happened. Our crew was down on the 'Battle Order'[19] and we had to go out in the afternoon to do a flight test in the Lancaster we would be doing our first op in. This was mainly for the pilot to test the engines. We reported for briefing at about 6:00pm, to find out about the operation. All leave was cancelled and telephone contact was cut off. No one outside

---

[18.] *It was originally Bomber Command policy to send new pilots along with an experienced crew for their first one or two Ops to see what an Operational Mission was like. As crew losses mounted later in the war this was less likely to occur.*

[19.] *This was the list that was posted up, detailing the names of the all the aircrew that would be taking part in the nights operation.*

F/O Les Brodrick (L. Brodrick)

this briefing room was to know where we were going, and there was even an armed guard at the door. I learned later that the Germans always knew that we were coming, but they didn't know where. The increased W/T activity before a raid, across aerodromes all over England created a lot of additional wireless transmissions, which were picked up by the Germans. From this they could calculate the numbers of aircraft that would be involved, but obviously they did not know where the intended target was to be.

Lancaster Bale Out

Briefing room (J.N.M. Haffer)

The whole squadron was seated on collapsible chairs in the briefing room. The room was full of cigarette smoke and aircrews would be laughing in a jittery sort of manner. There was an air of expectancy, as we wondered where we would be going. When the squadron commander entered everyone stood to attention until told to sit. Wg. Cdr. Searby[20] strode onto the platform, with his underlings, and the cover over the huge map was removed. "The target for tonight is the 'Lorient', U-boat pens." There were some sighs of relief from some experienced crews. "It must be an easy one", I thought. Our bomb load was to be 11 x 1,000lb armour piercing bombs, to penetrate the concrete of these pens. Take off time was to be 9:30 pm.

---

[20] *Wg Cdr John Searby went on to lead 83 Squadron Pathfinder Force and was the master bomber on the successful Peenemunde raid on 17/18 Aug 43.*

10.
1st Op - Target France

After briefing we went to our barracks and lay on our beds, or wrote letters home. It was a quiet barrack really, we all seemed to be deep in thought. Time seemed to drag. Eventually we drifted off to the dining-room, where we were served by the Women's Auxilliary Air Force (WAAFs), with a bacon and egg meal. It felt like the 'Last Supper'. After our meal we went to our locker rooms and collected our kit, and most importantly our parachutes. The navigators in particular seemed to be weighed down with equipment. In addition to their flying clothing, they also carried a green canvas bag of gear. After a long wait our transport arrived, with a WAAF driver, to take us to our Lancasters, which were standing silent at their dispersals.

Out to the Dispersal (Mrs M. Claridge Collection)

The ground crews were already there - it seemed as though they actually lived there. We all climbed aboard Lancaster R5492, 'S' for sugar, up the metal ladder at the rear of the fuselage. "Should I go into my position or not," I thought. We had been told that it was

Lancaster Bale Out

inadvisable to go into the nose for take off and landing. "Well," I thought, "if we're going to crash I may as well be in the nose as anywhere else in the plane!" So down I went into the nose.

Into the Aircraft[21] (Radio Times Hulton Picture Library)

One by one Lancasters would be lumbering out of their dispersals, and slowly heading for the control tower, where there was usually a crowd of airmen and WAAFs waiting to wave us off. Quite a thrill actually. There was my NAAFI girlfriend waving to me, and I waved back through the Lanc's Perspex nose. I felt quite a hero! I had a fascinating view out of the nose, but when it came to take off, I was beginning to wish I hadn't. One after the other the Lancasters took off with their deadly loads. The Lancaster in front of us was half way down the one and three quarter mile runway and still hugging the concrete. With a roar of engines we started off after them. At first we were crawling, but then the speed built up faster and faster. The Lancaster in front of us took off eventually, but then disappeared down into the valley of the River Trent at the end of the runway, only to come staggering, it seemed, back into view.

---

[21] *Pilot Sgt John McIntosh's crew, L to R, F/E Sgt Seeley, Rear Gunner Sgt Middleton, Nav Sgt Nicholson, Mid Upper gunner and B/A Sgt Ball*

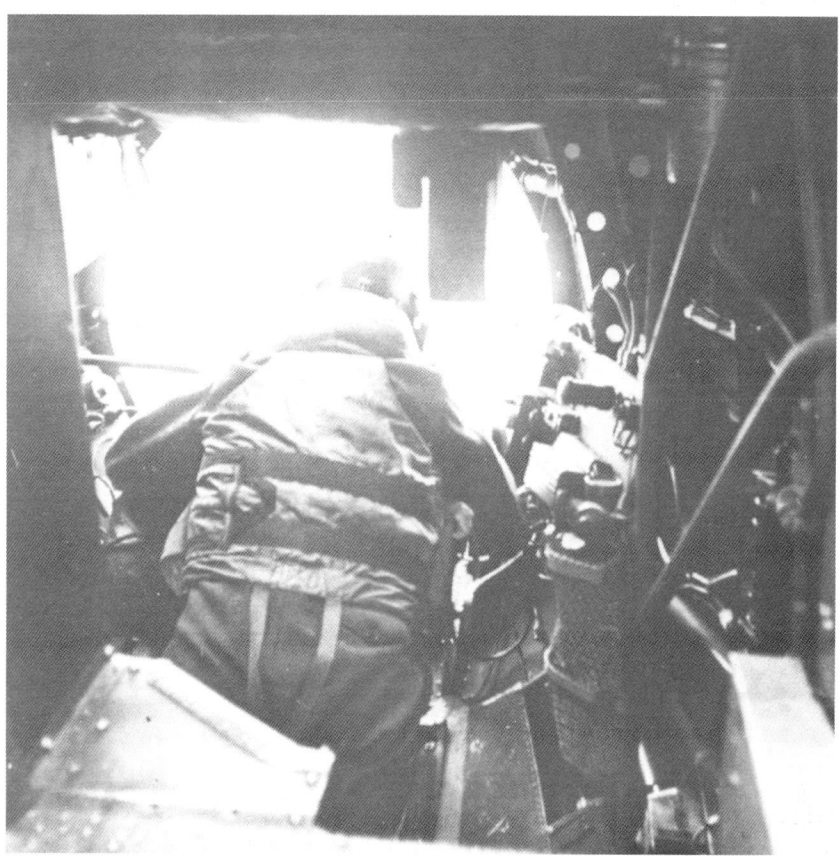
Bomb Aimer position (Portsmouth and Sunderland Newspapers)

I heard the skipper say,
"Through the gate, Ted," meaning push the four throttles into the extra boost position. This position apparently could only be held for a few seconds during take off. At 100 mph the end of the runway came nearer and nearer, until at 120 mph we lifted off, airborne about four feet off the ground. To prevent stalling, the nose up position was flattened out so that airspeed could be increased to a safe level. I wondered if we had also disappeared from the view of the Lancaster behind us, down into the valley. At the south coast we had still not reached our operational height of 20,000 feet. On later operations, we used to fly on a course, or courses, for an hour before reaching operational height, when we'd rendezvous at a vertical searchlight fixed on the East Anglian coast, around about Lowestoft.

Lancaster Bale Out

Lancaster wireless operator position[22] (Paul Popper)

This time however, we were flying straight to the target - Lorient. I think, however, that our Lancaster didn't want to go, because over the English Channel we experienced a most frightening judder. In addition, the intercom went off, so none of us knew what was happening! Coming from my position in the nose, I found Ted Amor and the skipper shouting at each other over the noise of the engines. We ended up writing notes to each other, "should we carry on or not?" We had stopped climbing by now, and after a written debate among the whole crew it was decided to return to Syerston. How did we all feel coming back home instead of carrying on? Feelings were really mixed. Would we be branded as cowards we wondered, but then, with our Lancaster behaving as it was, and without any intercom communication between the crew, what was the alternative?

---

[22] *Wireless Operator Sgt John Hyde adjusts the tuning on the R1155 Receiver at the Lancaster's port Wireless position.*

Lancaster Bale Out

We therefore turned round and headed back to Syerston, only to find when we reached there that we could not even talk to the ground. Messages were sent by Jack Hougham, in Morse code, explaining our predicament.

"How much fuel have you left?" asked the ground.

Ted Amor read the fuel gauges, gave the answer to Jack who signalled it to back to base.

"Fly on a course for an hour," we were told. This action was to use up some of our fuel, and reduce our weight. The maximum landing load for a Lancaster was 60,000lbs, and we still had our 11,000lbs of bombs aboard. We flew for an hour over blacked-out England, and returned. We were then instructed to fly for another half-hour. On our second return we were given permission to land. What a thump when we touched down. That landing gear must have been made of the best of materials. We kept rolling along the runway at a great speed. Rosner could not brake too hard or we might have tipped over on the nose, or burst a tyre, but the end of the runway came ever nearer and I was down in the nose, petrified. The Lancaster wouldn't stop rolling in time to prevent us going off the end, and down into the valley of the Trent.

Into the Trent[23] (E. Dickinson)

[23.] *An example of what could happen to Syerston crews if they had problems during take off or landing. F/O Peter Todd and crew crashed their 61 Squadron Lanc, DV232 QR-K, in the River Trent, after engine problems on landing returning from Mannheim, 6 September 1943.*

Lancaster Bale Out

At the very end of the runway, while still rolling, Rosner must have applied full left rudder, and heaved the control column to the left, because the Lancaster slewed in a huge arc to the left, and we came to a standstill on the grass.

Lancaster Rear Gunner position (K. Delve)

We were now facing in the opposite direction, with our port wing tip sheared off by coming into contact with the steel lamp-post at the end of the runway. The tail wheel was also pulled out of the fuselage by the massive swing to the left. Arnie Turner in the rear turret had the fright of his life and said so in some Canadian vernacular. We all laughed with relief as we made a speedy exit. So ended our first operation. We weren't criticised in any way for returning early, but I never found out what had been wrong with our aircraft.

11.
Onslaught -
The Air Battle of the Ruhr

We had no time to recover from our first op, as the next day - 3rd April 1943 - we were on the Battle Order again, but this time we were pitched headlong into the Ruhr[24]. We attended our second briefing, for what was to be our first operation over Germany. We all stood to attention again, when Wg. Cdr. Searby entered the smoke-filled room. After we all sat back down again, the cover was taken off the huge wall map to moans, whistles and cries of dismay.

Crews waiting for take-off, Syerston 1942 (J.F. Wickins)

"Not again," was muttered from numerous quarters.
"The target for tonight is - Essen, in the Ruhr valley." Drawn on the map were two thick coloured bands, red and blue, showing the German defences of the Ruhr industrial area. Blue was a searchlight

---

[24] *The Ruhr and Wupper valleys were the industrial heartland of Germany producing steel and munitions for war production. Essen, Dortmund, Wuppertal and Duisburg were all clustered around there because of the coking coal, iron ore and the River Ruhr, a tributary of the Rhine. It was Sir Arthur Harris who referred to this period as the 'Battle of the Ruhr'.*

Lancaster Bale Out

barrier and red for the anti-aircraft barrier. From the muted conversation amongst the experienced crews, it was evident that this was a tough one. It was to be a 'Parramatta'[25a] type of operation, where the Mosquito pathfinders[25] would mark the target with a huge, red, splash marker. Backer up pathfinders would aim at this red splash, with other green splashes, to form a pattern of red and green markers, at which we were to aim our bombs. Our load was one 4,000lb high explosive bomb, known as a 'Cookie', plus twelve cans of 11lb incendiary bombs totalling three hundred and sixty incendiaries. Take-off time was to be 10:30 pm, when we would fly on a course until we reached operational height, and rendezvous at a vertical searchlight on the East Anglian coast, where we would circle until zero hour. There were to be some three hundred and fifty[26] bombers on this raid, arranged in four waves. We were in the first wave, after the pathfinders. Until zero hour for our wave arrived, we did a left-hand circuit around the searchlight. Left-hand circuits were the rule, but some pilots seemed to ignore this and would do the opposite, much to the consternation of ourselves and other aircraft. At zero hour, all noses were pointed east, and some two hundred or so Lancasters headed out over the North Sea. All navigation lights were turned off, and we were alone, so it seemed. Our colleagues were there, but, except for the occasional glow of exhausts here and there, we were on our own heading for the Dutch coast, to be followed by other squadrons of Halifaxs, Stirlings, and maybe some Wellingtons. We tested our turrets and guns half way over the North Sea, and reported them to be in order to our skipper, who then told us to keep a sharp lookout for German fighter planes who might venture out to meet us. I settled down in my nose position to search. I could see everything from there, and could quickly get into my front turret if and when necessary. We crossed the Dutch coast at, or near, Flushing. From a height of 22,000 feet we could see all the Schelde Islands below, laid out like the pieces of a jig-saw puzzle. I gave Bailey, our navigator, a fix on one of the islands, and

---

[25a.] *Parramatta was the code name for an operation in which navigation aids were used to mark the target on the ground.*

[25.] *Pathfinders were special squadrons that dropped red or green flares over the target to mark it, so that the following aircraft could drop their bombs more accurately.*

[26.] *Bomber Command War Diaries details the number at 348 aircraft, 225 of which were Lancasters – this being the first time that over 200 Lancasters were used on the same op*

after a few minutes he gave the skipper an alteration of course, to take us north of the Ruhr. On this course the Germans would think we were bypassing the Ruhr, so it was thought. Flushing was said to be a hot spot to be avoided, and we experienced our first time under enemy fire. Some of our colleagues had crossed the coast further north, and were being targeted from Rotterdam, while others had crossed further south and were receiving a massive barrage from Antwerp. The flak we received however from Flushing, was really mediocre, and we were lulled into a false sense of security. We actually received very little attention, because Rosner was weaving like a man demented. We had heard the term "get weaving" but if this was what was meant, I didn't like it at all. However, it was fatal to fly straight and level. Just before we reached our turning point to fly south to the Ruhr, I could see out to starboard a seemingly solid wall of searchlights, interspersed by puffs of black smoke and jagged red flashes. This, I assumed, was the Ruhr defences. It seemed that our pathfinders had awakened a sleeping monster.
"Turn 90 degrees to starboard skipper," called Bailey, our navigator. It was all right for him, he was enclosed in his navigator's position and could not see what he was sending us into. We turned and headed south for Essen, some 50 miles ahead. "How are we going to get through that lot," I thought. As we flew nearer I was reminded of 'The Charge of the Light Brigade' which I had learned at school:

> Stormed at with shot and shell
> Boldly they rode and well
> Into the jaws of death, into the mouth of hell
> Rode the six hundred.

Only this time we were some three hundred and fifty heavy bombers, and I was not on a charger, but in the nose of a Lancaster which Rosner was throwing about all over the sky. "He must be practising aerobatics," I thought. Wherever Essen was it must have been burning because all I could see below were fires. The pathfinders must have also dropped incendiaries.
"Can you see the markers, Smookie?" yelled the skipper.
"Not yet," I answered,
"I'll keep weaving then," he replied. We were buffeted by exploding shells, blinded by searchlights, and it seemed, being hit by shovelfuls

of gravel. In the distance I spotted our red and green pattern of markers, and I tried to get them in my bomb-sight, but due to Rosner's weaving antics they kept shifting from one side to the other. To cries of dismay from our gunners, I shouted to Rosner, "You'll have to fly straight and level." This period of straight and level flying seemed endless. We were sitting ducks. Eventually I got the markers in my bomb-sight, "Open the bomb doors," I called. They opened with a thud.

"Keep her steady," I shouted, then "Left, left, right[27], steady, hold it." Would the target never settle down I thought, and then eventually I pressed the bomb 'tit.'

"Bombs gone," I yelled and my bomb switches went out one by one. "Bomb doors closed," called the skipper, and immediately started to weave again. We continued to fly south, into quieter, although still highly dangerous waters. I was air-sick for the first time, and spilled the contents of my stomach into the Lancaster's nose.

"For God's sake, let's go home," I thought. Arnie Turner, our rear gunner, reported that he could still see Essen burning when we reached the Belgian coast. After crossing the coast at 20,000 feet, Rosner had stopped weaving, and put the nose down, so we flew home across the North Sea at about 300 mph. On crossing our own coast, he was calling base, asking to land. We were still a good 100 miles away. Due to the fact that all aircraft were returning at roughly the same time, we had to queue up to land, and the sooner one called in the better the position in the queue. Lancasters were stacked at intervals of 500 feet, circling the aerodrome, until told to land. After what seemed like an eternity, we were finally given the 'all-clear' to land. What a relief! We'd done our first full operation and survived, albeit a more thoughtful and chastened crew. "Only another twenty nine to go for our first tour," I thought. The raid was generally quite successful although 106 Squadron lost one Lanc, ED 542 - Sgt. Tom Ridd and crew. It had been only their second operation.

The next week we stood down and trained again doing practice bombing runs and fighter affiliation exercises. This came to an end on the 10th April, when we were rostered for Frankfurt. This raid

---

[27.] *The word left was always repeated twice so that there was more chance of the instructions being understood over high levels of background noise.*

Lancaster Bale Out

Lancaster Pilot position[28] (Radio Times Hulton Picture Library)

turned out to be a total failure due to cloud cover in the target area but for us this trip was uneventful.

Three days later we flew our longest trip - a place called La Spezia, in Northern Italy. At this time, 1943, the Germans were retreating before the 8th Army in North Africa, and many German troops, who had retreated as far as Tunisia, were said to be at Cape Bon, waiting to be evacuated. According to intelligence reports, there was supposed to be a fleet of ships assembled at La Spezia, in preparation for this evacuation. We attended briefing for this operation, and learned that some two hundred Lancasters were to fly to La Spezia and destroy this evacuation fleet. There was 10/10 cloud over the whole of France, and the cloud was at such a height that German fighters would not be able to reach us. The target area however, we were told, would be clear. If we had any difficulty, shortage of fuel etc., we could fly on to North Africa to land and our navigator was

---

[28] *Pilot Sgt John McIntosh adjusts the seat in the Lancaster's port Pilot position.*

Lancaster Bale Out

given the necessary details for such an emergency. I knew however, that our skipper would not entertain such an idea. He would come back home regardless. We took off from Syerston at 10:00 pm and climbed to operational height en-route to La Spezia. Sure enough, France was completely blotted out by cloud, and we saw very little, until we reached the French Alps. What a sight to see. Snow clad peaks gleaming in the moonlight, it was almost ethereal, and here we were on a mission of destruction. On reaching the Mediterranean coast we reduced height to 5,000 feet and turned east to La Spezia. I had never visited La Spezia, but I could imagine it to have been a little coastal town, nestling at the foot of tree-covered hills, and a Mediterranean beach in front. Now the whole place was on fire. Any boats in the harbour were also on fire. I don't know if there was an evacuation fleet there or not, but I dropped my bombs in among the burning fishing boats. What a contrast this was to the targets in Germany. The only attempt at defence, was one gun pointing into the air - it could not even reach us and we were down to 5,000 feet. We turned towards home, on a reciprocal course to that which we had come, and I felt absolutely wretched. Over Germany it was easier not to have such a conscience; at least they were trying to kill us, but, this bombing at La Spezia was awful. Our course home was north west, over cloud-covered France, and I was no help at all to Bill Bailey, as far as map reading was concerned. We were flying on his dead reckoning navigation, where any change in wind speed or direction could adversely affect our course. We continued flying on this course seeing nothing, no fighters or other Lancasters, not even a searchlight to light up the clouds over which we were flying, and perhaps give us an indication as to our position. We seemed to have been flying forever. I think the Germans must have had an idea of our predicament because they remained silent, until suddenly over the intercom we heard a voice,

"Hello Swordfish, hello Swordfish, this is Seagull calling. Circle aerodrome at 500 feet."

"Who the hell is that?" was the cry. It was none of the crew, so who could it be on our intercom? The voice was persistent,

"Hello Swordfish, hello Swordfish. Circle aerodrome at 500 feet." It repeated.

"Hey, Bailey, where are we?" called the skipper to our navigator.

Lancaster Bale Out

"Well," he answered, "according to me we're somewhere over France."

"Can you get a fix on the Gee Box?" asked Rosner.

Bailey did his check as requested. The Gee Box, which was an early type of radar navigational aid, had its limitations though, because according to Bill Bailey it placed us over Leicester, his home-city. We could not be over Leicester, unless we'd had a terrific tail wind.

Lancaster Navigator position[29] (Radio Times Hulton Picture Library)

The voice on the intercom continued telling us to circle the aerodrome, but to my mind it had a German accent. I'd never spoken to a German in my life, but somehow I knew it was not an English accent, and could only be German.

[29.] *Sgt Iain H. Nicholson puts on his C-Type flying helmet in the Lancaster's port side Navigator's position.*

Lancaster Bale Out

"Have you got the TR9 switched on, skipper?" I asked.

He checked. "No," he said.

"Well then how can anyone talk to us from the ground?" I asked.

The Germans must have tapped into our intercom frequency. Bailey was desperate to find out where we were, and suggested that we come down below the cloud and have a look. I was one of the oldest members of the crew, being twenty-seven, and up to six years older than most of the others; I felt that I should give some fatherly advice. I advised us to carry on flying, until according to Bailey's dead-reckoning navigation we were at the position over the English Channel where we were to turn north for home. This advice was accepted, and we left our German operator's friendly voice behind. At the ETA at our turning point, over the Channel, Rosner brought us down through the cloud, and the first thing I saw was a white beacon flashing the letters 'BX'.

"Hey, Bill," I called to the navigator, "there's a white beacon in front flashing 'BX'." His 'dead-reckoning' navigation had been spot-on. The beacon was at Dungeness on the south coast. Navigation lights were switched on, and because our fuel was by now so low, we all wanted to land at the first aerodrome we came to - except Rosner. He was going home regardless. That is the way he was, a gum-chewing Yank, but a boy in blue just like us.

The return flight to La Spezia had taken us 10 hours 15 minutes and we landed at Syerston with empty tanks. We heard later that one Lancaster, which had kept flying north west over France for too long, had turned north eventually, and had ditched in the Irish Sea[30]. Another had also ditched off the coast of Cornwall off Falmouth.

The next night we were back on ops again, this time to Stuttgart, which again was reasonably lightly defended and therefore one of the easier targets we flew to. In the words of F/O Walter Thompson, "We were provided at briefing with a map of the target area of Stuttgart and I then began the practice, and asked the bomb-aimer to

---

[30.] *61 Sqn Lancaster ED717 that ditched around 7:45 am off the Isles of Scilly. The crew were in their dinghy for sixty-three hours before all of them were picked up safely. See 'Thundering through the Clear Air' by Derek Brammer, Pages 95-98 for details.*

do the same, of committing the target map to memory. Stuttgart had a good-sized river running through it, with two distinctive bends. The route in and across Germany brought us to a point north and a little east of the city. The night was clear and the visibility was excellent. I could see the river glinting in the moonlight as we approached. Then I saw some yellow and then some red target indicators dropped at the northerly end of the two bends of the river. They were about thirty degrees to starboard off the course we were flying and they didn't look right to me. I dropped altitude from 20,000 to 14,000 feet where I could see better. We could still see the river ahead and the southerly bend of it near the aiming point, which was about 6 miles to the left of the target indicators. I asked my bomb-aimer what he thought. "I think the Target Indicators are wrong and we are right" was his forthright reply.

"Good", I said, "We'll bomb where I think it should be, OK?"

We continued on our run in, slightly south west, altering course a little to port as we went. The bend in the river, which we were approaching, seemed to me exactly as it did on the target map. We ignored the target indicators and dropped our bombs where no other aircraft had bombed. I wondered briefly on the way back to England how we were going to explain this one. The intelligence officer shook his head when we told him at de-briefing. He called Searby over to our table to hear what had happened. Searby said nothing. The next day's photos showed that the Pathfinders had marked the wrong bend in the river. Fortunately for us we had been right.

F/L Brodrick[31] in ED752 did not return from Stuttgart. His empty bunk beside mine was hard to believe."

We were next sent to Pilsen, in Czechoslovakia, on the 16/17th April[32]. We were forced to return again to base as there had been a severe shuddering of the airframe. The bombs were jettisoned and the mission was abandoned. It was entered in our log-books as DNCO - Duty Not Carried Out. It didn't count as an operation for first tour purposes, but in my mind it had been just as hairy.

[31.] *F/O Brodrick and and 2 other crew members spent the rest of the war as POWs, the remaining members were killed. See Appendix B.*
[32.] *See 'A Shaky Do' by Peter Cunliffe for an in depth account of this Operation*

Lancaster Bale Out

It was Bomber Command policy to award crews ten days leave every six weeks and our turn came on 19th April 1943. Generally most crew members would head off back to their home towns and villages, dispersed throughout Great Britain. The Commonwealth crew members though, usually had no such luxury and were resigned to staying on the base, with friends or long distant relatives. Bill Bailey would often take Jim and Arnie back to his family home in Donisthorpe with him. For the families it was a welcome relief to see their loved ones but very few knew, or would have been able to comprehend, the horror and sheer terror of flying at 20,000ft through a wall of flak over an inferno of a burning German city. Many a family found it hard to come to terms with the loss of sons whom they had seen one day and were lost the next, such was the policy of taking the war to German soil.

Going on leave after a night's operation was tiring, but I would rush to Newark and catch the train to Darlington or Durham city. I would arrive home just in time to hear the one o'clock news, being announced by Frank Phillips. "Last night a force of our heavy bombers carried out a raid on Duisburg."
"I was there," I would announce proudly, but then Frank Phillips would say, "Thirty five of our bombers failed to return." I am afraid my poor old mother was not impressed.
"You could have been one of the thirty five," she would say. She was right of course. Losses of this magnitude were common after every operation over Germany. Up until now we had been lucky, six times over enemy territory, and most of them to the Ruhr. Even though one of them was a DNCO, our lives had still been at risk. Losses at Syerston were not excessive, although the six empty beds in our barrack had been occupied twice and now a third crew was in occupation. I learned that an aircrew was at very high risk on their first operation and also crews going on leave after an operation or flying an operation after returning from leave seemed to spell danger. Something untoward happening, to disrupt the natural sequence, often brought about a crew's down-fall.

Lancaster Bale Out

Sgt. Jack Hougham, home on leave (C. Smith)

Lancaster Bale Out

Jim Calder's letter home (April 28, 1943):

"Well we have been on leave the last nine days and I haven't had much time for writing. We are having beautiful weather here so we have been out around seeing the part of London we didn't see last time. We've really been having a swell time. I suppose it is nice and wet at home now but over here everything is green and has been for a month now. The blossom is all just about finished and it has only rained twice in the last three weeks so that is pretty good for this country. I guess we're kind of getting used to it now. Well as usual we are broke now but it doesn't matter as we have to go back tonight anyway and Friday is payday so it isn't too bad this time.

I guess I had better finish this letter now; I am back in camp I didn't get around to finishing it in London. When I got back to camp (last night) there were cigs and quite a few letters for me. I was real glad to see the cigs. Arnie had three parcels, so we had quite a little lunch before going to bed.

Well Mom there is a big dance in the camp here tonight so I guess I will get dressed and go. I haven't much I can write about. I have lots I would like to tell you but the censor wouldn't let it through anyway."

When we returned from our leave, we were tasked to fly to Essen again on the 30th April/1st May. We next flew trips to Dortmund on the 4/5th May and then Duisburg, a week later on the 12/13th May.

The next night ops were on and we were tasked for Pilsen again. As we had done previously, we carried one 8,000lb bomb - a 'Blockbuster'. This bomb was like a small 'Lancashire boiler' or to be more precise, a huge cylinder, with three detonators in one end. Due to the size of it, the bomb doors of an ordinary Lancaster would not close properly, and therefore some Lancs were specially adapted to carry it. These aircraft were known as 'pot-bellied Lancs due to their distorted shape. It didn't seem to affect the performance however. After I had dropped our bomb on what I believed to be the Skoda works, and we were on our way home, Rosner told us over the

Lancaster Bale Out

intercom, that he was going to 'climb as high as she would go', for our return journey across enemy territory. He eventually climbed the Lanc to 27,000 feet, but after that she wouldn't go any higher. It was a fairly long trip to Pilsen - 7 hours and 50 minutes - but we returned safely. We found out later that the operation had been a failure again.

Jim Calder's letter home (May 14, 1943):

"I have lots I would like to tell you but of course can't write about it. We've had it very quiet for the last ten days but as you know by the news we had a little excitement the last two nights; I had a pretty good time. I see you are following me around on the map, well as you see none of the moves have been very far apart but this is about the nicest part of England I think. I also got the parcel with the other shirt in it Mom. There is one thing you don't have to send now and that is coffee. We don't have anything to make it up now and don't bother to send any more of that stuff I asked you to send for Bill, I would sooner have lots in the parcels. I never thought to tell you she was brunette but it won't make much difference. Never mind trying to send stockings because I know you can't get them O.K. I still am not getting many cigs; I have only had two lots since I came here to this station. You mentioned a watch, well as you know I smashed the one they gave me and now I can't get another one, can't even buy them over here and I sure need one bad.

Well I am glad to hear that Ralph[33] didn't join up, he is alright at home. I don't see any need for two of us to get in this, although I can see it must be awful now with the taxes and no one there to go around with. He says he doesn't think he will bother again, so I am glad to hear that.

I suppose the snow is gradually leaving now and everyone is talking fishing, eh? Arnie and I were in London for Easter, but it is just the same as any other day over here. I went into Newark the other night and went to a dance, had a good time, the best dance I have been to since I came here. I met a girl who could really dance, so I am going

---

[33] Ralph Calder was Jim's younger brother

Lancaster Bale Out

back there more often now. We are having a big dance in our mess Sunday night (if there is nothing else to do) and she is coming out so I expect to have a good time. As a rule these dances are generally terrible as I can't find a girl who can dance the way we do, but this one sure can, so I think I will just hold on to her. She is a real nice looking kid too (Oh boy, a blonde)!

There is one thing I want to ask you Mom, could you get along O.K. if I cut my allowance? We are allowed to draw our full pay now and I could sure use some more money. You see I am just drawing fifteen dollars a month more than you are getting and over here it really goes so would it be O.K. if I cut it down to twenty? Then again before I get your answer I may have had a promotion and if I get it I won't need to cut it down. Arnie and I were up to headquarters when we were in London and all Canadian promotions have been held up for three months. I should have had my first promotion four months ago, but everything is mixed up so I don't know when it will come through now."

Jim Calder's letter home (May 21, 1943):

"I am glad to hear that you are getting the watch, as I really need one. In my last letter I mentioned that I might cut my allowance. Well I have decided not to. I figure I can get along but I may have to wire for some money for my next leave, which comes up about the end of June. There are a few things I need Mom, if you can get them. They are braces, shorts, soap and socks (light ones like the last ones). Mom never mind sending any more of that stuff for Bill, that will be plenty that is on the way now. I would sooner have stuff for myself. I haven't had any cigs for a long time and Arnie and I are both about out. He had six hundred two weeks ago and they are just about done so I am hoping to get some soon. So Ralph has increased his bond eh? He will have lots of money when I get home, won't that be nice. At present I am exactly broke and it is still a week to pay day, but I know a cute little blonde in Oakham who just loves to spend money. She's making more than I am so I guess she will just have to spend it for the next week! We went to a dance here on the station last night and had a pretty good time, but came home early as we had to fly all morning and part of the afternoon today.

Well Mom as you know I have been on operations for quite awhile now and really enjoy it. I have had some real good trips, as I told Ralph in his letter, but the best was the one over (place censored) and then a couple to (place censored) but at the end of (censored) hours flying a fellow is pretty glad to get down and into bacon and eggs and then to bed for the day. I suppose you have heard about the raid earlier in the week, when the two dams were bombed. It really was a wonderful feat and it will certainly be remembered for a while. It has really slowed him down a lot and he has lost a lot of his most important industrial centres. The people in the Rhur are sure kicking up an awful fuss now, so I don't think myself they can stand up to too much more of this that we are handing out to them now.

I have had a couple of letters from girls in Montreal. I guess they are kicking up an awful fuss because they can't get liquor over there now. They were telling me that even Montreal is getting dead now so I guess it must be bad. I am just as glad I did come overseas although I have lost an awful lot of pals in the last couple of months. We got word last night that one of our best pals (Arnie's and I) had gone. We just left him before we came here and we thought he was coming here too but he went to another squadron so we missed him.

Well Mom I guess that is all for now, I have completely run out of writing material. One other thing I could use is writing paper, the stuff we get here now is no good at all."

We went back to Dortmund again on the 23rd/24th May and then Dusseldorf on the 25th/26th May. Our third trip to Essen, the home of the Krupps[34] armament factories, was on the 27th/28th May and then Wuppertal on 29th/30th May. All these ops passed without any major incidents.

We were now due some leave again, so after a quick shave and clean up, I headed straight for Newark, to board my train for home. It was beautiful summer weather and on some daylight evenings - we were

---

[34.] *The armament factory of Alfred Krupp known as the 'Weapon Smithy of the Ruhr' produced over 2,000 heavy guns during the course of the war and was therefore a prominent target for attack by Bomber Command.*

Lancaster Bale Out

on double summer time - near my home, scores of Halifax bombers could be seen heading north in a nose up attitude. "Where will they be going?" I was asked. These aircraft were from Middleton St. George and Croft, near Darlington.

"They are climbing to operational height," I would explain, "before going out over the North Sea." Sure enough, after about 15 to 20 minutes these bombers returned, higher, levelled out and heading south.

I didn't want to go back after this leave, but I had to. I bade my parents farewell, and hid my reluctance to go as best I could.

Jim Calder's letter home (June 13, 1943):

"Well as you see by the paper I am on leave again. Arnie and I got in last Monday and it is now two weeks since I last wrote to you, so I suppose you are beginning to wonder if something has happened to me? I am still O.K. and having a great time but as you know I never did write too many letters. I got your ten dollars two days after I sent the cable for money and boy it sure came in handy. We are going back to camp tomorrow because our finances have run out, however we have had a week and really have had a swell time. We were going to go down to Bournemouth but we didn't get around to it, so we'll go down there next time I guess. It is really lovely weather here now and I suppose they are beginning to talk beach at home now although I think it will be pretty quiet this year and I doubt if there will be very many who will bother going at all.

I received two parcels (April 15th, May 3rd) just before I came on leave so I am hoping the watch will be there when I get back. I received three hundred cigarettes also just before I came and boy was I glad to get them. As I told you before never mind sending any more of that stuff for Bill, but send me some writing paper will you? Mom this stuff we get here now you can't even write on it. I understand Mom that it is getting pretty tough now for you to get stuff yourself, so don't worry too much about parcels.

The first day I was in London I met Danny Adams again, he only had two days left of his leave but boy did we have a good time those two days. He is just as funny as ever. Never a dull moment all the while we were with him. We went up to Hyde Park one afternoon and rented a boat. What a time we had, we were all soaking wet but we had some fun. We met Jim Rushton and Benny Livingston at the Beaver Club. Two nights ago I was going up town to meet Gene (our pilot) when who do I run into, but Ronny. He had just got in.

I haven't had my picture taken yet but we took some snaps of the crew so if they turn out I will send them on to you. I am still going around with this girl from New York, but it is nothing serious on my part anyway. She is a really nice kid and a good looking. I will send you a picture of her later.

Well Mom I suppose you are hearing and reading about all these heavy raids now, well for the next while I will be taking part in those. It really is nice to be able to see all those bombs going where they will do the most good. Bombing may not win this war but certainly is playing a big part in it. As you know those last two Islands were practically taken by bombing. They had to surrender, and Germany itself is certainly beginning to feel the weight too now, as he is getting pounded from all sides, he is trying to move some of his industries but he just can't do it. He always said there would never be a bomb dropped on the Ruhr Valley, but he was certainly mistaken and before long that place will be wiped out completely. As you know Bomber Command is getting stronger everyday and thus there is only one thing the raids will be bigger and bigger until he is wiped out completely.

Well Mom I guess I have run out of news for now. I suppose you are having a great time with the kids now that vacation is almost here. Well Mom give my best regards to all at home."

Once leave was over again we returned and flew to Krefeld on the 21st/22nd June, Mulheim for the second time the next night and then Wuppertal - Elberfeld the night after.

It was on the next raid to the Ruhr, on 25th/26th June, that we were nearly shot down. The target was Gelsenkirchen, not too far from

Lancaster Bale Out

Essen, and it was to be a 'Wanganui'* type operation. This type of operation as opposed to 'Parramatta', was performed when there was 10/10 cloud. Instead of bombing at coloured markers dropped on the ground by the pathfinders, parachute flares were hung in the sky. Flying east and tracking north of the Ruhr as usual, we would see a white parachute flare, where we were to turn south. A green flare further on would indicate our track, and eventually a red flare would be my aiming point. I had to put special settings on the bomb-sight for this type of operation. All went well for a while, but suddenly the cloud had disappeared, and the searchlights were probing the sky. To our consternation, Arnie Turner in the rear turret, shouted that the red flare, which was to be my aiming point, was behind us. By misfortune, we must have passed the pathfinders. We obviously were alone over this heavily defended area, and then suddenly out of nowhere we were coned - caught in the apex of a number of searchlights. We had seen other aircraft coned in this manner, and had watched transfixed, as the pilot had twisted and turned in desperation, to get out of the blinding light, only to be eventually set on fire, and plummet to the ground. Rosner had learned a trick or two though.

"Jettison the bombs, Smookie," he yelled.

"Open the bloody bomb doors then!" I yelled back.

The bomb doors opened with the usual thud. I hit the jettison switch and we dropped our bombs on what I believed to be Essen. Our Lanc must have risen a thousand feet but the searchlights still had us in their grasp. Rosner now shoved the nose down, and we dropped in a screaming dive to about five thousand feet. We had lost the searchlights at last, but now we were disorientated and lost. We decided to fly west, in the general direction of the North Sea. Fortunately Bailey's course for home had been good, and we got back to Syerston. We were extremely relieved to be back after this op, we knew we had been lucky this time, but was our luck running out I wondered? Gene Rosner's usual practice, after landing and taxiing to our dispersal, was to grab a torch from one of the ground staff mechanics and minutely go over our Lanc looking for holes in the fuselage. He was actually hoping to find a piece of flak to keep as a souvenir. This time however, he found a hole, high up near his

---

* *Wanganui was the code name for an operation in which navigation aids were used to mark an unseen target in the sky.*

cockpit. At the left side of the pilot's position was a Perspex blister, large enough for the pilot to put his head in, in order to look to the rear. The Perspex blister had disappeared. If his head had been in there when a piece of flak had spattered it, his head would have been blown off too. He never did find his souvenir, but he did find quite a few holes.

Jim Calder's letter home (June 26, 1943):

"Just a note to let you know I am O.K. I suppose you heard about the four raids we did through the week and I suppose you were wondering about me. Well Mom, I sure got my fill of excitement last night. We really got shot up bad, that was the first time we really got hit bad. We had just dropped our bombs when we got hit the first time and it came right through the bomb bay and hit our oxygen supply so we had to dive from 20,000 to 10,000 feet, because we couldn't stay up there without oxygen. Well we got hit several times more on the way down and when we got home the plane was just like a sieve. None of us were hurt at all, but I'm telling you I don't want to come any closer than that. Of course that doesn't happen very often, that was the first time in twenty trips that we got hit, so it is not bad, eh?

Well Mom I am getting two days off this week so Arnie and I are going to London again. As I told you before we have a Yankee pilot, well he is transferring to the American Air Force so he has to go down to London for a couple of days to get his new uniform etc, so we have that time off. He is one of the best pilots that ever (censored) into a plane and I'm telling you he has gotten us out of more than one tight spot (censored) flying over here. As soon as he (censored) he will be going to the (censored) Air Force and the rest of (censored) be going on some other station (censored) instructors.

Yes, Mom I need a new pair of shoes very bad, size 8, and I would like them the same as the last ones if you can get them. If not a pair with no toe cap just the plain toe. I got the money you wired me O.K. so it will come in handy on these two days I have off.

Lancaster Bale Out

Arnie and I went into Newark last night but Arnie doesn't dance, so he went to the show and I had a date with a little blonde I know there so we went to the dance. We had a good time but I missed the last bus and had to walk home[35]. Boy, never again. I'll make sure I get that last bus from now on. Well Mom I guess I am running out of space I will have to close for now. I have about four more letters to write. I had a letter from Gord yesterday he is still O.K."

Lanc Flight Engineer position[36] (Radio Times Hulton Picture Library)

[35] *This was a distance of around 6 miles so probably would have taken him a couple of hours*
[36] *Flight Engineer Sgt Ron Seeley of 207 Sqn adjusting the controls on the Lancaster starboard panel.*

Lancaster Bale Out

On the 28th June 1943, we were briefed for an operation on Cologne. It was to be a 'Parramatta' type of raid, with pathfinders marking the target with a regular pattern of red and green splashes. While the defences were not so fierce as the Ruhr, they were hot enough. Were we becoming complacent though? We were beginning to adopt a "nothing will happen to us" attitude. During all of our eighteen raids, the two gunners and myself had never actually fired our guns in defence.[37] We had seen enemy fighters, but they always seemed to be, fortunately, after other aircraft. We had been hit by flak, blinded by searchlights, but had always got back home unscathed. This operation again followed a similar pattern.

Sgt. Eugene Rosner (LAC Canada)

---

[37] *It was extremely rare for the nose guns in a Lancaster to be used for defence, as attack from enemy fighters was usually from behind and below.*

12.
Op 20 - Return to Cologne

Rosner had been pestering the United States Army Air Force (USAAF) authorities for a while to accept him into their ranks, and when we met him the next day at our crew room, he announced that he was going to London to re-muster and he would try to arrange a weekend pass for us.

F/O Gene Rosner, on leave in London (R. Schwartz)

He had joined the American air force before the war as a trainee pilot, but had been washed out, as there was no requirement at that time for any more pilots. When the war started in 1939, and Canada had come into the war, he had gone over the border and joined the RCAF, where he had proved his own mob to be quite wrong. Now at last the USAAF had agreed to accept him, although he was to finish his tour of duty with us at Syerston. Somehow this was a bad omen I thought. My fellow crew-members commented on my silence, so I forced myself to cheer up. After a week, during which we did nothing but lie about in our barracks, Rosner returned in his new regalia. This consisted of an olive-green tunic, with a pair of wings on each breast (RCAF and USAAF), light fawn trousers and an American peaked cap.

"I liked him better when he was in RAF blue, albeit the darker Canadian version," I thought. Somehow, he was now a stranger to me, although he was still our pilot. Soon after he was back he got permission to visit an American air force base in Norfolk, and we all flew with him. He wanted to get some USAAF flying kit. It was bad weather, operations were postponed for the time being, and when we flew over the American air base we could see all the B-17's wrapped up in tarpaulins. When we commented on this seeming lack of action at this American air force base, it was amusing to hear our skipper criticising his American countrymen.

"These guys can't fly when the weather is bad," he remarked.

We were given permission to land, and our big, black Lancaster became the focus of attention from these Yanks.

"Are these guns loaded?" asked an officer to Arnie Turner.

"Yes, Sir, they're always ready for action," he answered, whereupon the officer ordered a notice to that effect, to be placed on his four rear Brownings. Rosner left us, and went off with an officer. He went to the officers' mess, and to the stores to see what he could purloin in the way of American flying kit, or maybe shoot a line or two about his operations against our common enemy, I thought. The rest of us were escorted to the sergeants' mess where we had a meal, 'Yankee style'. We all sat at one table, adopting an air of arrogant know it all, and listened to the ribald chatter of our comrades in arms. I think the only kit Rosner managed to get was a pair of American flying boots, not much different from ours. All in all, I think it had only been an excuse to show his countrymen how wrong they had been

Lancaster Bale Out

Lancaster	Time Up	Time Down	Duration	Pilot	2nd Pilot	Flight Eng	Nav	Bomb Aimer	Wireless Op	Mid Upper	Rear
ED 720	22:10			Rosner	Disbury	Amor	Bailey	Smooker	Hougham	Calder	Turner
ED 919	22:10	03:50	05:40	Crowe		Flower	Crewe	Feltham	Keill	Dunn	Christie
EE 191	22:10	03:50	05:40	Browne		Neal	Lynn	Pepworth	Hayhurst	Williams	Berry
DV 182	22:15	04:10	05:55	Robertson	Read	Ingram	Fairweather	Willett	Taylor	Moseley	Tysall
R 5665	22:15	04:30	06:15	Stephens	Cole	Garbett	Bayne	James	Grimes	Holton	Taylor
ED 358	22:20	04:55	06:35	Hoboken		Lucas	Jenkins	Graham	Read	Rutter	Broome
R 5573	22:20			McLean		Leigh	McLeod	Muir	Barrett	Johnson	Handel
ED 360	22:25	01:40	03:15	Bristow		Scattergood	Johns	Hazel	Worthington	Murphy	Sims
R 593	22:25	04:45	06:20	Harvey		Brownjohn	Neale	Bull	Edgecombe	Bell	Mantle
R 5614	22:25	01:40	03:15	Browne		Hebbes	Archer	Browne	Cleeve	Astwick	Cubitt
DV 181	22:30	04:45	06:15	Hayley		Horten	Hevinen	Miller	Rathbone	Ball	Hambling
ED 303	22:35	04:40	06:05	Ham		Gale	Pitman	Jones	Weight	Waller	Higham
R 5609	22:35	04:25	05:50	Whetter		Grey	Johnson	Worsdale	Cameron	Woolf	Smith
W 4242	23:30	04:30	05:00	Charters		Slack	Jordan	Roche	Maben	Doyle	Davies

Cologne Battle Order (C. Smith)

in washing him out before the war. He was now a 1st Lieutenant in the United States Army Air Force, but he still had to finish his tour of ops - thirty in all - with the RAF.

The weather at the beginning of July 1943, had been too bad for operations over Germany, but by Thursday July 8th, skies had cleared, and we were scheduled for briefing once more.

Our old Squadron Commander, Wg.Cdr. Searby[38], had left and we now had a new Wg. Cdr., called Baxter. Our briefing was for a return to Cologne, only this time it was a 'Wanganui' type of operation, since the target was predicted to be covered by cloud. There would be nearly three hundred[39] bombers on the raid, and the Lancasters would carry one 4,000lb bomb, twelve cans of incendiaries plus a 500lb bomb in each corner of the bomb bay; our load had been increased by 2,000lbs.

P/O Geoff Disbury (M. Disbury)

[38.] *He had left on 9th May 1943 to join 83 Squadron, Pathfinder Force.*
[39.] *This was primarily a Lancaster only raid, with 282 aircraft detailed, according to the Bomber Command War Diaries.*

Lancaster Bale Out

On this trip, in addition to our own crew, we would also be taking along a 2nd trainee pilot whose name was Geoff Disbury[40]. He was a Sergeant pilot and was going with us to gain experience of operational flying before flying his first Op with his own crew. What a combination I thought. This was our first operation after returning from leave; Rosner had just become a 1st Lieutenant in the American Air Force; Wing Commander Baxter had just taken over the squadron; and for the first time we had a second pilot on his first operation. I was becoming superstitious. Bill Bailey used to carry a little mascot for luck, and Rosner always carried his gold cigarette case and lighter.

Over the Target[41] (Imperial War Museum)

[40.] *Geoffrey Francis Disbury was the son of Robert and Frances Gertrude Disbury of Whitby, Cheshire. He was born on 11th June 1922. He had studied history at Manchester University and then after volunteering for the RAF, was sent to Oklahoma, America, to carry out his initial pilot training.*

[41.] *A photoflash picture captures another Lanc over Hamburg on 30/31 January 1943.*

Lancaster Bale Out

We were flyng Lancaster ED 720 'R' for Robert, the usual kite of P/O Fred Yackman. Take off was 10:10 pm and our trip over the North Sea was uneventful. Sure enough as we went over the Belgian coast we were above the clouds, that the met. men had predicted. We continued on our track until a point north of Cologne, where a white flare was dropped and we turned south for the target. Then things began to happen. Searchlights turned the clouds into a dazzling, white sea of snow; I felt that I could get out and walk on it. We began to see that we were not alone on our journey of destruction; in front and to either side could be seen the black silhouettes of our accompanying Lancasters, from whom no help was possible in the event of a disaster. The illuminated clouds were now beginning to be splashed with jagged, cherry-red flashes, which disintegrated into red-hot coals. The green flare appeared directly ahead. We were right on track - and so was the flak. The jagged flashes were now all around us, and I could feel my insides begin their usual churning and my flesh and skin began to tighten. All my instincts told me to cringe and curl up into a ball. We cruised at some 220mph towards our aiming point. The pathfinders had hung a number of these red flares, so that we wouldn't all be heading for the same one, and risk a collision. Rosner told me our airspeed and altitude over the intercom, while I busied myself setting the special adjustments to the bombsight. By now we had ceased our continuous climbing and diving, weaving to port and starboard, and we were flying straight and level over a white shiny carpet mottled with an angry red glow. On my instructions the bomb doors were opened, to expose some five tons of high explosive and incendiary bombs, to the hail of red-hot metal being thrown at us. It seemed an eternity before the red flare came into my sights and I literally screamed,
"Bombs gone!"

Our Lancaster leapt 1,000 feet higher on being released from the load in her belly. Within seconds we had the bomb doors closed, but we had to continue to fly straight and level until the photoflash had been released, at which point the skipper again started our Lancaster doing its jiggling and weaving as if our lives depended on it - which they did.
As we continued south, the worst of the holocaust was beginning to retreat behind us, and my taut nerves began to unwind as my brain

Lancaster Bale Out

told my body to stop pumping adrenalin into my bloodstream.

"Keep a look out for fighters," called Gene to the gunners and myself. I lay on my stomach in the nose, gazing out of my huge Perspex dome. When we reached the turning point on our south track, we turned on a westerly course, over Northern France, for home, as plotted by Bailey. We were at some 22,000 feet.

"Hello, skipper," called Ted,

"The starboard outer is heating up."

"OK, Ted. Keep an eye on it," replied Rosner.

Minutes later;

"Hello, skipper, the starboard outer temperature is worse and still climbing."

"OK, Ted. We'll have to feather the prop. Stop the engine and fly on three."

After a while on three engines, the inside temperature of the plane became extremely low, and I found that one of my feet had numbed with the cold. Crouching in my bomb aimer's compartment I slipped off my boot and massaged my foot back to life.

"Hey, you guys," called the skipper,

"I'm going to fly straight and level to keep up with concentration."

Lancaster Mid Upper Gunner position (Imperial War Museum)

Lancaster Bale Out

This concentration, although invisible, consisted of two hundred or so other Lancasters carrying out the same tactics as ourselves. All were flying at more or less the same height and airspeed, to prevent the German defences picking up on any individuals. As we were now only flying on three engines, our airspeed had dropped and we were becoming more vulnerable.

"Hey, Smookie," called Gene, "can you get at my feet and give them a massage?" Of course I could if I stood up in my compartment, his feet on the rudders being just at my shoulder height. I pulled my left boot back on, undid the zip fasteners on his boots and commenced the massaging operation on the skipper's feet - his feet being more important than mine in this situation. After five minutes or so, my own left foot was numb again, so I asked Ted if he would come down and take over, while I re-attended to my own. I think the skipper and I must have had damp socks, because no one else complained. While Ted was doing his stuff and I had my left boot off again, there was a terrific, sickening crash. The Perspex dome in the nose of the Lancaster disintegrated and a blast of ice-cold air gushed in, swirling target maps and other sundry items about the place.

"There's a fighter!" yelled Jim, from his mid-upper turret. I scrambled up into the front gun-turret but the controls and hydraulics were dead. I was helpless.

"The starboard inner's on fire," yelled Jim.

"OK, Ted," said the skipper calmly. "Get back up here."

Ted went back up the steps to his usual position at the pilot's right hand side to operate the fire extinguisher and feather the engine.

"Turn to port," yelled Jim again. Rosner threw the Lancaster into a corkscrew* dive and the two port engines started to speed up in an increasing crescendo until they were almost screaming like banshees.

"Hey, you guys, we've got to bale out," screamed Rosner. "Somebody get me my chute. Bale out! Bale out! Bale out!"

Our two screaming port engines suddenly stopped dead, and then came the most sickening of sensations - falling like a stone out of the sky in a dead aircraft. I could not believe it even as I grabbed my chute and clipped it on. It was impossible! It could not be

---

*The corkscrew was the standard defensive manoeuvre consisting of a series of steep diving and climbing turns in alternate directions

Lancaster Bale Out

Lancaster loss (P.B. Browning)

happening! I pulled at the handle of my escape hatch in the floor upon which minutes ago I had been squatting. The square hatch then wedged itself across the hole, and when kicking it free I realised that I still only had one boot on. Even then I was expecting the engines to restart. I didn't want to bale out, but to stay meant death. Gripping my ripcord handle in my right hand, I went feet first into the gaping hole in the floor. My legs were swept under the belly of the Lancaster and away went my one remaining boot. My Mae West had inflated inadvertently and had me stuck fast in the hole. I managed to wriggle and writhe free and with one hand still on the ripcord handle I dropped out into the darkness.

13.
Home Front - Kent

Living in Kent, through the days of the Battle of Britain, John Hougham would have been used to spitfires and hurricanes flying overhead. Three years later, he would have been hearing the more familiar sound of bombers overhead flying to and from enemy occupied territory during the night. He had been working that morning on the railway with his brother George, at Betteshanger Colliery. He had cycled home for lunch and was now preparing to return for the afternoon shift when there was a knock at the door. He went to answer it and was greeted by the sight of the postman standing there handing him a small buff envelope. John Hougham knew immediately what this meant and his heart sank as his wife Ada came into view. He opened the envelope slowly and read the message "Deeply regret to inform you that your son Sgt. I. Hougham[42] is missing from Operations night 8-9 July letter follows"

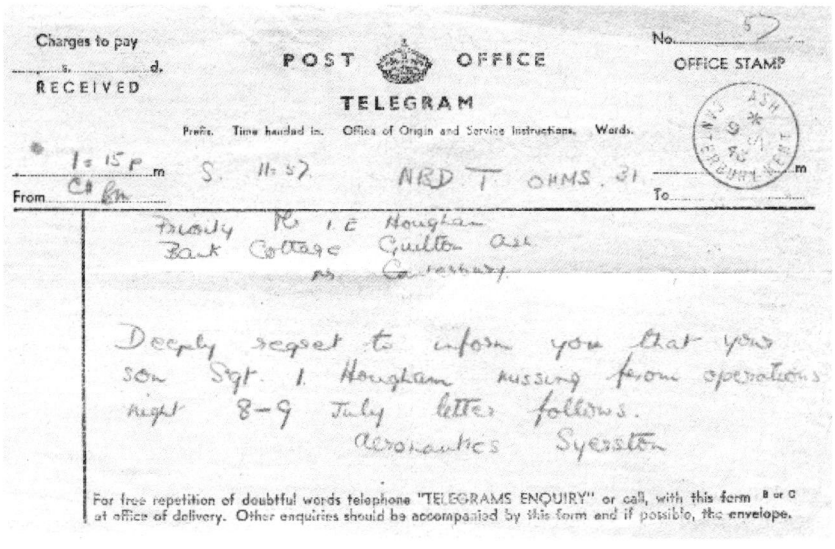

Missing (C. Smith)

---

[42] The initial 'I' on the telegram was incorrect and should have been 'J' for Jack

Lancaster Bale Out

Up and down the country a similar scene was playing out to numerous other families. It would take longer for the information to reach the American and Canadian parents.

The Squadron Commander would often write personally to the parents of the missing airmen and would sometimes provide details of the next of kin for the other crew members too so that they could write to each other. At least it was some consolation that other families were going through the same worrying times, although human nature often clung to false hopes.

```
Gerrard 9234
                                                    Casualty Branch,
                                                    73-77 Oxford Street,
                                                    London.W.1.
P.406129/6/43/P.4/A2.

                                                    31st July, 1943.

        Sir,
               I am commanded by the Air Council to express to you their great
        regret on learning that your son, Sergeant Jack Houghan, Royal Air
        Force, is missing as the result of air operations on the night of 8th/9th
        July, 1943, when a Lancaster aircraft in which he was flying as wireless
        operator set out to bomb Cologne and was not heard from again.
               This does not necessarily mean that he is killed or wounded, and
        if he is a prisoner of war he should be able to communicate with you in
        due course. Meanwhile enquiries are being made through the International
        Red Cross Committee and as soon as any definite news is received you will
        be at once informed.
               If any information regarding your son is received by you from any source
        you are requested to be kind enough to communicate it immediately to the
        Air Ministry.
               The Air Council desire me to convey to you their sympathy in your
        present anxiety.
                                        I am, Sir,
                                             Your obedient Servant,


        J.E. Houghan, Esq.,
             Bank Cottages,
                Guilton,
                   Ash,
                       Canterbury,
                             Kent.
```

Standard Casualty Letter (C. Smith)

14.
Down in France - Evasion

I didn't count to ten - I just pulled the handle. I felt the plane pass over me, then I was whirling in space, cringing as if expecting a sudden violent shock which would jar the life out of me.

The sudden shock came - but I was still alive. However, I had a burning pain in my groin. I was hanging beneath my parachute. I very gingerly reached up with both hands to grasp my shoulder straps and ease the weight off my groin. The chute gave a lurch and my heart almost stopped, then thud, I hit the ground. I lay on my back, and looking up I could see my parachute canopy slowly collapsing on the ground in front of me. I stood up, and immediately my legs gave way. My ankles were lifeless. "God," I thought, "my ankles are broken." Some 500 yards away I gazed in shocked disbelief at my blazing Lancaster in an adjoining field.[43]

Lancaster Wreckage[44] *(J. Alwyn Philips)*

---

[43] *ED 720 'R' crashed into a field of wheat, adjacent to the Cambresis railway station at L'Epinette, north east of the village of Quiévy.*

[44] *Lancaster ED 781 from 57 Sqn, was shot down on night of 24/25 June 1943 returning from Wuppertal. The circumstances of the loss were very similar and as can be seen the aircraft crashed into a wheat field at Lantin, near Liège, Belgium. Only the bomb aimer, Sgt Lambdin, survived to become a POW.*

Lancaster Bale Out

Then came the awful doubt that surely no one else could have got out in time? Overhead, the continuous droning of Lancasters. Come and get me I prayed. Then reason returned. What could I do? I could help none of my comrades. Instructions came to the fore. Hide your parachute and get away from the plane before the Germans come to investigate. I got to my feet again and this time stayed upright. Thank God, my ankles can't be broken, only sprained. Hobbling about I bundled up my parachute into a ball, but where could I hide it? I was in a field so, pulling up some long grass, I laid the chute in a hollow and covered it over, not very well hidden, but I was going to have enough to do to walk, without lugging a parachute with me until I found a good hiding place. "Get away from the plane," I thought. I turned my back on the blazing Lancaster and with great difficulty, hobbled away in my socks, gasping with pain as I went, until all was quiet. No burning Lancaster, no droning Lancasters overhead, only me in a field in the north of France at about 3:30 am. I continued to hobble across fields, skirting one in which frightened cattle were milling about, until it was breaking daylight. I climbed over a fence into a narrow country lane. Crossing the lane, I climbed another fence and was hobbling through a cornfield when I decided to lie down and rest in the corn. I immediately fell asleep.

When I awoke the sun was high in the sky and I had a raging thirst. The full course of events which had happened passed through my mind and I started to cry. My parents would maybe now have had a telegram to tell them I was missing. Were all my crew really dead? I didn't know for sure. Surely Jim had managed to get to the door in the fuselage[45] - and Jack and Bill? Rosner must have got out of the top escape hatch[46] I thought. I was on my own here, in a cornfield in German occupied France.

It must have been raining while I was asleep, so to quench my thirst I sucked rain from the ears of corn. We were issued with an escape kit for operations, containing various supposedly useful items of assistance. Horlicks tablets, maps of Europe, in the form of silk

---

[45] *The Lancaster was the most difficult of the heavy bombers to get out of in an emergency because of the positioning of the escape exits, followed by the Stirling and then the Halifax.*
[46] *The Escape hatch above the cockpit on a Lancaster was only supposed to be used when ditching on water and therefore Rosner would have had to exit via the front hatch in the nose*

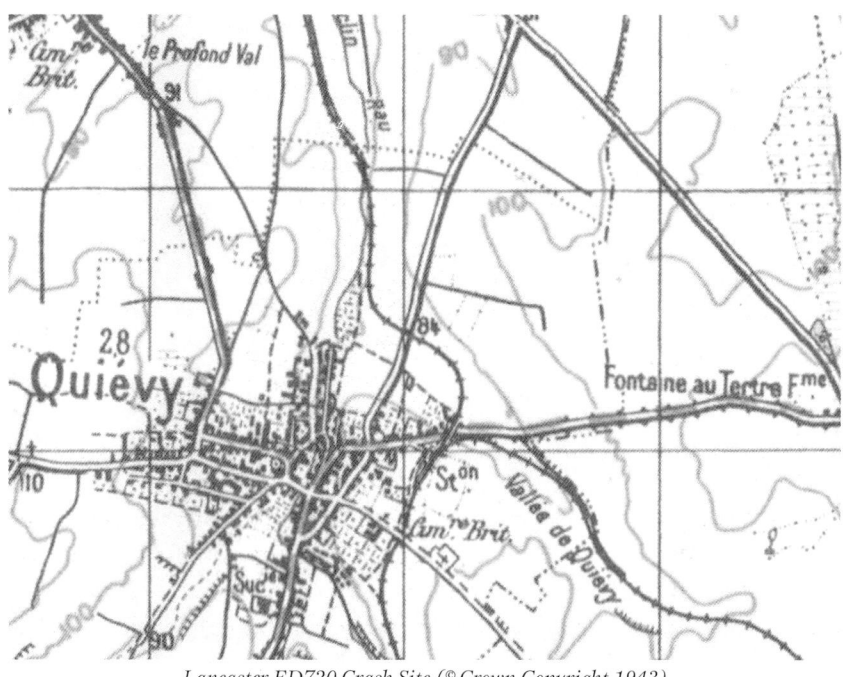
Lancaster ED720 Crash Site (© Crown Copyright 1943)

handkerchiefs, a small hacksaw blade and a rubber water container. I also had a small, sealed, can of orange juice on my person, but I could not open it because I had no tin opener or a knife, and I still had a raging thirst. I dared not stand up in case I was spotted, so I poked my head over the top of the corn, and found that it was only a square patch that had not yet been cut. About 100 yards away some women were gathering stalks of corn which had been left by the reaper. I thought of calling out to them to help me, but I decided against it in case they might give me away. Next to an area of corn in another direction I saw a patch of potatoes, and further on a water trough. I lay down and went back to sleep again.

When I next awoke it was dark. I tried to stand up, but I could not because my ankles were swollen to a terrible size. My flying trousers had elastic braces so I cut them off, with the hacksaw from my escape kit, and bound my ankles. I could still not stand and actually crawled on my hands and knees, out of the corn, and over the potato patch to the water trough. My thirst was terrific so I had a good drink from the trough. I filled my water bag, but it was useless

- I could not carry it with me because it was just an open rubber bag, so I threw it away in disgust. Using the trough as a support I managed to get onto my feet. I realised I would not be able to walk on rough ground so I decided to get on to the country lane which was smoother. Walking on the lane was easier, so I had the idea that I could walk to Switzerland. I must have been delirious. After a while, maybe 15 minutes, I heard the clip-clop of horse's hooves. It could be a mounted policeman I thought, or a German on horseback. We had been told that there was a curfew in France, everyone had to be indoors by 10:00 pm. I didn't know the time but I thought I had better get off the lane, so back into the fields I hobbled agonizingly. I don't know how long I suffered but eventually while negotiating another cornfield I fell down, and said words to myself to the effect "sod this for a lark" and remained lying in the corn, where I went to sleep again.

Upon awakening again it was daylight, and under normal circumstances one would have thought what a beautiful summer morning it was. It was now Saturday, July 10th, and the only thing I could think of was, I needed a drink, I was extremely thirsty. I managed to stand and noticed, near a gate in the cornfield, there was a water tank on wheels with shafts for a horse to pull it. I hobbled out of the corn towards the gate and found this tank had a tap on the end where I again quenched my thirst. I seemed now to have come to my senses. I could never walk to Switzerland, and I had to either give myself up, or get some help. I went out of the gate and sat down on the bank of a country lane. After a while I heard voices - French - and soon two men on bicycles came along. They passed me and then stopped in their tracks. They came back to me and I pointed to my chest and said "Angleterre." I know little French, but they jabbered on together "Avion, quatre moteurs, etc." One of them offered me his bread, but I refused. I was not hungry only thirsty. As I said I know very little French but I understood when they said that they had to go to work. I was disappointed at first, but then one of them pointed across the fields and said "Petite ville, pas Allemands." I looked where he was pointing and could see a large square tank up on a high girder framework. I took this to be a water tower, and after they had wished me "Bonne chance" they cycled off. I was on my painful way again, heading for this water tower. Eventually I arrived, and found myself at some gardens. I climbed the fence and walked down someone's garden path. I will not say hobbled again, it goes without saying.

On reaching the end of the garden, I came into a cobbled street of cottages and there leaning on his back door post was a man smoking a cigarette, and taking in the morning air. He saw me, and motioned with his arm for me to go to him, as if he was expecting me, and disappeared inside. I walked to his house[47] and entered, and found him pacing the floor smoking furiously. It was a peasant cottage with a brick floor, and in the corner was a hand pump for water. It really was quite basic inside.

"Monsieur," I said pointing to the pump, "Can I have a drink?"
He came out of his fright then and said,
"Oui, oui, Madame, café" he then disappeared through another door which I assumed led to a bedroom. I went to the pump and drank my fill, and then sat down on a chair. When he returned he was followed by his wife, who was still in her nightdress. When she saw me sitting she crossed herself as a Catholic would and I thought the poor woman was about to faint. Being the gentleman I am, I stood and said
"Madame, sit down." She refused and somehow made some coffee, which we drank, while she and her husband conversed together in French. Then she disappeared, and returned dressed for going out, and tried to tell me something that I could not understand. After she had left, her husband and I tried to converse in our two languages. We didn't learn much, although I assumed that his wife had gone to get the nearest police officer. The man was called Jean Baptiste Bauduin[48], although I was not told this at the time, and was the Garde Champétre - the village policeman.

The lady returned later accompanied by a huge man wearing a butcher's apron. He spoke some English.
"My name is Chamberlain," he said,
"Have you your papers?"

[47.] *The cottage was at 41 rue Voltaire, Béthencourt.*
[48.] *Jean was born on 18th December 1886 so was 57 years old*

Lancaster Bale Out

Monsieur Bauduin and Family (S. Besin)

"I have no papers", I answered, "but I have my identity discs," which I showed to him.

While he was interrogating me the lady was proclaiming,

"Il est Anglais, Il est Anglais." The reason for all this, I learned later, was because the Germans used to carry out such a charade, just to find out which French people were helping Allied airmen. In addition to my dirty dishevelled appearance, I found that I had a swollen mouth and had a gash on the inside of my cheek. Thinking it over, I realised that I must have forgotten, in the panic, to unplug my intercom, and disconnect my oxygen mask before baling out. When I had dropped from the plane, the whole lot had been whipped from my mouth. I was lucky that I hadn't been suspended from my helmet. Chamberlain was finally satisfied that I was English and told me that I'd have to get rid of my uniform, indeed everything English, even the woollen pullover which my mother had bought for me, and which I wore under my battle-dress blouse.

Juste Caullery, alias 'Chamberlain' (S. Besin)

I was then ushered up a flight of stairs - brick steps really - and into a room containing a double bed, with old iron bed ends. The window had no glass, just a wooden shutter. This was indeed a poor peasant's cottage; but who was I to be so fussy. I got into bed in my underwear, and Chamberlain told me that I could stay there for a while and left with my clothes, promising that he would get me back to England in five days time. 'Chamberlain' was in fact the code name for Monsieur Juste Caullery, who was the Mayor of Béthencourt and an active member of the local 'Réseau' - escape line.

Lancaster Bale Out

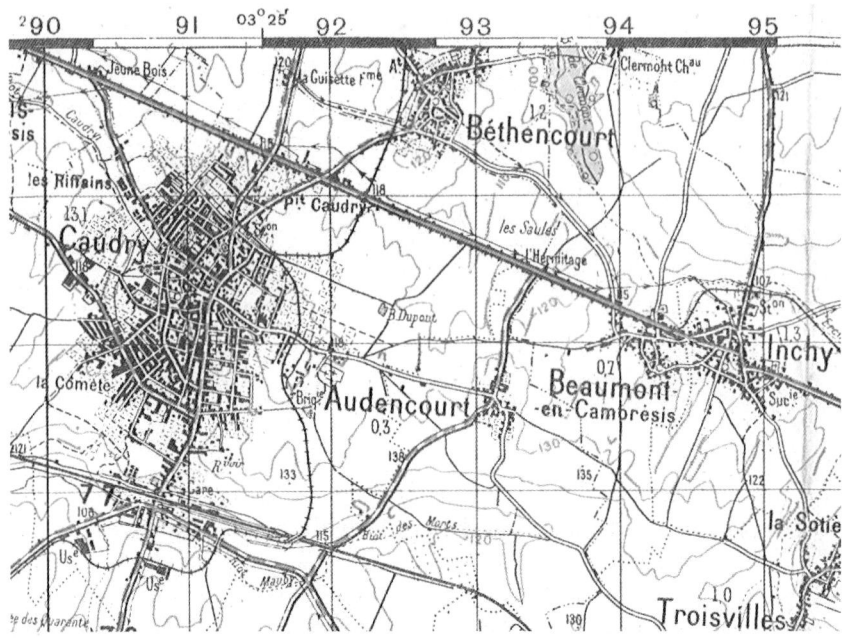

Map of Béthencourt and Caudry (© Crown Copyright 1942)

Soon I was asleep. I was awakened about midday, by my old friend, with a plate of chips, meat of some kind, and a bottle of French beer. Never had I tasted anything so good, at that time. My old friend, who I learned was the same age as my own father (fifty-seven), sat with me and we tried to converse together. I never discovered his name as I have said for security reasons, but he could not have been kinder if he had been my father. He produced some kind of oil and massaged my ankles. He asked me if I wanted a shave, and produced a cut-throat razor, soap and a shaving brush. When he saw I was having trouble with the razor, he offered to do it for me instead. During my stay there, he even emptied my chamber pot. I often have said that it seemed as if he had been standing at his door, that Saturday morning, waiting for me to arrive. I discovered that the name of this village was Béthencourt, but I saw very little of it.

The next day was Sunday and I was awakened by the sound of church bells, and the voices of children. Looking out of the partly open shutter, I could see some children[49] playing on a haystack, so I immediately got back into bed. The old lady had been to church, and they told me my "avion" had crashed near the town of Cambrai. Six bodies had been recovered, and the people of Cambrai had scattered flowers over the site. The Germans, however, had stopped this because they said the French people didn't do the same for crashed German planes. I was extremely saddened by this news, but at least there was some hope that I was not the sole survivor - I excitedly told my friends that another of my fellow crew-members must have got out of the plane in time.

I stayed with this elderly couple for five days, which meant five days in bed for me. I grew very fond of them. On the fifth day, as promised, 'Chamberlain' arrived in the morning with some new clothes for me and asked me if I could walk 5 km. I answered that I would try. He then gave me a pair of black pin-stripe trousers, an old shirt, old mackintosh, a pair of large oversize brown boots and a black beret. I was worried about looking like a civilian in case I was thought to be a spy if caught, but I thought I would be all right as long as I still had my identity discs.

Chamberlain returned at about 6:00pm in the evening, and told me to follow him, but to stay 25 yards behind him. I felt heartbroken. It was a tearful farewell from my friends and I could not express my gratitude in French, all I could say was
"Vive La France."
I was hugged and kissed on both cheeks. It was a very emotional goodbye[50].

Chamberlain kept at a slow pace as I followed behind him. I was still struggling with my ankles. Eventually we arrived at the outskirts of a town. A teenage boy on a bike cycled past us in the same direction, and five minutes later we caught up with him, as he had stopped to pump up his tyres. Here and there in the streets, women were

---

[49.] *One of these children would have been Genevieve, the Bauduin's only daughter who was seven at the time. Fred was not told about her though - probably because the Bauduins were afraid that she might give him away. Genevieve Pointeau died in 1999, and was still living in the same house that Fred had been sheltered in.*
[50.] *In fact the Bauduins never forgot this "Anglais" whose memory was so dear to them.*

Lancaster Bale Out

standing gossiping in the summer evening, and seemed to gaze at me as I passed by, probably wondering who the young tramp was. We turned into a street and Chamberlain disappeared into a doorway[51].

Lucien Janssoone (S. Besin)

Gilbert Janssoone and fiancée Jacqueline[52] (F. Smooker)

[51.] *The house was at 12 rue Zola, Caudry.*
[52.] *Gilbert subsequently married Jacqueline after the war but she was tragically killed in a road accident in 1976. Gilbert still lives in Cambrai today.*

Lancaster Bale Out

Fred and Janssoone[53] (F. Smooker)

When I arrived, I also entered - the door was open, but it immediately closed behind me, and from behind the door there stepped a small man, who shook me by the hand and said,
"Good evening, my name is Janssoone[54]. The first thing we will do, is have a cup of English tea."
He was the Headmaster of a local school, and the town where he lived was called Caudry. He introduced me to his wife, Yvette who was also a school-teacher, but could not speak English. His son Gilbert was seventeen, and he was the boy who had cycled past us,

---

[53] *Note the French-English dictionary on the table.*
[54] *Lucien Janssoone. Born 23 march 1898 at Ghyvelde (Nord) would have been 45 and was part of the Réseau Castille*

Lancaster Bale Out

before we got here. Janssoone's first name was Lucien and he too was a very ardent member of the escape movement. After bidding me farewell, Chamberlain left, and I think he was relieved to have rid of me. I never saw him or my old friends from Bethencourt again. Janssoone got a doctor to examine my ankles, who, after a cursory examination, proclaimed that my ankles weren't broken and hurriedly disappeared. This man was a Doctor Victor Lesage, a friend of Janssoone's and he was taking a very big risk going round there.

Dr Lesage (S. Besin)

At the Janssoones, I was made very welcome, well fed, and given my own bedroom. I was instructed, however, to remain very quiet in my room, as Monsieur Janssoone said,
"We have a maidservant who comes in daily, while we are at work. She is trustworthy, but the fewer people who know you are here the better."
All day long therefore, I was locked in my room and could hear the servant working. I read numerous books in English. One book I remember was 'Three men in a boat' by Jerome K. Jerome. The Janssoones were very anxious to know when the English and

Americans were coming to liberate them. As if I knew? All the time Janssoone was talking to me in English, Madame Janssoone would ask,
"Qu'est ce qu'il dit?"
On one occasion I burst out laughing at this, and Janssoone asked me why I was laughing. I said in French,
"Quand je parle avec Monsieur, Madame toujours dit, qu'est ce qu'il dit."
I didn't want to seem ungrateful, and accepted the applause in good humour. I felt like a small child who had just said its first words. I did begin to talk some French after that. Dressed as I was I felt very scruffy in that household, which was quite a well-to-do residence. However, they were very kind to me. I had a bath and a shave, and they fitted me out with some decent civilian clothes, and shoes. They also fed me well during the ten days I was there, in spite of the severe rationing of food - of course I didn't have any 'coupons'.

Gilbert and Fred (F. Smooker)

Lancaster Bale Out

While I was there, one night, a little old lady arrived, dressed in a long, black, coat. I don't know how old she was, but I guess about seventy. She could not speak English, but proudly showed me a medal, which she claimed was presented to her by King George V, after WWI, when she had been working with Nurse Edith Cavell[55]. She talked and talked - in French. Janssoone produced an identity card for me in the name of 'Petit George'. He told me that at night when they heard our bombers passing over en-route, or returning from Germany he used to go out into his garden with a torch and flash the 'V' sign into the sky. He also invited one of his neighbours from across the street into his house to see me and we discussed the progress of the war.

In fact Fred was not the first RAF evader that Janssoone had helped. A 9 Squadron RAF Wellington (W5703) had crashed nearly two years previously on 27 August, 1941. Janssoone had harboured two of the crew from that aircraft - Sqn. Ldr. H.E. Bufton[56] and Sgt. W.F. Crampton[57]. Both returned safely back to England, in November 1941.

Sqn. Ldr. Bufton, Janssoone and Sgt. Crampton (S. Besin)

[55.] *Edith Cavell was born in 1865 in Swardeston, Norwich, and in her twenties moved to Brussels and began a nursing career. After the start of the First World War, she began helping wounded British soldiers to avoid capture by the Germans, and certain death. She had aided over two hundred men, before she was caught and arrested by the Germans. Tried, and sentenced to death by a military court, she was executed by firing squad on 12 October 1915. Her death caused worldwide condemnation and turned her into a martyr.*

[56.] *Sqn Ldr 'Hal' Bufton later became the first person to bomb a target using the Oboe electronic aid, on 20th/21st December 1942 flying a Mosquito with 109 Squadron.*

[57.] *Sgt Crampton survived this incident only to be killed on the first 1,000 bomber raid to Cologne, on 30/31 May 1942.*

Janssoone told me in confidence, about the little old lady in the black coat, that they called Madame Souris - Mrs Mouse. She was in fact Madame Balési (alias Madame Blanche) and owned a café in the 'Coron de Viesly' area of Caudry.

All in all, on the Friday of my ninth day there, I was pleased when Janssoone told me I'd be going on the train to Paris the next day, Saturday July 24th. Early next morning he took me into his back garden, and told me to hide in the summer house. He went through the gate and stood in the back lane, anxiously checking his watch. I could see that he was worried. Eventually a canvas topped van arrived with a driver and a passenger in the front. The passenger was called Richez, but I'd never met him before. Janssoone told me to quickly get into the back of the van, while he and Richez conversed excitedly in French.

Commandant Richez was the head of the L'organisation Civile et Militaire (OCM), the escape organisation, and he lived in Le Cateau. He had a small textile factory, the firm was called TISCA Ltd., and had two offices in Paris. The driver, Maurice Thuru, also lived in Le Cateau and was an electrician by trade. Because of this, the German Police had given him an 'Ausweiss', which was very useful for his main role as an active member of the escape lines. The canvas topped van had been used on many previous occasions for transporting escapees.

Edouard Richez (S. Besin)

Lancaster Bale Out

Maurice Thuru (S. Besin)

15.
No. 9 Squadron - Bardney

9 Squadron Lancaster ED 480 'U' took off from Bardney at 10:30 pm Friday 9th July 1943 - target Gelsenkirchen. The journey was relatively uneventful, but after dropping the bomb-load the aircraft was hit by flak. The wing tanks were holed and the Lancaster began losing petrol fast. The skipper, Sgt. Duncan, decided to head for France knowing that they had no chance of getting back to base. The bale-out order was given at about 3:00 am near Le Cateau Cambrésis, Northern France. The exit was a controlled one, all the crew had time to clip their parachutes onto the harness, unlike in an emergency escape. Sgt. David McMillan[58] - 'Mac' - the rear gunner was the last but one to leave the aircraft, the skipper followed.

Lanc ED480 'U' Uncle[59] (N. R. McCorkindale)

All the seven crew made a safe landing, Mac coming down in a large grass field about a mile south west of the town, although badly spraining both his ankles on landing. He hid his flying gear and parachute[60] under some brushwood and had to sit for a while, as his legs were quite numb from the shock. When he could move them and walk freely he headed in the direction of some clock chimes, believing the sounds to be coming from a church where he could summon some help. He knew that the plane had crashed not far away[61] and thought that if he walked too far, he would come up

---

[58.] *David Basil McMillan was born on 3rd April 1922 and came from Hamilton, Ontario, Canada.*
[59.] *Lancaster ED480 at Waddington in February 1943. The pawnbroker's symbol was quite a popular emblem on many a 'U' Uncle.*
[60.] *Mac actually wrote to Irvin, the company that made the parachute, after the war thanking them for their product that had saved his life.*
[61.] *The plane crashed outside Troisvilles at a place called Borne Bleu*

Lancaster Bale Out

against the cordon, which by now the Germans would have had round it. He decided to hide somewhere quite near. While passing through the outskirts of the town, he heard someone whistling and scaled a low wall to get out of sight. In so doing he made a noise and found himself covered by the rifle of a young German soldier. There was no way he could escape and was marched with his hands above his head to a guardroom nearby. He was searched by a more senior soldier, who handed him back his escape kit, purse and pencil, but confiscated his cigarettes, watch, matches and a ten-shilling note. He also overlooked his escape compass button on his battle-dress. He then made him write down his name, rank and number on a piece of paper before telephoning someone to get some transport. As none was available, he was then marched off again by a German private. His ankles were still very swollen and giving him a lot of pain, so after walking for a little way, he sat down on low, stone, wall and took off his flying boots. He pointed to his ankles and begun to rub them. When the private showed signs of impatience and wanted him to put his boots back on, he turned round to reach one off the wall and accidentally knocked it off. In feeling over for it in the darkness his hand came in contact with a large stone. He pretended to be in considerable pain and held up his hand for the soldier to pull him up with, and as the soldier obliged, Mac crashed the stone against the side of his head. The German went down with a clatter. He then tried to get the bayonet off his rifle, but failed. Searching him he managed to recover his watch and cigarettes, but found little else of any use. The German was still quite senseless, bleeding slightly from his nose, so he bundled him over the wall. He was feeling quite shaken now and his only thought was to get out of the town, although he was tempted to go back and get the German's boots.

He got onto a main road and according to his compass began to travel south. One time he was forced to hide in a ditch to avoid a German motor cyclist. He started out at 04:30 hours and by 09:00 hours had reached a village called Busigny, on the Le Cateau to Cambrai road. He then went to the local railway station to see if he could catch a train. There was an elderly French clerk at the booking office and he asked him for 'Un Paris' putting down four of the fifty Franc notes from his escape box. He gave him the ticket without any comment

Lancaster Bale Out

Flt. Sgt. David 'Mac' McMillan (J. McMillan)

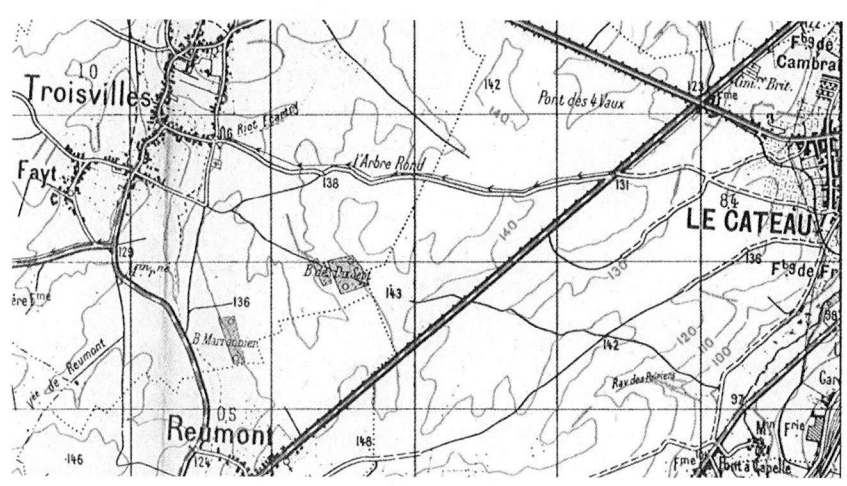

Map of Troisvilles and Le Cateau (© Crown Copyright 1942)

Lancaster Bale Out

and handed back two of the notes and some small change.
He asked, "Train quelle heure?" and the clerk wrote down 4:30 on the back of the ticket. He then left the station with the intention of passing the time hiding somewhere. Just outside the station he passed a farm cart upon which three young Frenchmen were sitting. They called out in French to begin with and when Mac did not reply, one called out in English. He then told them who he was. They took him to a small field outside the village, before going off to get some food. After an hour, two of them returned accompanied by a middle-aged Frenchman, who spoke English. He was a Doctor Bernard and he advised against providing any civilian clothes saying that Mac could be shot as a spy if caught.

Madame and Monsieur Bates (S. Besin)

Lancaster Bale Out

Mac was left hiding in the field for the rest of the day, but towards evening the man returned accompanied by Maurice Thuru. He then drove Mac in his van to Catillon, where he was hidden at the house of a Monsieur René Sents, a farmer and member of the escape organisation.

Navigator, Flight Sergeant Henry 'Harry' Thomas Brown, upon baling-out of the stricken Lancaster ended up landing in a tree near a village called Pommereuil, about three miles East of Le Cateau. He cut himself free from his parachute, which was entangled in the tree, and then ran off. After about three miles he went into a wood and slept until 5:00 am. Taking off his tunic, he was in the middle of cutting off his Sergeant's stripes when he heard German voices quite close by. He hurriedly pushed his tunic into some undergrowth and ran off again. After a while he came to a farmhouse and decided to knock at the door and ask for shelter. The farmer was a Monsieur Durieux. Harry Brown spoke no French, and after much difficulty managed to convey to the farmer that he was English. The farmer then went off and returned in the afternoon accompanied by a man who did speak English. This man asked Harry if he knew anyone that could help him, or if he wanted to give himself up to the Germans. He replied that he had no friends in France and stated that it was his duty to try to get back to England. The man left and returned later with a complete set of civilian clothes for him, accompanied by a woman who spoke good English. This woman was Madame Bates; a French lady married to an Englishman. She took down his details, such as name, rank and number, and took away his escape kit and the remains of his uniform (anything that would betray him as being an RAF airman) and told the farmer to destroy it.

On the evening of the 10th July Madame Bates took Harry by car to Richez's house at 17 Rue de La Gare, in Le Cateau. He spent the night there, and the next day, at 7:30 am Richez and he left by train for Paris. They went to his office in Paris where he left Harry while he went off to make contact with the escape organization. Richez returned later in the day but said that he had been unable to find anyone to help and that they would have to return to Le Cateau, which they did.

Lancaster Bale Out

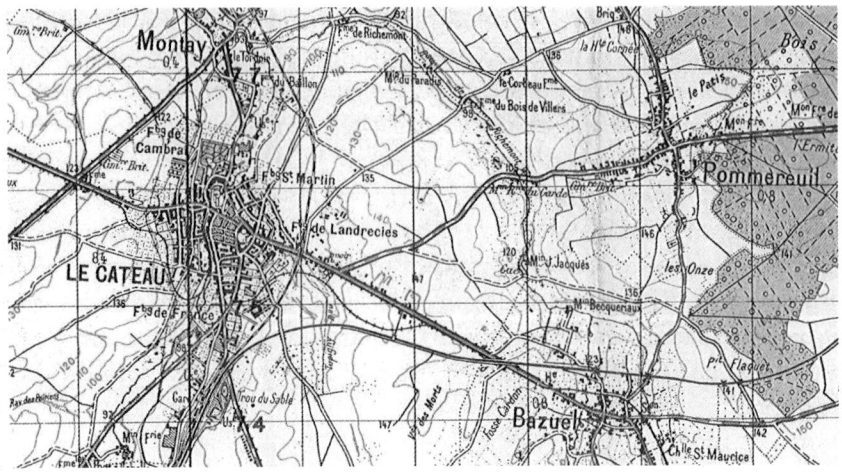

Map of Le Cateau and Pommereuil area (© Crown Copyright 1942)

On the 12th July, Madame Bates returned again to see Harry and told him that Richez would continue to try and find an organization in Paris and in the meantime he was to be moved to Monsieur Delporte's house in Montay, north of Le Cateau. Maurice Thuru again provided the transport and drove him there where he remained for eight days. Madame Bates also told him that Sgt. McMillan was being sheltered at Catillon and that Sgt. Blunden (the Flight Engineer) had been injured and taken to hospital.

On the 20th July he was taken back again to Le Cateau, this time to Maurice Thuru's house. Two days later Mac joined him and they were both given false identity cards produced by Theophile Boyer, another resistant and expert forger. On the 24th July Mac and Harry were loaded into Maurice Thuru's van and driven the six or seven miles to Caudry, accompanied by Commandant Richez.

Lancaster Bale Out

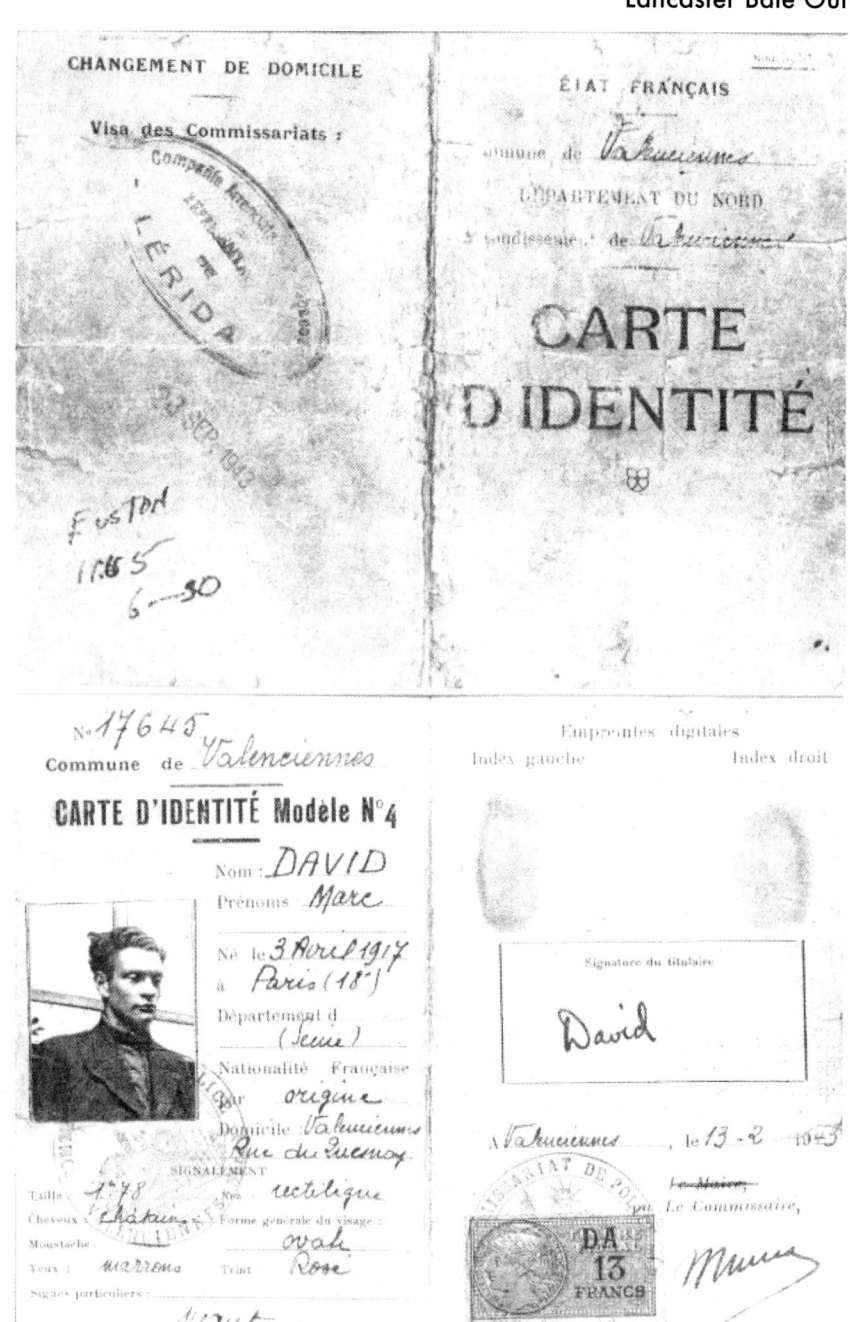

Mac's Identity card in the name 'Marc David' (J. McMillan)

16.
Friendly Faces - RAF Company

When I got into the van, I was surprised to find that there were two RAF airmen already in there. We introduced ourselves and exchanged stories of our evasion. One of the airmen was called Harry Brown, and the other, a Canadian, I knew only as 'Mac'. I was relieved somewhat that I was no longer alone in my plight; now there were three of us.

Harry Brown (1st left), Mac (2nd left) and crew[62] (J. McMillan)

We drove off at high speed, leaving Janssoone behind. We sped through country lanes, going like the clappers, and after a while we heard a car horn blaring behind us. Looking through a chink in the canvas top, I saw a taxi tearing after us. It pulled alongside, trying to pass, and I spotted Mrs Mouse in her long, black coat seated next to the driver. She talked to Thuru, who was driving our van, as

---

[62.] *L to R: Sgt Harry Brown (Nav), F/Sgt David McMillan (Rear gunner), unknown (Pilot), Sgt Sidney Hughes (W/Op), unknown (Bomb Aimer). This photo was probably taken at OTU whilst training as a crew of five.*

Lancaster Bale Out

we sped along, and eventually the taxi went ahead. After a further hair-raising ride we stopped outside Arras railway station. I could see Mrs Mouse talking to a porter outside of the station, and then she came to our van and climbed in front with Richez. Off we went again up a side street and then we stopped. Mrs Mouse and Richez came to the back and told us to get out, which we did. Richez then got back into the van and off it went leaving us with Mrs Mouse in Arras.

The plan was that we would get on a train here to take us to Paris. We would be looked after on the train by a woman from Arras. I never knew whether Mrs Mouse was going with us or not, but the Arras woman had other escapees with her, so it seems reasonable to think that Mrs Mouse would also have been going too. However, what happened was that she'd overslept, and due to the delay at Caudry we'd missed the train and now we were left in Arras with little old Mrs Mouse for chaperone. She smiled encouragingly at us, and told us that it was her fault that we'd missed the train, but she would look after us. Mac, the Canadian, said that he could speak French, and he wanted us to go off on our own. The old woman vetoed the idea, and said that we would stand a better chance of escaping by staying with her. So we followed her, for what seemed like ages, up and down streets, rubbing shoulders with French shoppers and numerous German troops - the latter took no notice of us at all. The town seemed to have a central circular area, with streets radiating off like spokes of a wheel. I was beginning to think that the old lady was lost but eventually she seemed to have got her bearings as she headed up a long street with buildings on both sides. We quickly followed her - like detectives tailing a suspect. She eventually disappeared into one of the buildings, and when we arrived a few seconds later, we found it was a church. When we entered, we saw Mrs Mouse at the front, kneeling at the foot of the image of the Virgin Mary, counting her beads. Canadian, Mac, muttered quietly,
"I suppose she's saying a prayer for us."

Her prayers completed, she came towards us anxiously, placed some offering into the collection box and motioned us to follow her. Again we were out into this long street, and maybe 100 yards from the

Lancaster Bale Out

Church, she disappeared into a house, and when we arrived, in we went, to find her talking to the lady of the house. This woman was a Madame Mendlicott and the address was 135 Rue de Bapaume. This lady, we learned later, was married to an Englishman who had been interned by the Germans for the duration of the war. It must have been an awful dilemma for her to have three RAF evaders thrust upon her. We could see that she was not keen to have us - she had no room - and in any case, how would she be able to feed us? Mrs Mouse however, was very persuasive and despite the lady's anxiety, she finally agreed that we could stay for a while. Mrs Mouse then left us, telling us that she would return at regular intervals. Where she went or lived I do not know. The house was terraced; with two rooms downstairs, a living-room and a sitting-room. I don't know what was upstairs, because we never went up there. The toilet was outside in the back yard. I think that there was only one bedroom, because the sitting room we were finally shown into, had a double bed in it.

The lady had two young daughters at home. The eldest called Lily was about seventeen or eighteen, but the other girl was only a youngster, of school age. Fortunately for us Lily spoke English - unlike her mother. Lily told us that we had to stay in the sitting-room because, as neighbours will in terraced streets, they used to call in for a chat. She used to tell us when they had company, and then we had to keep very quiet, as no one was to know that we were there. We spent a week in this house - some periods of utter boredom, and other periods of hilarity. The three of us slept in the one double bed, and usually it was Lily who would bring our meagre breakfast in on a tray in the morning. Mac would occasionally grab hold of her and pull her into bed with us to squeals of protestation. Her poor, petrified mother would then rush in and tell us to be quiet. Harry and I being British though never did such things.

Mrs Mouse, as promised, returned regularly, bringing food coupons and money, so that this lady could feed us properly. Mrs Mouse must have had connections unknown to us. Occasionally, when neighbours arrived, Lily would enter and hold her fingers to her lips to indicate that we should keep quiet. After we'd been there a week, it was now Saturday, 31st July according to my reckoning, (It will be

Lancaster Bale Out

Mrs Mouse (S. Besin)

noted throughout, that we were always moved on a Saturday) it was about midday when the panic started. The lady of the house - I never found out her surname - rushed into our room and in her excited French told us we'd have to go. Lily came in and explained that the Gestapo were further along the street, searching and ransacking a house, and they were frightened that they might come here. Guess who arrived next? - Little old Mrs Mouse! She calmed the situation down. It appears that we'd been lucky to have missed our train from Arras the previous Saturday, because the house being searched was that of the other woman who was on the train that morning, with her brood of escapees. They must have been caught.

Nevertheless, our landlady wanted us out now. She was persuaded however to allow us to stay until 9:30 pm, when Mrs Mouse would return and take us away. To go now while the Gestapo were in the street would be foolhardy. Common sense prevailed, and Mrs Mouse left again. I don't know where she got the energy to be running about like that at her age[63].

[63.] *Mrs Mouse was born in 1879, so would have been about sixty-four in 1943.*

Lancaster Bale Out

She returned at about 9:00 pm and told us that we'd have to walk about 20 km. We thanked our reluctant landlady for having us, and at about 9:15 pm off we went following Mrs Mouse again. After a short walk we left Arras behind, and were out in the countryside. After being confined for so long, the three of us set off along the country road at a brisk pace, leaving the little old lady behind. Looking back and seeing her struggling to keep up with us, I dropped back, and she took my arm. Mac dropped back once, and said jokingly,
"Who's your girlfriend?"

We walked a little further, when Mrs Mouse called a halt and reminded us of the 10:00 pm curfew. It was strange I thought, that we hadn't met a single other person on this country road. I think she had spotted a convenient haystack in a field, just off the road, and it was here that she decided that we should spend the curfew hours. It was easy for us young men to climb up on the stack, and bury ourselves in the hay for the night. We each took a running jump at the haystack and ran up the sides and on to the top. It was too much for the old lady however, so she settled herself down on a pile of hay at the bottom. Looking down from the top of the haystack, I thought Mrs Mouse was well named. She lay there, curled up with her long black coat wrapped around her ankles, looking like a little dormouse lying asleep. It was quite chilly in the evening air, and I felt so sorry for the old lady. I had a rain-coat, made of some synthetic material, given to me by Monsieur Janssoone, so I slid down off the hay and covered her with it to help keep her warm. We were quite warm up top, but we didn't sleep much, it was too prickly and dusty.

Come the dawn we assumed that we'd be safe, as the curfew would be over by now. No one seemed to have a watch, but we set off again regardless, along this country road, never seeing another soul until we entered the town of Bapaume. Imagine; early Sunday morning, 1st August, an old lady and three, stalwart, young RAF men all covered in hay, unwashed, unshaven, and looking quite grubby! We'd had no breakfast either. The church bells were calling the faithful to prayer, and it was a lovely summer's morning. The first man we met seemed to be a bicycle repairer, who was working in a shed at the entrance to the town. Mrs mouse engaged this man in conversation. I think she was asking him directions, because he answered her and pointed in a certain direction, meanwhile looking at us in a very inquisitive fashion. We followed the old lady up a street, and eventually we entered a gate into some grounds. Walking up a short drive, we came to the front of a big house, whereupon Mrs Mouse rang the doorbell. A young woman dressed in a maid's uniform answered the door, and after a brief conversation with the old lady, we were invited inside. From the little English the maid knew, we discovered that the master of the house was in Paris, visiting his sick wife who was in hospital there. He would be back home in the evening, and she assured us that he wouldn't mind us staying there for a while. Meantime we could get cleaned up, have something to eat and go to bed if we wished. We were all very tired actually, after our restless night on the haystack, and in separate beds - for a change - we slept until the afternoon. When we left our beds, we sat around chatting and we met a young lad aged about sixteen, who I think worked in the grounds of this big house. I don't know his name so I will call him Henri.

When the master of the house returned later on, he made us welcome and invited us to have a meal. I do not know who he was or what he did. He didn't speak English, but Mrs Mouse gave him all the details. We had a good meal, and sat about talking amongst ourselves until it was night-time, and we were wondering if we would be staying there. It was not to be however. Young Henri came rushing in, quite agitated and sweating, proclaiming that he had been followed on his way here, perhaps by the Gestapo. There was an immediate panic amongst our French hosts
"Quick, quick; Out the back," was the cry.

With young Henri in the lead, and Mrs Mouse following him, we rushed out the back, down the garden path to a barbed-wire fence. Henri went through unscathed, Mrs Mouse followed on her hands and knees. As she crawled under the fence her long black coat became snagged on one of the barbs. She tugged and tugged trying to get free, but she lost her balance and rolled over, causing her coat to become more attached to the offending barb. Mac, who was next in line to crawl through, muttered, "I'll soon fix this!"

Lancaster Bale Out

Pulling out his pocket-knife, he slashed the bottom off the old lady's coat, freeing her from the entanglement. Harry Brown and I, who were behind, were engulfed in peels of laughter. We all got through this fence, and found ourselves on some waste ground, where we all crouched down in a hollow, with young Henri peering over the top, as if looking for the enemy. This situation was so bizarre. Here we were, RAF escapees, lying in a hollow on some waste ground with a sixteen year old boy, and a elderly woman for company. We were helpless with laughter, as we remembered Mac with his knife liberating Mrs Mouse from the wire. I don't think the old lady knew yet how she had got free. Henri, our young leader, held his hand up for silence, as he peered over the top of the hollow, like an Army Officer in WWI looking over the trenches. There was not a soul in sight, and through the gloom of the night, we could see houses, not more than 100 yards away. Henri then waved us on, and we left the hollow and proceeded over the waste ground towards the houses. We entered a street with dwellings on each side, and Henri stopped at a house. From the bedroom window of a house on the opposite side of the street, there was a French woman leaning out and she wished us, "Bonsoir."

We entered the house where we'd stopped, and this was to be our next resting place. The lady that we'd seen at the window was called Madeleine Eele, and was married to an Englishman, who had been interned. Young Henri was their son, and was therefore half English. The house we had entered belonged to Madeleine's sister, who was married to an Englishman too, but both her and her husband had been interned, so our house had been unoccupied for a good while, and it certainly showed.

I had never realised before, just how primitive rural dwellings were in France. I had not been brought up in luxurious surroundings, but my parent's colliery cottage in Durham was a palace compared to this place. This house consisted of one room and a kitchen downstairs, and one bedroom upstairs. The staircase was actually in the downstairs room, which also contained a bed. The fireplace was a big black cast iron affair, but unlike the one back at home, this one was dirty and beginning to rust, due to it not having been used for so long. First Henri left, and we didn't see him any more, and then Mrs Mouse left, promising to return daily to cook some food for us. We were now on our own, so we bedded down, with nothing to do but talk, play cards and wait. The toilet happened to be out in the back yard. We never knew if we had neighbours or not, but we never heard anyone next door.

The first few days were not too bad. Sure enough the old woman came daily and brought us some food, and even cooked for us, mainly French fries. Occasionally we had a visit from Madeleine and she and Mac - who could speak some French - used to bandy a few words together, which Madeleine took in good fun. During the latter part of week, things really began to get on our nerves though. Mac developed jaundice, and one day when Mrs Mouse was frying some chips he said he wanted them hard and crispy. I joined in and remarked that I didn't like them too crispy, at which he snapped,
"I suppose you like them all soft and soggy?"
"Well I haven't got jaundice!" I replied.
Harry Brown burst out laughing at this remark, and I thought that Mac and I were going to have a real physical go at each other.
We didn't however, but it illustrates the tension we were under, living like this. Mrs Mouse sensed it and towards the end of the week, she told us she was going to take us out.
"Are we going home?"
"Non," she replied, unfortunately.
I remember it was the weekend, when she told us that she was coming back at night to take us out, before the curfew. It was dark when she cautiously checked the street, and out we went. We followed her for about 15 minutes, until she went up to a large house and rang the doorbell. The door was opened by a Frenchman, who invited us in. The inside was very dimly lit, by an oil lamp on a table, around which were seated two young men, one of whom greeted us in English. He was a Pilot Officer - from a Spitfire - who, he told us, had been shot down in the area of Dunkirk. He had stolen someone's bicycle and had cycled all the way here, where he had been sheltered by our host, the Mayor of Bapaume. The other young man was a Russian who had been in a forced labour camp near Duisburg. During one of our raids on that city he had escaped, and walked here. We all sat around the Mayor's table, drinking his wine. Mrs Mouse and the Mayor conversed in French, while the

Lancaster Bale Out

four of us RAF men exchanged experiences. The Russian however, sat morosely by himself. All in all, it eased the tension and was a pleasant interlude to our confinement.

Eventually, Mrs Mouse said it was time for us to go, before the curfew hour. We invited these other escapees to come with us, but the Russian declined. I think he knew where he was better off. The pilot did come with us however, but I think that when he saw how we were living, he wished that he hadn't. Mrs Mouse now had a brood of four. Another mouth to feed, but I think she was enjoying herself.

It was Saturday, 7th August when our stay at Bapaume ended abruptly. In the early morning Janssoone and Richez arrived, and told us to get ready quickly; We were going to Paris! Actually we were already prepared, because we had nothing to pack. The only belongings we had were what we wore, and which we'd been living and sleeping in for weeks. We were hurried out of the back door, where again, the canvas topped van was waiting in a back lane. I didn't even have time to say goodbye to Mrs Mouse. We were again taken charge of by Janssoone and Richez and told to quickly climb into the back of the van while they went up front with the driver. It seems strange to say the four of us, since it had been only three a week ago. I can't remember the Pilot Officer's name, indeed I don't think that he mentioned it. We didn't call him 'Sir' though. After a short journey we arrived at the railway station at Albert. Our train tickets were bought for us, and we boarded the train for Paris. The train was full of country folk, taking some of their wares to sell at Paris markets. There were even baskets of chickens in our compartment. Janssoone sat next to me, and told me that the body of Arnie Turner had been found by farm labourers, lying dead in a cornfield, on 31st July. He didn't know whether his parachute had opened or not. I was a very subdued young man suddenly, who had just had it confirmed that I was the only one to survive out of a crew of eight. I didn't weep, I just wondered how it could have happened to me, and why I had been so fortunate. I was very quiet during that journey from Albert to Paris, and Janssoone must have thought that I was not pleased to see him.

On arrival in Paris, we left the station, and went down some steps into a white-washed tunnel with some lights set into the roof. At a bend in the tunnel we were stopped by two French policemen. While Janssoone and Richez argued with them, Harry Brown and I sneaked past, and made our way up the sloping tunnel towards the exit. We were very worried in case arrests were being made, but fortunately our companions soon caught up with us. Janssoone assured us that the police weren't looking for us; they were stopping people at random, looking for black market goods. Why they should have stopped us I don't know, because we weren't carrying anything, although Janssoone and Richez did have some parcels.

We went up some steps, and were now out in the streets of Paris, in sunshine and fresh air for a change. We would like to have lingered, mingling with the Parisians and German troops, who were strolling about, but our two guides hurried us along. A group of six people hanging around together, was too conspicuous for comfort.

We left the crowded streets, and entered a more residential area. Along one street, Janssoone and Richez entered a building and after a few words with the Concierge, we got into a lift and travelled up to the top of the building, where we entered a flat. The residents of this flat were two young people - man and wife - who seemed to have been expecting us. The man was a Monsieur Templier, an electrician who owned two shops. The couple were having an animated conversation together in French, while we stood about, more or less tongue-tied. Shortly afterwards, a middle-aged lady arrived, followed a few minutes later by a pretty young woman. She was about 4'11", very willowy and looked no older than about twenty one. Her name was Susan Lacombe.[64]

Janssoone and Richez then left, wishing us, "Bonne Chance!"

[64.] *Susan Lacombe was the code name for Simone de Cormont, an active member of the Resistance. She lived in a large apartment in Rue du Rocher, near Gare St. Lazare and helped at least eight Allied Airmen during the course of the War. She was part of the Comet Line until betrayed and arrested in February 1944. Interrogated by the Gestapo she was sent to Fresnes Prison, but was fortunate to be released two months later. She survived the rest of the War and died in the mid 1990's.*

Lancaster Bale Out

We were looked over quizzically, and then the middle-aged lady took the pilot away with her. It seems as though we were being assessed as to our suitability for something, but how could that lady have recognized an Officer? We were all in civilian clothes, and I'm sure that he was no different looking than us. However, Mac, eyeing the pretty young woman, turned to us and said, quite loudly,
"I hope I get to go with her."
To his obvious delight, Susan Lacombe walked over to him, and answered him in English,
"You are to come with me."
She told Harry and me, that we had to stay there, until the next day, which was Sunday. Off she went with Mac, and I never saw him or the Pilot Officer again.

17.
Separation -
And then there were two

I had now been left with Harry, the Londoner, for company. We were both quiet, unassuming types. Indeed, I think that I was the more talkative of the two.

The young couple whose home we had invaded, tried to converse with us but they could not speak English, and our French was very limited. The flat we were in consisted of one L-shaped room, diner and lounge combined, and a curtained-off alcove where there was one double-sized bed. I was wondering where we would all sleep at night, and also where the toilet was. Feeling embarrassed, I sheepishly asked,
"Où est le toilette s'il vous plait ?" hoping that it would be somewhere in the passage outside the main door. But no; it was in a cubby-hole near the curtained-off bed space - but I had to go.

After a very tedious day, during which our hosts seemed to be very nervous, we retired to bed. Harry and I shared the double bed in the alcove, while they slept on a put-up bed on the other side of the curtain. Next morning after a meagre breakfast, we sat about waiting. The young couple were very apprehensive, as if expecting a thunderous knock on the door, or perhaps it being jackbooted down.

It was about midday, when a knock did come, and with a sigh of relief our male host answered the door. He returned with a tall, young man wearing glasses. He introduced himself as Olivier Richiet, and told us to go with him. We bade goodbye to the relieved young couple, and out we went into the streets of Paris, with Olivier. Fortunately he spoke good English, and told Harry and me that he was also on the run from the Germans. He didn't tell us why he was a wanted man, but he said that the Gestapo had come to arrest

Lancaster Bale Out

him, and because he was not at home at the time, they had arrested his mother. Now he daren't go home. I thought at the time that he ought to go home and face the music, so that his mother might be released, but who was I to criticise, we were now in his care. We walked the streets of Paris all day and were beginning to think that Olivier didn't know what to do with us. Eventually, late in the afternoon, we entered what to me, seemed to be a fairly well to do residential area. Again, we went up in a lift to the top storey, where Olivier rang the doorbell of a dwelling. We were admitted. Olivier knew the residents, a smart middle-aged man and his wife, who made Harry and I welcome. They also could not speak English, but they told Olivier that we could stay there for the night. However, since this gentleman had to be about his business in the morning, we'd have to leave then. Olivier then left. We never knew where he went, but we knew it wouldn't have been back home.

The lady of this abode cooked us a good meal, after which Harry and I got cleaned up a bit, and had a shave. During the evening, this gentleman tried to teach us how to play mah-jong, but because we could not converse with each other and the fact that Harry and I were worn out with walking, it was a failure. We retired to bed; this time we had one each.

Next morning we had a continental breakfast, before Olivier arrived to take us away. Once again we walked the streets of Paris, and Olivier told us not to walk in step as we looked too military. He also told us that if we saw any Germans in black uniforms, we were not to stare at them, as they were SS soldiers, and we should just move casually out of their way, in case we collided with them. In actual fact we didn't see any SS but there were plenty of others in field grey and jackboots. If it was not for the constant hunger I was feeling, I realised that I was actually quite enjoying this adventure - I would however have liked to have known where we were going.

We entered a district where I noticed a signpost, telling us we were in Pigalle. Olivier took us to a house, occupied by three adults and a couple of children. These people agreed with him that we could stay there for a while. They seemed in awe of us, especially the children. Olivier then left, promising to be back in about two and a half hours. We sincerely hoped that he would, because it was very tense in that house. We could not communicate at all, but we did however, have a small meal while we sat uncomfortably on our seats. What would we do if Olivier didn't return we wondered? My fears were unfounded however. Olivier returned and took us away. It may seem to be ungrateful, but I would rather have been walking the streets, instead of sitting uncomfortably in a stranger's house.

Olivier took us to the underground station (Metro) where he bought our tickets. We boarded an underground train, and were speedily on our way, to Barbes. When we reached our destination and left the station, we found ourselves out in the countryside. Olivier took us to a large country house set in its own grounds. It was actually some sort of hotel on the Boulevard de La Chapelle. After ringing the bell we were admitted, and Olivier introduced us to the lady of the house. This lady greeted us in perfect English. I can't remember her name or where her husband was, but I think he was an army officer who was in a POW camp in Germany. This lady was a real anglophile. Her two small daughters spoke English, and she told us that although they were French, they spoke only English in their home. She explained that she could not accommodate us until now, because her house was used by German officers at the weekends, as a country retreat. This was probably the reason we fed so well the two days that we were there. If it hadn't been for our earnest desire to get back home, I think that Harry and I could easily have stayed there until the end of the war. We were very comfortable.

Sadly, after two days there, we had to go. We didn't know why. One can only assume that we weren't the type of English that this lady was used to mixing with, or perhaps she was worried that her two young daughters, who liked talking to Harry and I, might disclose to the German officers, that two British airmen had been staying there. In that case it would have meant a firing squad without a trial for her. Olivier had pointed out to us, on our wanderings around the streets, notices in French, stating that anyone caught assisting, or harbouring Allied airmen, would be shot without a trial. Not a very nice prospect for our Allies, if we were caught together. Why did they do it, I wondered? Perhaps they were very sensitive about France's capitulation in 1941.

Lancaster Bale Out

Olivier took us back onto the Metro, and after a while we got off the train at another station, where Olivier met three of his friends. He didn't introduce us but he must have told them what Harry and I were, because they stared at us in amazement. Across the other side of the electric rail there was a man standing, in a long, black leather coat with a Homburg hat - obviously a Gestapo type. This man was smoking a cigar and Olivier's friends were making catcalls and pretending to inhale the cigar smoke, wafting across from the opposite platform. Harry muttered to me quietly
"This lot will get us caught."

Fortunately, another train arrived and we all boarded it. We were glad when Olivier's friends left us. We got out a couple of stations further on and once more we tramped the streets of Paris. I think that poor Olivier didn't really know what to do with us, but he didn't say anything. We stuck to him like glue.

Walking along one street, Olivier met a girlfriend, from his college days I assumed. She was a very small girl, and as she and Olivier chatted together he must have told her who we were, because she looked at Harry and me with sympathy. She and Olivier set off along the street, motioning us to follow them. I don't know how Harry felt, but I personally felt somewhat like a stray dog, who had found some friends and was being encouraged to follow them home, where I'd be looked after. We followed Olivier and his slight young girlfriend along two or three streets and eventually came to the inevitable block of flats. After climbing the steps this time, we entered a flat where Olivier's girlfriend was arguing with a lady, who apparently was her mother. She was a lady in her late thirties wearing a low cut dress, and was very well painted and powdered. Olivier's young friend was quite vehement with her mother and was insisting that she let us stay there. The mother finally agreed, but to our ears she was expecting a visitor that evening. To our astonishment, Olivier and the young girl left us here with the mother. She was not too bad really and tried to make us welcome. From the little we understood of French, we gleaned that she was not very well off. People in France could not afford to feed guests in those days, unless they bought food on the Black Market, and to do that, one had to have money.

AVIS[65], warning to French helpers (C. Smith)

She did cook Harry and me a meal of sorts - French fries and some kind of meat, which we wolfed down. This flat was identical to the first one that we had been in (an L-shaped room with a curtained off bed space) and again we wondered about sleeping arrangements. Early in the evening the lady's visitor arrived. He was a middle-aged man, who looked at Harry and me as though we were usurpers. He was quite affable though, once our hostess explained the

---

[65] *See Appendix G for a translation of this notice.*

Lancaster Bale Out

circumstances and we sat around, forcing conversation in our two languages. Later, after looking at his watch, he suddenly said that he had to go - because of the curfew - and bade us goodbye.

Harry and I were to sleep in the double bed in the alcove, so we retired there. Harry decided that he would have a drink of water before we settled down to sleep. He went to the small kitchenette and returned hardly able to stifle his laughter. While he had been in the kitchen, the window had been opened from the outside, and the gentleman friend climbed through. He had the shock of his life when he saw Harry standing there. Our hostess explained to Harry, that he had had to return because of the curfew, and would have to stay the night. We could not sleep for laughing.

When the next morning came the gentleman had gone. Olivier arrived after we'd had our meagre breakfast. He was carrying some parcels and a couple of lengths of French bread.

After a long walk, we arrived at a seemingly neglected part of Paris, and off one street, we entered a passageway with brick walls on either side, and doors let into the walls at intervals. We walked down the sloping concrete floor, and at the end of the passage Olivier led us into a room, through one of the doors. This room was fairly big, and had the appearance of being either a lecture room, or a place of worship. At the front, there was a kind of stage, with a dais where a lecturer or preacher might stand. The floor sloped fairly steeply to the back, and on each side of a central aisle there were rows of wooden benches. Also at the back, near the roof, was a gallery with wooden benches. It appeared that we were in a lecture room, and this was a college complex. Outside in the passage, Olivier showed us a toilet that also had a cold water tap. He told us that we'd be safe here for a while and that the parcels contained some food which we'd have to make last until he returned. He might not be able to come every day, but he would come as often as possible with more food. We now had a great deal of faith and respect for Olivier, but how long would it be we wondered before we would be back to Blighty. Chamberlain's promise that he had get us back to England in five days, had now increased tenfold.

Olivier left Harry and I in that lecture room, where we idled the days away, lying on the benches, climbing onto the stage or up to the gallery, spinning yarns and telling each other jokes. True to his word Olivier returned at intervals with more food. One day he brought us a circular cheese, which stunk to high-heaven. We scraped it and washed it under the cold water tap, but we still could not eat it. We eventually flushed it down the toilet. Our clothes hadn't been changed for weeks now, and with our beards, we must have looked like two tramps. We tried to keep ourselves clean by bathing under the tap. One day when I was out there in the passage, I met a man, who I assumed to be the caretaker of the college, but we didn't acknowledge each other. I was a little worried actually, in case he started talking, but nothing happened. I think that he knew we were there, and who we were. We became bored stiff with the situation, and to quote a phrase - absolutely cheesed-off. Despite our enforced confinement, Harry and I got on famously, not a cross word passed between us. Actually we were doing our duty as laid down by the authorities at home, 'Don't give yourselves up, you must try to escape.' Help was available in the occupied countries. To our helpers on the other hand, we were really a firing squad waiting to happen. We were walking disasters.

After nine days in this complex - according to my reckoning, August 22nd - Olivier arrived at about midday, all smiles
"Come with me" he said "You are going home."
We went out into the streets. I wondered how Olivier dared to walk with us, in our unkempt state. However, the ordinary residents of France at that time didn't look 'chic' either, so perhaps we were not too conspicuous.

Olivier led us into a shopping area, and we followed him into a ladies' hairdressing salon, where people were sitting having their hair permed or whatever. Harry and I stood sheepishly just inside the door, while Olivier went out and talked to a smart looking lady in her mid-thirties. I think that she was either the owner, or manageress of this establishment. She was very pretty, and Olivier introduced us and then shook our hands, wished us the best of luck, and then went on his way out into the streets of Paris. Our new helper was called Madame Marie Christine Bodin. She went to the

Lancaster Bale Out

cloakroom and returned with a large, woolly, black dog on a lead. He was called 'Peerat' or pirate in English. Marie Christine could not speak English. We followed her along the street, where she called at two or three shops, buying goods. She was having trouble carrying her parcels and at the same time holding Peerat's lead, so I took the lead from her. Peerat didn't seem to mind at all. I think that Harry was quite shy in the presence of such a pretty lady. She took us to her flat, which was better than those we'd been in before. She gave Harry and I some clean underwear, a clean shirt and a tie each. I think these clothes belonged to her husband, who was not there at the time - unfortunately she was married. Harry and I each had a bath and a shave while Marie Christine cooked us the best meal we'd had for weeks. During the meal, we gleaned from her, that she was taking us on the train at "neuf heure est demi" from "La Gare du Nord." We were going to the south of France, to a place called Dax, where we would change trains. Later she would pay some guides to take us over the Pyrenees into Spain.

After our meal was over, Marie Christine asked to see our identity cards. She examined Harry's card and said,
"Bon," but when she saw mine she said
"Vous peut-être non"
"Pourquoi?" I asked agitatedly
I could not understand, but she held up her hand, and tried to tell me not to worry, she would try to get me a new identity card. I could not believe it, what was wrong with my identity card? I assumed later that the card that Janssoone had given me was an older type that didn't need a photograph on it, as Harry's did have his photo on.

Marie Christine took us out into the streets, and we arrived at more luxurious residences. We were admitted into the flat by a big, buxom, lady, to whom Marie Christine was explaining my predicament. This lady introduced herself to us as Miss McCartney. She was Irish, and taught English at a Paris school.
"You know," she said, "we Irish are supposed to be neutral in this war, but we aren't really. When you get home, you must write to my sister. Her address is Miss McCartney, Kilkarney, Ireland."
"Is that all?" I asked

"Oh yes, that will find her," was the reply.
Then she told me to go to the station, to catch the 9:30 pm train as arranged, and she would try and get me a new identity card. If successful, she would meet me at the station.

We returned to Marie Christine's flat where we rested, until it was time for us to go to the station. I was very worried on that walk to the station. "Let Miss McCartney be there" I prayed. What would I do if she didn't come, I wondered? When we got to the station, I was amazed that the train was already waiting, and besides the French travellers on the platform, waiting to board, there were at least half a dozen people who weren't what they seemed. If the Gestapo had been on the alert, they would have netted quite a few escapees. One little guy, obviously a Yank, was in a passionate embrace with a French woman who wore glasses. He was a USAAF airman called Alan Robinson.

I glanced anxiously around, looking for Miss McCartney, while Marie Christine went amongst the travellers, sorting out her brood of escapees - Harry included. "Please come," I prayed, but she was nowhere to be seen, and people were boarding the train. The little Yank, had said his good-byes in typical Yankee manner, and Marie Christine was now standing arguing with the woman whom he had been embracing.

18.
Solitude - Despair

I said goodbye to Harry. My last link with home was leaving me behind, and I was in deep depression. Marie Christine brought the little Yankee's woman to me, whose name was Annette, and to my surprise she spoke good English. She told me that I could stay with her, until Marie Christine returned in a week. Marie Christine looked very upset for me, and tried to tell me that she would collect me in a week, and in the meantime I could stop with Annette until she returned. She then left and boarded the train. My depression deepened.

Harry, Marie Christine and Alan Robinson travelled via Bordeaux and arrived at Lourdes at about 12:00 hours on 25th August 1943. Marie Christine took them to a restaurant and introduced them to a guide who was to arrange their journey over the Pyrenees. They stayed there until the 27th August, and at 5:00 am left for Tarbes, where they caught another train to Bagneres, arriving there at about 08:30 hours. They waited there for some time, but as the guides failed to turn up they had to return to Lourdes. The following day they made the same journey to Bagneres and this time the guides were there and they set out at about 10:00 hours on 29th August to cross the Pyrenees. The crossing took them two days, and before they had reached the border the guides left, after giving a few vague directions for the last part of the journey. By this time the party had split up and there was only Harry, Alan Robinson and an Englishwoman that had joined them at Bagneres. They met some shepherds who took them almost to the frontier. On 31st August they were arrested by the Spanish police and taken to a civil prison at Bielsa. On 2nd September they were moved to Barbastro prison, where they remained for a week. On 9th September they were taken, by a Spanish Air Force Officer, to Alhama de Aragon and then on 16th September a Group Captain Vincer took them by car to Madrid leaving for Gibraltar on 22nd. Harry Brown left Gibraltar on 25th September and arrived back in Bristol on 26th September 1943. He had been missing for two and a half months.

Annette hurried me away, and on the route back to her house, she told me that she had not wanted to take me, because she was supposed to be going for a week's holiday. Imagine my feelings; Annette was only taking me because Marie Christine had told her that it was her patriotic duty to shelter me. I felt unwanted and alone. It was nothing personal she told me, but she had been sheltering the little Yankee for weeks now and they were more or less engaged. After the war, he had promised to come back and marry her. I doubted it myself, and thought that she must be naive. I felt like going off on my own, but knew I was a danger, not only to myself but to those who had helped me.

Annette led me to her home, which was quite a nice house. She was a teacher, but the schools were still on holiday, so we sat around and chatted about the war, and how the French were suffering under the German occupation. My depression continued; what if Marie Christine was arrested on the train with her gang of Allied Airmen and didn't return? What would Annette do with me then? I was miserable company. Annette was very concerned about my mood, and asked me what was wrong. I told her that it was now almost two months since I had been shot down, and my family wouldn't know whether I was dead or alive. They would only have been told that I was missing. Thinking it over, she then said that it might be possible to inform them that I was still alive. French civilians were allowed to write to English civilians, via the Red Cross, but only on a special type of postcard, upon which space was limited. I brightened up at this suggestion, and Annette went out to obtain one of these Red Cross cards.

When she returned, we sat at the table together and discussed how we should word this short correspondence with my girlfriend. We decided not to use the name Smooker on the address, in case the Germans knew that a Smooker was on the run. Perhaps my name had been on my parachute, Mae West or even my boots. Very unlikely really, but we decided not to risk it. I chose my mother's maiden name - Jane Ramsay - and then wrote in block capitals:

> HOW ARE YOU? FRED AND I ARE SAFE
> AND WELL, AND HOPE TO RENEW
> OUR PRE-WAR ACQUAINTANCE SOON.

That was all there was space for. Annette chose a name out of the telephone book, and we signed it in that name.

My girlfriend actually received this card, and took it to the Citizens Advice Bureau in Crook, where she was apparently told to do nothing, "Your boyfriend is in hiding." He certainly was, and he wished that he wasn't.

I tried to cheer myself up after this, but I was still worried about what would happen if Marie Christine didn't return. I suddenly realised, that now I didn't even have an identity card. Miss McCartney had kept my old one. Although Annette, who had been very reluctant to have me at first, was now becoming quite friendly, I didn't think that she was capable of getting me back home. She merely took in Allied boarders; if somewhat reluctantly.

September 12th was a great day - Marie Christine returned; her mission apparently completed, without any trouble. Perhaps it would be my turn next Saturday, I thought, thinking that she carried out her dangerous missions on a weekly basis.

We said goodbye to Annette and Marie Christine took me back to her flat, where I met her somewhat irate husband. Although I don't think he was pleased to see me, he didn't make me feel unwanted. He and Marie Christine had quite an argument though, his anger tempered only by my presence, I think. After all, the poor fellow had been left alone for a week with only Peerat for company, and then when his wife did return she brought another incriminating RAF man with her to stay in his flat. He spoke a little English, and told me that he didn't agree with what she was doing, it was too dangerous. If she was caught, he would also be held to account, and he wanted no part of it. He was however disregarded by his wife, who was the domineering partner. I noticed that when he shook hands with me at our introduction, he did so with his left hand. He appeared to have a withered right arm, which was probably why he had not been in the French armed forces. I must admit, that I also wondered how he managed to get such a good-looking wife. They had no children.

I had hoped that I'd be on my way on the following Saturday, September 19th, but it was not to be. I spent three weeks there at No. 33 Rue des Petits Champs[66], the only address that I knew. I was well fed, and able to bathe, shave and in general keep myself clean. I had my own bedroom, but I think that Peerat used to have the bed before me, because I was often bitten by fleas. I was still, more or less a prisoner there. Both Marie Christine and her husband went out to work everyday. I don't know what he did, but of course she had the hairdressing business. I was alone all day, and tried to keep myself fit by doing physical exercises, press-ups, sit-ups, running on the spot and sprinting from the lounge along the hall, past the kitchen and bathroom and back again. It was a frightful bore really, and I was constantly whining, until I think Marie Christine became fed up with me, and told me how lucky I was not to be in prison. I learned a great deal about this lady during my stay there. She hated the Germans, and was vehemently anti-Communist too. On one occasion, when I expressed an admiration for the way the Russians were fighting the Germans, she told me that I shouldn't complain about Peerat leaving a few fleas in my bed. Since I had communist views, I should be glad that I was getting a fair share. I sometimes thought that she had no regard for the English or the Americans either. She was just using us as a weapon with which to hit the Germans. She was a De Gaullist, or to coin a phrase, she was the reincarnate of Joan of Arc, with the enemy this time being the Germans, not the English.

One Sunday she and her husband took me out to the cinema, where we sat through a German propaganda film, amidst raucous catcalls

---

[66.] *By a strange coincidence this was the address of Henri Paul, the driver of the car in which he and Diana, Princess of Wales were killed, in 1997.*

Lancaster Bale Out

from the audience. We were in a darkened cinema of course. Another day she came home from work early and took me out into the streets - brave woman. We walked under the Eiffel tower, where some German soldiers were taking photographs of each other, probably to send home to their families. After a while we entered a large sort of supermarket. I was told to stand just inside the entrance and Marie Christine then went to talk to one of the shop assistants. She must have told this lady who and what I was, because I was gazed at with a great deal of interest. I was then ushered into a small booth, where I had a passport photo taken, before we returned to her flat. Things were beginning to move at last I thought. One Friday, October 1st, Marie Christine came home from work early. I thought she had brought the vicar to see me, as she was accompanied by a young man, dressed in black pin-stripe trousers and jacket, with a white shirt. This was not a clergyman however, it was a Flight Lieutenant Geoffrey Ball[67], a Typhoon pilot.

Geoffrey Ball next to Typhoon, 2nd from right (RAF Museum)

---

[67] *Flt Lt Geoffrey Francis Ball (89410) was flying with 182 Squadron, Fighter Command, when on 19 Aug 1943, during a fighter sweep over France, his Typhoon was damaged by flak and he force-landed at Blagny around 12:30pm.*

154

She looked very nervous, and was peering out of the window into the street below. She had the feeling that they had been followed home. Indeed, she was so worried that she took the Flight Lieutenant and me, along the passage, and placed us in a cupboard under some stairs. Geoffrey Ball and I spent the rest of the day in this cupboard, but I learned very little about him. I think he was annoyed because I called him Geoff, and not sir. We were let out of the cupboard when Marie Christine and her husband came home again, and we all sat around the table having our evening meal. The next day, October 2nd, was to be a great day as we were going to be on our way. That Friday night was the first time that I'd shared a bed with a Flight Lieutenant. I don't think Geoff Ball liked it, but then neither did I. In any case, I was there before him.

On the Saturday, Marie Christine took Geoff and I to see Miss McCartney, who presented me with my new identity card. We were briefed about our forthcoming journey that night, at 9:30 pm from La Gare du Nord. In addition to Geoff and me, there were to be three Americans and also two young Frenchmen who were leaving to join the free French forces. All our seats on the train were booked in advance - as indeed was the German rule. Geoff Ball and the three yanks would be in one compartment with Marie Christine and one of the Frenchmen, while I would be in another compartment with the other Frenchman and Susan, the girl that had taken Mac previously. It took an English speaking person to brief us. We were told that we must not talk on the train, even if we could speak some French, as we had English accents. If anyone asked us where we were going, "Où allez vous?"
and we were forced to answer, just to say, "Je vais à Lourdes."
We weren't told how to deal with further conversation. I should mention that there was only Geoff Ball and me at this briefing. I don't know who was briefing our three Yankee Allies, indeed I didn't even know who or where they were. Before we left Miss McCartney's place, she handed me a small brown paper parcel for the journey. I didn't know what was in it and I can't remember if she also gave one to Geoff or not.

We left her house in high glee, practicing our French phrases. We had lunch back at Marie Christine's flat - her husband was missing

Lancaster Bale Out

- and in the afternoon, Susan arrived, and introductions were made and phrases again exercised. I think Susan was very nervous, even though she had made this trip before. Geoff and I could not wait; we were both impatient to be off, but we were told to calm down, it was not too far to walk to the station. I should mention that we'd also been told that the danger point would be at the border, with Vichy[68] France, where we would have to show our identity cards.

---

[68] *When France was invaded by the Germans during the war the new French government agreed to collaborate with the Nazis and give them control of the northern part of the country, what became known as the occupied zone, and they would control the southern, unoccupied 'Vichy' zone, under Marshal Petain.*

19.
Another Journey by Train - Freedom

The four of us, Marie Christine, Susan, Geoff Ball and I set off early for La Gare du Nord. I assumed Marie Christine had a briefcase full of money. She was followed closely by Geoff. With my new identity card and with my brown paper parcel under my arm, I dogged the foot-steps of Susan.

On arrival at the station, the train was again at the platform, waiting for passengers to board. Marie Christine went among the passengers, sorting out her three Americans from amongst the throng. She eventually found them and was followed onto the train by four young men. Susan was busy talking to a young Frenchman, who I assumed was one of those also leaving. I never let her out of my sight, and when she boarded the train I was close behind.

I followed her along the corridor and entered the same compartment. I sat down next to her, but we never acknowledged each other. The young Frenchman was sitting directly opposite me. The compartment was one of those claustrophobic types where four people sit looking at each other. I placed my parcel on the rack above my head and sat with folded arms, trying to look like any bored, young Frenchman. The compartment soon filled up, and people were talking amongst themselves. I was dreading someone starting to converse with me, so I just sat staring out of the window. Marie Christine, with her four escapees, was in a compartment about six along from us.

"Will this train ever move?" I thought, surely it was 9:30 pm by now. I had no watch and I seemed to sit like a dummy for ages before we moved off with a jerk. Susan and I were in the middle of our side, and we had our backs to the engine. I gazed out of the window and watched La Gare du Nord and Paris retreat behind us. The train picked up speed and we headed south through blacked out France.

Lancaster Bale Out

To discourage anyone from talking to me, I sat with my arms folded, dropped my head onto my chest and feigned sleep. Susan just ignored me.

After about an hour the ticket collector arrived, but I just sat as though asleep, until someone nudged me. I looked up startled. The man across on Susan's right had reached over and shaken me. I looked at him and the ticket collector vacantly, as a deaf and dumb mute might have done. The man who had woken me, showed me his ticket, and indicated that I should do the same to the collector. I feigned stupid comprehension, and produced my ticket, which was dealt with in the usual manner. From then on, everyone in that compartment had the impression that I was deaf and dumb - except Susan of course - which suited me nicely. I sat feigning sleep all through that long night. In fact I think that I did actually fall asleep at one time, and was woken by excited conversation. It appeared that the train had stopped at the border with Vichy France, but no one had come on to the train to inspect our identity cards, as had been expected. The other passengers seemed highly delighted about this, and I wondered to myself whether they were all escaping.

Morning arrived and it was breaking daylight, but I still maintained my sleeping posture. To my surprise, an hour or so after daybreak, Marie Christine arrived at the door of our compartment, followed by Geoff and the three Yanks. She opened the sliding door, and told Susan that she was going to the dining-car, and would she care to join her. She agreed, left her seat, and went out into the corridor to follow. I just sat there, but she stopped and motioned to me to follow her, while making eating motions, with her hand to her mouth. Again I feigned stupid comprehension, and followed her along the corridor to the dining-car for breakfast. Susan and I sat at the first table inside the dining-car, while Marie Christine and her brood of four were further along.

Our breakfast was a handful of black grapes and a hunk of brown bread. While we sat there a German soldier entered and sat next to me at our table. I believe that he was more uncomfortable than I was, because he didn't stay there very long. Soon our train stopped at Bordeaux, and we sat looking out of the window at the crowded

Lancaster Bale Out

station. Passengers started to leave the dining-car as the train steamed out of the station. Our group was led out by Geoff Ball - looking more like an English vicar than ever. He was followed by one of the Americans, and then Marie Christine looking more attractive than ever. I followed Susan out, and along the corridor. There was quite a queue and we moved slowly on our way, back to our individual compartments. The queue suddenly stopped, and peering over Susan's shoulder, I could see that Geoff had been stopped by a tall man, with close-cropped blond hair, who seemed to be demanding to see his identity card. I then heard his raised voice shouting, "Où allez vous?," at which Geoff seemed to be stumped.

He was roughly manhandled into their compartment. It was the Yankee's turn next, and he suffered a similar fate. Marie Christine was next and she seemed to pass the inspection. Of course she had her own story, and she knew all the answers.

I was surprised to hear an American voice behind me suggesting that we should hide in the toilet. It was one of the Yanks that had loitered behind, probably as worried as I was that there were too many escapees in one compartment. His plan was foiled, as from the dining-car end came the clatter of hob-nail boots and raucous shouts of, "Hinein!"

We were all marched into our compartments by armed German soldiers, as the train sped on towards Dax. I sat in stunned silence next to Susan, and saw Geoff and the three Americans being marched past our compartment, back towards the dining-car end. "Perhaps they had checked all the identity cards now" I thought, maybe they wouldn't bother any more. My hopes were dashed though. I heard sliding doors being opened and shut, as men of military age were being checked. At last a German civilian policeman arrived. He was a middle-aged man dressed in sports jacket and slacks. He looked around the compartment, spotted the young Frenchman opposite me, and demanded to see his identity card. The young man produced his card, and was asked the usual question, "Où allez vous?"

This young man obviously understood everything asked of him, and passed the muster. The German then turned to me and demanded

Lancaster Bale Out

to see my identity card. I tried my deaf mute act, but the man on the right of Susan showed his card to me, and again I feigned stupidity but produced my card. My photo had come loose inside the card and was lying upside down.

"Où est photographie?" the policeman yelled and then turned it the right way up. A woman in the window seat, on the opposite side of the compartment, said to the man, "Monsieur, il est blessé." She pointed to scars on the left side of my neck, which I'd had since childhood and indeed had even forgotten that they were there.

Not to be outdone, the German produced an envelope from his inside pocket and wrote on it
"Où allez vous?"
He handed it to me with his pen, and I wrote
"Je vais à Lourdes"
and handed it back to him. He then wrote
"Pourquoi?"
I had to think quickly, why was I going to Lourdes?
"Je visite ma famille" I scribbled, hoping it meant what I thought it did.
He then asked me where I was wounded and I responded with
"La Guerre." All the time I was writing answers to his questions he was barking questions at me, and I was becoming confused. He then asked me when I was wounded
"Quand?" he wrote.
When was France in the war I wondered, so I wrote, 1941.
His next written question had me puzzled. I didn't know whether he was asking me where I lived, where I was born or where I'd boarded the train.
My response was Paris, but unfortunately I not only wrote but spoke it as well.
"Aha" he cried as he pulled a handgun out and took the envelope from me. I reached for the ceiling. He started smiling as if he had won a childish game of noughts and crosses, so I smiled sheepishly back at him. He raised his gun and playfully pretended to hit me with it, but didn't. He asked me if the parcel was mine and I admitted that it was and had completely forgotten about it. He grabbed Miss McCartney's parcel off the rack, and backed out of the door, motioning me to follow. I could not or dare not refuse.

20.
Back to Paris - Capture

He took me along the corridor and I was shoved into a compartment, where Geoff and the three Americans were already, sitting dolefully. There was a German soldier in each corner. Those nearest the door had their jack-booted feet on the seats opposite. The civilian German stood in the corridor and tore open my brown paper parcel. From it he produced half a dozen packets of Players cigarettes, and some bars of Nestlés chocolate. He was very pleased with his discovery. He shoved the cigarettes into his pockets, but handed me the bars of chocolate which I shared out and we ate there and then, while the guards watched on enviously. As it happened I was a non-smoker at that time so the loss of the cigarettes didn't bother me anyway. We sat in silence as the train sped on towards Dax.

When the train arrived at Dax, we gazed out of the windows, hoping to catch a glimpse of Susan and Marie Christine. I didn't know at that point whether either of them had been arrested or not, but I learned later that they hadn't. Marie Christine did get arrested about a month later though. This information came from Miss McCartney's sister in Kilkarney in 1945. While the train stood in the station I felt like saying to the guards,
"Excuse me, but I have to dismount here", but I knew that it would be useless. The train moved off taking us with it.

Our next stop was Bayonne, where we were ordered off the train by three civilian Germans carrying Lugers. One of the Germans asked each one of us in turn
"What are you, English or American?"
When it came to my turn, I assumed an air of arrogance and proclaimed with pride - that I didn't feel
"I am an Englishman."
After a while two taxis arrived and we were told to get in. They took us to Biarritz, where we stopped outside a hotel. We were marched into the lounge which although carpeted was unfurnished

Lancaster Bale Out

except for an odd, small table or two. Hanging on the wall was a large picture of Hitler.

"God" I thought, Gestapo headquarters and I started to sweat.

We were lined up and stood with our hands tied behind our backs, while one of the Germans sat on the edge of a table with his leg dangling over and his Luger held loosely in his hand.

I thought we were going to be shot in the back of our heads. My imagination ran riot, these people had such a ruthless reputation. I could feel the sweat trickling down my back, under my shirt.

After a while one of these Germans appeared through a door in the wall facing us. He beckoned with his finger and said,

"Ein mann soll kommen!"

The end man went over and through the door. I don't know how the others were feeling, but I teased and strained my ears, to listen out for him screaming. I could hear nothing. The same man appeared at the door again and repeated the order. Again I listened intently, perhaps they were shooting us one at a time? I was next in line, but to my relief when the man appeared a third time he said

"Alle mann hierkommen!"

The remaining three of us went over to the door and down some stairs into a basement room. We were told to take all our clothes off, while the first two of our colleagues were busy dressing themselves. When we were standing naked the Germans carried out a minute search of our clothing, even running their fingers along the hems of our under garments. They even did a body search. I had sweated so much while upstairs that I was extremely thirsty. I asked one of the Germans - in French,

"Can I have a drink of water?"

"Ja ja" he said.

I quenched my thirst at the tap at the wash basin.

We were then told to get dressed. They produced some forms, for us to fill in our details of number, name, rank, mother's maiden name and civilian occupation. I wrote that I was a gardener, naively thinking that if I wrote 'coal miner' I would be sent to work down a German coal mine. After all these details were completed, we were led back upstairs and out of the hotel into two waiting taxis. Not a finger had been laid upon us, I had sweated for nothing.

The taxis, with our German civilian captors in attendance, took us back to Bayonne, where we were put in prison. Maybe there was no prison at Biarritz, I don't know. This prison was horrible. As usual the warders were German soldiers and our captors left us in their care. I was put in a cell with one of the Americans, while Geoff and the other two Americans were put in another cell. I don't know why they did this, because as far as I could make out we were the only residents. It was one of those slopping-out-type of prisons, with only one ground floor arranged around a central concrete courtyard and a drain in the middle. My American cell-mate and I had a bunk each, with a straw or wood shaving mattress and there was a bucket in the corner for toilet purposes. We had no cutlery, and the food that we got - brown bread and black meat - we ate out of our hands. We spent four nights in this prison, nights where we could not sleep for being eaten alive. I thought that they were fleas, but I learned later that there are such things as bed bugs. The only way we could avoid being bitten was to cover all exposed skin. Trouser bottoms were shoved inside our socks, and coat sleeves were pulled down and grasped in our fists, to keep our hands covered. Our coat collars were also pulled up around our necks, the only exposed part left was our faces. The American used to cry in his sleep, or perhaps he thought I was asleep and wouldn't hear him. Neither of us slept much at all.

On the fifth day we were rescued by four German soldiers, one of whom seemed to be an NCO. We were bound by the wrists, by a kind of light dog chain in our two cell groups. I think it was Geoff who had a chain on each wrist, and we were marched back to Bayonne station, where we had a reserved compartment waiting for us on the train.

We sat squashed together, still chained up, with a German soldier sitting in each corner. Again those near the door had their booted feet across the seats opposite. Our side was not too bad but the others, having an extra body, were very cramped. It was still daylight and the station platform outside was quite busy. A young girl knocked on our window, and held up a packet of French cigarettes. The German NCO opened the small window up top, and took the gift. He must have known that they weren't for them, and being honest, he handed them to us. That act made me think that perhaps the Germans weren't so bad after all.

The train left the station while still daylight, but most of the journey back to Paris was in darkness, so we could see nothing outside. The German guards chatted amongst themselves for a while. It became very hot in that compartment, and our guards unbuttoned their uniform jackets, secure in the knowledge that their prisoners were chained together. They even closed their eyes and feigned sleep. I had my hands resting in my lap, and because it was so warm my hands were sweating. This enabled me to slide the chain from my wrist and by moving it a fraction of an inch at a time I got it over the ball of my thumb and was free. I held the loop of chain in my hand and thought to myself
"What now Fred?"
The two soldiers by the door still had their eyes closed. They had opened the sliding door to let some air in. I toyed with the idea of trying to get into the corridor, but the train was travelling very fast and I would have to step over the guards' legs and they might not even be asleep. I might be shot trying to escape and besides I felt too tired and lazy to be attempting anything drastic. Accusing myself mentally of cowardice, for not taking a chance, I slipped the loop of chain back onto my wrist and settled down with my eyes closed, telling myself that I would have to suffer whatever fate awaited me.

We arrived in Paris during the early morning, where a German military truck awaited us. We were ordered onto the back of the truck while two armed guards sat at the exit. After a while we arrived through the gates of a prison, and were escorted into the reception area, whereupon our guards removed our chains, and left. They didn't wish us "Auf wiedersehen."

I didn't know at the time, but we were in a prison called Fresnes[69], situated in the Val-de-Marne area of Paris. It was used during the war by the Germans to hold political prisoners. It was fortunate

---

[69.] *Fresnes prison was built in 1898 and was unusual at the time for its adoption of the telegraph-pole layout (in which the cell houses extended crosswise from a central corridor), designed by Francisque-Henri Poussin.*

for me that I didn't know of the terrible things carried out here, as I would have been more worried than I was[70]. The reception area was bedlam. There were numerous French prisoners milling about and talking loudly, probably protesting their innocence. The five of us stood about like lost sheep. Clerical German soldiers sat at trestle tables, taking details from the French prisoners. Looking around, I noticed in a square part of this reception area some tall wooden boxes about 7' high and 2'6" square. I wondered what they were and was soon to find out.

Fresnes Prison Block (J Tickell)

Amidst the clamour, we heard a raucous voice shouting in German. An officer had come out of an office along the corridor and like a man demented, was bawling and shouting at the prison guards. They pushed everyone who was standing around, towards these boxes, and one by one we were locked in our own individual waiting rooms. Goodbye Geoff and the three Americans, I never saw any of them ever again.

Inside my box there was a wooden seat, but if one sat on it one's knees were up against the door. Over the top of the box there was a steel mesh. After a while I stood on the seat and called out
"Are you there Geoff?"
but I got no answer.

---

[70] *A number of SOE agents were sent to Fresnes and horribly tortured by the Gestapo. Two of the most famous ones being; Violette Szabo, who was later sent to Ravensbrück concentration camp and executed in January 1945 and Odette Sansom (later Lady Churchill) who was also sent to Ravensbrück but survived until her death in 1995.*

Lancaster Bale Out

"Hey Yank, are you still there" I called
But there was still no answer. It appeared that I was now on my own, unless they had not heard me. I began to wonder if I was going to be kept in this vertical coffin forever, God forbid.

Being an ex-coal miner I was used to being in confined spaces, but it must have been a nightmare for anyone who suffered from claustrophobia being in these boxes for any length of time. I guess I must have been in there for about half an hour, before being let out by a German soldier who pointed me towards one of the trestle tables. I realised that they had been bringing prisoners out one at a time. The clerical soldier at the table asked me in English
"What is your name?"
How he knew I was English I don't know. Maybe they had been watching us when we first entered.
"I am 1048639 Sgt. Smooker F H" I replied
"Where is your watch?"
"I don't have a watch."
"Oh, you must have a watch," he said,
"all English Airmen have watches?"
"Well I don't have one" I answered.
I was then told to stand over in the corridor with some other prisoners, but I didn't know what nationality they were as we were not allowed to talk. When there were ten of us standing there in line, we were marched away along the corridor, with an armed soldier at the front and the rear. We went through a door and down some steps into a tunnel, which reminded me vividly of a coal mine tunnel. It was dimly lit by electric lights set in the roof, and there was a narrow gauge rail track laid on the floor. What frightened me most, was that there appeared to be cells along one side. I was horror-stricken. "Surely not," I prayed, "they can't imprison us down here?" I was very relieved to come to the end of that horrible tunnel. We went up some steps, through a door and into the main prison complex. In contrast, this seemed to be brilliantly lit and had a polished wooden floor. We were marched to the head warder's office and lined up in front. I think he was a German NCO.

I didn't have much time to survey the place, but it seemed as huge as a cathedral, minus the pews. We were ordered to remove our shoe

Lancaster Bale Out

laces, trouser belts and ties and were led one by one to our rooms. All around the perimeter there were metal catwalks with stairs leading up to each one. I think there must have been five or six and each one had numerous wooden cell doors along them. Holding my trousers up with one hand I was led up to the 3rd floor and shown into my cell. The door was wooden and arched, about $2^{1}/_{2}$" thick and had a spy hole at the top so that the guards could look in, but a flap on the outside prevented us from looking out. I entered the cell and the guard pulled the door shut behind me and locked it.

I surveyed my new abode. This cell was different to the last one in Bayonne; it seemed clean and more modern. In the corner, to the right of the door, was a porcelain basin with a metal pipe leading out of the wall and a button to press for water. In the left corner there was a wooden shelf upon which rested a tin basin and spoon, with only half a handle. Also on the left was my bed, which was fixed to the wall. I had a thin mattress, one blanket and a small bolster-type pillow. On the right hand side wall there was a wooden table fixed to the wall and a heavy wooden stool chained to the floor. The window, opposite the door, was of corrugated, frosted glass and the

Fresnes Prison, Cell House (J. Edgley)

outlines of steel bars could be seen outside, but nothing else. The floor was polished wood. All in all the place looked clean, but I was still a prisoner.

I was very tired and hungry, and I sat on my bed and pondered my fate. How long would I be here I wondered? I felt awfully lonely and sad, and not a little frightened. None of my friends knew I was here, except for Geoff Ball, and I doubted if he would even remember my name. I didn't know where he was, or the Americans, but they were in here somewhere. After I had been sitting for about fifteen minutes, I heard the 'V' sign being tapped out on one of the walls ••–, ••–, and traced the sound to the corner beside the toilet bowl, where it looked as though some plaster had been pulled away. I heard a voice calling
"Hello, hello."
It was a Frenchman in the next cell.
I sat on my toilet bowl in the corner and returned my next door neighbour's call through the wall. I called back
"Hello, hello."
He became very excited
"Was I English or American?"
I answered of course
"Je suis Anglais."
Again came the inevitable question
"When are the English or the Americans going to rescue us?"
The conversation continued in pidgin English and French and he told me that if I heard the guard coming I should quickly leave my listening post. If the guard heard us talking our soup would be stopped. The thought of soup reminded me that I had not eaten for some twenty four hours and I remembered my hunger again. I went and sat on my bed and waited. Eventually I heard the keys in the door, and the guard outside motioned me to get my tin bowl. This was then filled with some sort of soup, from out of a zinc container. I don't know what sort of soup it was, but I devoured it with my half-handled spoon.

My French neighbour conversed through the wall for a week or so, and he told me that he had been arrested for committing sabotage

on the railways. One day he told me that the following day he was going to Paris for his tribunal. I heard the guard come for him early the next morning and he was taken away. After a long day without company, I heard him being returned to his cell. Listening for the guard to leave I went immediately to my listening post, knocked the usual call sign and said
"Hello."
When he answered my call I asked him how he had fared at his trial, and his response struck me to the core
"Je suis condamnée à mort."
I was really stunned, and went and sat on my bed with my head in my hands.

Later I heard the guards come for him and they took him away. A young man who I'd never seen, but who had been a friendly voice to me. Feeling upset for my neighbour, I began to worry about my own well-being.

I had good reason to worry now. My French friend had been condemned to death for sabotage but I had done worse things by bombing their cities. I was pining away and had no one to talk to. I saw a guard only twice a day, and he wouldn't talk to me. He came sometime about midday with soup and he had a prisoner to push the container for him. I would have willingly done that job if I'd been allowed. The second visit was to issue me with a hunk of brown bread and a bowl of ersatz kaffee. Other than that all I saw was the guards eye looking at me through the spy hole.

One day the guard peered in, and seeing me sitting dolefully on my bed he unlocked the door. As he entered I stood up, holding my trousers up with one hand. He muttered something in German and motioned that I should polish the floor.
"What with?" I asked, I had no equipment.
Sliding his foot backwards and forwards on the wooden floor, he indicated that I should do the same. I did it for a few seconds until he left me, after which I ceased this fruitless task. To give him credit, I think that he was telling me in his way to keep myself busy, and not just sit around moping on my bed.

Lancaster Bale Out

I had kicked a chunk of plaster out of the wall, and was marking on the wall under the table each day as it passed. It was day twelve when the door opened and a Luftwaffe Officer was shown into my cell. "Good" I thought, movement at last.

The Officer was very tall and was wearing steel-rimmed spectacles. He was what we in the RAF called a 'Penguin', in that he had no wings on his tunic, and therefore never flew. He was an administrative type and was very suspicious.

"You stand over there by the window, and I will sit here" he said

"I will ask the questions, and you will give me the answers."

I went and stood by the window while he sat on my stool at the table and produced a notebook and pen.

"What is your name?" he asked

"I am 1048639 Sgt. Smooker F H" I replied

"Where were you shot down?" he asked

"I can't tell you that" I answered

"Why"

"I'm only supposed to tell you my number, name and rank" I replied

He looked at me with disdain

"That's all right Mr Smooker for those who are caught in their uniforms, but you have been caught in civilian clothes"

"Ah" I replied

"But I still have my identity discs"

and pulled them out from under my shirt to show him.

He was not impressed.

"Mr Smooker," he said

"your people are dropping agents with identity discs."

This answer dumbfounded me, was it true I wondered or was he merely trying to frighten me? I had to tell him something without actually helping him, but I had to help myself to get out of this place.

"Right" I told him

"I will tell you when I was shot down, and which raid I was on. That ought to prove to you that I am an airman."

So I told him that I had been on the raid to Cologne during the night of 8th/9th July. This information only led to more worrying questions, and he looked at me with feigned disbelief.

"July 9th Mr Smooker, but it is now the middle of October, where

have you been and what have you been doing?"
"I've been trying to escape" I answered
"But you people get from the North of France to the south in one week. Where have you been?"
"Sir," I said
"I've shown you my identity discs, I've given you my number, name and rank, and which raid I'd been on and the date," I nervously carried on,
"I would now suggest that it is your duty to get me out of here, and into a POW camp."
"Do you realize" he replied
"You are in Fresnes Prison, and in the hands of the German civilian Police. I would advise you to tell me where you've been all this time, and then I'll be able to get you to a POW camp."
"I'm telling you nothing else" I replied
At which point he got up, called the guard and left me in a more miserable frame of mind than I had been in when he arrived.

I think the Luftwaffe Officer must have interceded somewhat on my behalf, because within an hour of him leaving, the guard returned with a safety razor, some ersatz soap and a rough sort of towel. He indicated that I should have a shave. I don't know how many people had used that razor, but it was certainly a painful operation. I hadn't shaved for weeks, and what with only having cold water and soap, it took some time for me to remove my beard. The guard actually laughed at my antics - he was human after all. When I had finished he took the razor away, but left the soap and towel.

The next day, the guard motioned to me to go out of the cell and stand by the door with my soap and towel. He went further along the catwalk opening other cell doors, and bringing out other prisoners. When there were about a dozen of us, we were marched off down the stairs and into a shower block, where we all had a good bath. Afterwards, we were lined up again and ordered not to talk, or get within 5 yards of each other. Being very inquisitive to know who my fellow prisoners might be, I loitered and tried to talk to the man behind me, asking if he was French or English. I was frantic to know whether there were any other RAF airmen here. Suddenly there was a terrific yell from one of the guards who was escorting us

Lancaster Bale Out

back to our cells, and I heard the clatter of hob-nailed boots running towards me. I hurried forward to regain the stipulated gap but the guard kept coming and as he drew near me he lifted his foot to kick me on my behind. Unfortunately for him he missed me, and his other foot slid away on the concrete floor and he fell flat on his back. I think he must have hurt himself because nothing else happened, and I could not wait to get back in my cell. Someone is watching over me I thought.

About a week later, there came a further distraction. The guard again motioned me out of my cell.
"Good," I thought, "I'm getting out" but it was not to be. I was taken downstairs and out of a door on the ground floor where I found myself outside in the fresh air. I was still a prisoner, alone inside a walled-off courtyard, that was so high that I could not see over the top. I stood with the sun on my face for half an hour or so, while the guard, who was standing up on a parapet, watched me with a pitying look on his face. It was a great feeling to be out.

These were the only times that I was allowed out of my cell. According to my scratches on the wall, I had been there four weeks and began to think that I would be there until the end of the war, unless I was shot as a spy before then. I had no doubts as to the outcome of the War, and I thought that surely if they were going to shoot me that they would have done it before now. I began to think about what I would do after it was all over, and then I started thinking about my mining studies before the War.
"That's what I'll do" I thought, work out some mining problems, so I kicked out another lump of plaster and invented some mining problems to solve. I revised trigonometry and other mathematical equations on the surface of my table. In this way instead of sitting moping on my bed all day, I kept my brain occupied with more productive activities.

One day while doing my studies, I heard the guards footsteps outside. I cleared the plaster marks from my table, but he didn't come for me, he opened the door of the cell next door and moments later shut and locked it. It had been unoccupied since the French Saboteur had left, but now seemed to have a new occupant. I hesitated for a while,

Lancaster Bale Out

but then my longing for conversation overcame me and when over to the corner by the toilet and knocked the usual call sign, ••–, ••–, "Hello, hello" I called.

It took some time but eventually I received an answer, and to my delight it was another RAF airman. He was very cautious and suspicious, and didn't tell me very much, even though I had plenty to tell him. He was a Flight Lieutenant B.L. Kenyon[71] from Kensington Church Street in London. After we'd exchanged names and addresses, we promised each other to inform our respective next of kin where we'd met, if we ever got out of here. Whether he had been caught in uniform or not I don't know, but he seemed to leave fairly soon after.

Time dragged on, and one day I heard shouting in French. It seemed as though some French prisoners had their windows open and were calling out to each other. I got the false information that Turkey had entered the War on the side of the Allies. It was on my fortieth day of captivity that the guard arrived and beckoned me out again.
"Was I being freed?" I wondered, but it was not to be.
This time I was led up two flights of steps and into a cell on the top floor. This had been made into an office and seated behind a table was a civilian. To my horror, standing with his back towards me, hands clasped behind his back, was a huge SS man. He was gazing out of the window, in his immaculate all black uniform and shining Jackboots. He must have been 6' 6" tall and I noticed the silver piping on his cuffs and the words 'Der Führer'. I was scared stiff. Suddenly he spun round and, towering over me, barked out,
"You say you are an airman, why didn't you salute me when you came in?"
I must have looked pretty ridiculous, standing there holding up my trousers with my left hand, but discretion being the better part of valour, I gave him the best salute that would have done credit to any Sergeant Major. I left him in no doubt as to what I was.
"Sorry" I muttered
"but you had your back to me when you came in, and in the RAF we don't salute Officer's backs."
I think I must have impressed him, because much to my relief

[71.] See Appendix B for the circumstances leading up to becoming a POW.

Lancaster Bale Out

he goose-stepped out of the office. Although I had saluted an SS Officer, what I had done was to prove to him that I was an RAF airman. The civilian behind the table told me to sit down on the chair opposite him, which pleased me, as in my weakened state my legs were trembling.

"Now then" he said
"you were shot down on July 9th, I want to know all you have done since then?"

My brain went into overdrive, I must get this man away from the Béthencourt, Caudry, Arras area.

"Did you bale out?" he asked
"Yes" I replied
"What did you do then?"
"I started walking" I answered.

His next question caused me to shudder inwardly.

"Could you walk? Did you have a good landing?" he asked
Did he know something I wondered?
"Oh yes" I lied
"Where did you walk to?"
"To the west"
"Why to the west?"
"Because that is where my home is" I responded.
"Where did you get your civilian clothes?" he asked.

At this point my imagination served me well.

"I bought them"
"Who from?"

I didn't know if there were any canals in Northern France or not, but I think neither did he.

"I came to a canal" I told him
"and a bargee on this canal sold them to me and took all my money from me"
"Did you have money then" he asked
"Oh yes" I answered,
"We always carry money - French, Belgian, Dutch - and this bargee took it all"

He then came to his main question

"Where have you been staying in Paris?"
"I don't know" I answered.
"You mean to tell me that you have been staying in a house in Paris

for two months and you don't know where?" he said

Actually I'd been in Paris for six weeks only, but by lying it had extended it to two months.

"Yes, but I've been in more than one house" I told him, foolishly thinking that he would be more likely to believe my ignorance. Actually I did not know many names and only knew Marie Christine's address. I appealed to his good sense.

"Do you think that these people would have allowed me to know their names and addresses, knowing that they would be shot if found out?" I questioned

"They wouldn't even let me look out of the window."

I think he saw the logic in this answer.

"If I arrange to take you round Paris in a car, could you recognize the districts in which you were staying?" he asked

"No" I answered

"I can't do that"

At this he lost his temper and banged his fists down on the table

"You do not wish to help me Mr Smooker, go back to your cell and rot! You will never get out of here."

I can't remember the walk back to my cell, I was in a famished daze. I thought they were trying to starve me to death, or at least, mentally torturing me.

My bread ration had arrived by the time I got back to my cell, so I sat on my bed and ate it thinking about what state I would be in if they kept me in here any longer. The civilian Policeman was not interested in asking me about the RAF, all he wanted to know was where I had been staying in Paris. I spent my time thinking of convincing lies in case he called for me again.

Ten days later the guard came for me again, the fiftieth day of confinement. As I climbed up the steps again I realised how run-down I had become. I had to rest after each flight of stairs, much to the annoyance of the guard. I was pleased to see that this time my interrogator was alone, and I think he could see how distressed I was. I sat down and he asked me how I was enjoying my stay here. On the table in front of him were some white bread sandwiches and an apple.

"I'll tell you what" I replied
"I wouldn't mind having one of those sandwiches"
I think he was surprised at my audacity, and indeed if the guard hadn't been standing outside the door he might have let me have one.
"Down to business" he said
"You say that you have been staying in six houses in Paris"
"Not all houses, places" I interrupted
"What were you in first?" he asked
"A house"
"What were the people like and what sort of house was it?"
I thought of my father and mother
"They were in their middle fifties, and the house was a two bedroom terraced house"
"But you don't know their names?" he asked
"No"
"The second house" he asked
"Was that the same?"
"Oh no" I answered, and thinking of my eldest sister and her husband, replied
"it was a three bedroom flat."
And so it went on.
"How did you get to these places?" he continued
"I walked"
"Did you know where to go?"
"No, I was taken there by a short, stocky, dark haired, young man called Jack" I said describing someone just the opposite of Olivier.
"You mean his name was Jaques?" he prompted
"No, he called himself Jack. I think he was English, because he spoke perfect English."
I then said to him
"Do you realize that I can't tell you anything?"
"Oh yes" he replied
"Never mind, carry on"
The College complex I transposed into a Church, and at this point he put his pen down, put his hands behind his head and leaned back on his chair.
"Who do you think will win this war, Mr Smooker?" he asked changing the subject abruptly.

I felt a small glow of triumph inside me, he was fed up of listening to my lies. Not wanting to be too confident and state outright that we would, I said

"Well I can't see how Germany could win against the might of the British Empire, America and Russia"

"Yes, but the fighters in this war are your men, our men and the Russians. The Americans are to you what the Italians are to us."

He must have been trying to imply that the Americans were not doing much to help. He had had enough now and dismissed me back to my cell. I was now nearly at the end of my tether. I didn't sit on my bed, I lay on it.

On the fifty-sixth day of my stay at Fresnes Prison the guard came for me again.

"What now?" I thought.

This time I was taken downstairs to the ground floor and made to stand outside the head guard's office. There was already another man in civvies standing there

"English?" I muttered.

To my surprise he was another RAF airman. The guards gave me back my trouser belt and shoe laces.

"Good" I thought "We're going out."

We were given a bowl of the inevitable soup each, and we squatted together on the floor and slurped it out of our tin bowls. We sat there until the afternoon, when two Luftwaffe guards arrived and went into the office - no doubt to ascertain who we were.

One of the guards was about my age and build, with only a pistol on his holster, but the other one was a little fellow about 5' 3" and armed with a machine gun. We were given a hunk of dark bread and were then on our way. We were walked until we reached an open station platform and my prisoner companion was violently sick over the edge onto the rails. When the train arrived we were seated in an empty compartment, us two on one side and the guards at a seat behind us on the other side of the aisle. I began then to have stomach pains and asked if I could go to the toilet when the train started pulling out. The larger of the two took me and stood outside with the door open. My friend and I debated as to whether our soup had been doctored, but we were both weak already, even before we started to feel unwell.

21.
Back to Frankfurt - Dulag Luft

We travelled through the night and left France behind, not knowing where we were going. Next morning we arrived at a station in Germany. We got off the train and the station was very busy with commuters. Going through the barrier into the main complex, the little guard had his gun jammed against my spine. I think he was showing off in front of the German people, to show them what a tough guy he was. Two girls passed by and one of them called me an English Pig, and spat at us. I think that the guard was hoping that I'd make a run for it, so that he could shoot me in the back and show these girls what a dedicated Nazi he really was. In the condition that I was in, I could not have run for it even if I'd had the chance.

Over the station tannoy came the announcement that this was Frankfurt. How interesting I thought, I had bombed here nine months previously (10/11th April), but I could not see any evidence of the damage. I knew then where we were headed - Dulag Luft, Oberursel - a transit camp for Allied Airmen.

I had heard of Dulag Luft from lectures delivered to us during our training sessions at home. It was here that the Germans would interrogate us about RAF matters - what squadron we were from, who was our commander, what targets had we been bombing etc. All we were supposed to tell them was our name, rank and number. By refusing to tell them anything, it was possible that we would be subjected to the alternate sweat-box and cooler treatment. The former was a cell in which the heat would be turned up to an intolerable level, and the latter just the opposite. On reception at this camp, one would be left in a room with other RAF men and their conversation listened to, by means of a hidden microphone. Sometimes a stooge would be included in the company to get the conversation going. Fortunately, this camp was run by the Luftwaffe, although apparently there was always some Gestapo types around, to ensure that the prisoners weren't treated too leniently. According to the Geneva Convention, prisoners were not supposed to be held near military targets. The British complained about this camp being on the outskirts of Frankfurt, a legitimate military target, but the Germans ignored their protests.

It was bitterly cold on that station, and my friend and I were curled up as our guards led us across the station complex towards a German canteen. We were told to sit outside on some sacks, while one of them went in. "Maybe he'll bring us out a hot drink," I thought, but he returned empty-handed. His colleague then went into the canteen and he also returned empty-handed. We'd had nothing to eat except a bowl of soup and our bread ration for nearly twenty four hours. I still had some of my bread left, but kept it for future emergencies. The next thing I remember was standing on the Strassenbahn-Haltstelle; tram stop. I don't know how we got there, I must have been in a trance, but I assume we walked. After standing there a while, shivering in our thin French clothing, we boarded an electric tram, on which a number of German civilians were seated. At least we were out of the cold for a while. We experienced another sign of aggression from the conductor, who barked at us
"Wo sind ihre Uniformen?"
He carried on shouting and swearing at us, but the more decent one of our guards answered him by saying
"Nein, nein Soldaten. Sie sind Soldaten"
This mollified the conductor and he carried on his business of issuing tickets.

We dismounted the tram outside of a barbed-wire gate, leading into a camp complex. On entering, my friend and I were put into a room by ourselves and he immediately called out in loud voice
"Where's the microphone?"
It was exactly as we'd been shown on a film in the RAF, two prisoners alone in a room discussing RAF business, while the Germans eavesdropped on their conversation. We didn't talk at all, in fact my young colleague had told me very little about himself during our journey to this place. He did tell me that he had been in Fresnes prison for a month after being caught in a house in Paris. He had been lucky to escape with his life, as apparently there had been quite a battle between his helpers and the Gestapo who had

Lancaster Bale Out

Warning to airman about Dulag Luft (L.F. Lampitt)

stormed into his house guns blazing. His helpers had been firing back and he had been caught in the middle.

Since we were not talking, we weren't kept in this room very long before the camp guards came and took us away. I never saw my friend again. The next thing I remember was being in a cell. This was smaller than the one at Fresnes, in fact it was quite claustrophobic, but the main thing was that it was lovely and warm - the thing I desired most at the moment. I think I was ill, and I sat gratefully on the bed and almost fell asleep. Indeed I think I did drop off at one point because I heard the tinkling of teacups, and imagined I was at home, where my mother was setting the table for tea. "Perhaps they are serving tea," I thought as the tinkling noise continued. I sat up and started munching at the hunk of bread I still had, hoping that they would soon arrive with my cup of tea. The door of the cell opened and a Luftwaffe Officer entered. I noticed then that the tinkling of teacups that I had imagined was the bunch of keys carried by the guard as he patrolled along the corridor outside.

Remembering the SS Officer in Fresnes, I got to my feet to show a modicum of respect to this Officer. He was a very different type altogether, very charming and friendly, to my dazed eyes.
"Sit down," he said, "eat your bread."
I sat again and he removed his cap. I noticed that he was nearly bald, but yet quite good-looking.
"Where did you get your bread?" he asked.
"Oh, I brought it from France" I answered.
"Have you been in France?" he asked as if he didn't know.
"What have you been doing there?"
"I've been trying to escape" I replied
"How interesting" he continued
"Where did you get the civilian clothes?"
I told him the tale about buying them from a bargee, after which he told me what he would have done in a similar position
"I would have got some clothes off a scarecrow," he said.

"Where do you come from in England?" he continued.
I told him that I was from the county of Durham. At this he expressed pleasure
"I was at college with the son of the Dean of Durham" he said, "His father wanted him to join the church, but he wouldn't."
What a charmer this man was, talking to me like an old friend. Suddenly,
"What squadron are you from?" he asked.
I felt quite at ease with him and responded
"I can't tell you that"
At this answer he laughed
"You boys make me laugh. You all tell me the same thing and yet on your aircraft you have in huge letters your squadron codes."
He continued
"Indeed, if the fuselage was any bigger you would make the letters correspondingly larger."

Lancaster Bale Out

"Were your letters ZN?" he asked
I kept quiet and he answered for me
"They were weren't they?" he said, "106 squadron."

Lanc R5573[72] ZN 'B', October 1942 (Imperial War Museum)

At this I burst into hysterical laughter, and he asked me why I was laughing. I told him it was because things were turning out just as we'd been told they would.
"Was Wing Commander Baxter your squadron commander?" he asked.
I must admit that I told him that he was.
"Well," he said
"He's not there now, he's been moved"
"How on earth do you know all this?" I asked
"You have a magazine published, called Flight" he answered, "and it is available for sale in neutral countries. From this magazine we get all kinds of information."
From his briefcase this charmer produced a black coloured strip, about 15" long by 1" wide.
"Do you know what this is?" he asked.
I told him that I hadn't a clue, and asked him what it was.

---

[72] *This was another 106 Squadron Lancaster lost on the Cologne op of 8/9 July 1943, piloted by Sgt McLean and crew. All were killed.*

"Your people call it 'window'[73]", he answered, "Your bombers throw thousands of these out, to confuse our radar defences, did you never use it?"

"No, I answered, "does it work?"

"It did at first, but we soon found a way round it."

He then stood up to leave, telling me that I was of no use to him; I was too old-fashioned. He told me before he left, that I wouldn't be there long.

I was sorry to see him go really, it had been quite entertaining. Here I was feeling guilty about telling the Officer in Fresnes what raid I'd been on and the date just to prove that I was an airman, and yet this Officer knew squadron letters and even the name of my squadron commander. In addition, some of this information was being published - if I could believe my charming interrogator. As I was ill and must have been operating like an automaton, I had acquired from somewhere or other an Army uniform, cap, battle dress blouse, boots and overcoat. My trousers were American Army ones, and I had always believed that the Yanks were big, hefty men; but these trousers were extremely tight, even for me in my run-down condition. I next remember walking down a road with a squad of other men, some of whom were in RAF uniform, but one poor fellow was wearing a pair of khaki trousers which had been torn off at the knees. No wonder our guards were laughing. I was joined by a young airman, but didn't feel like talking to him. We did however exchange names as we walked along, and he told me that he was called Stan Cancea[74]. He was born in England, but his parents were Rumanian. The Germans had been puzzled by his name. How could a Rumanian be serving in the RAF? We walked along together until we finally came to some wooden barracks, surrounded by the inevitable barbed-wire fence with armed guards patrolling round it. Stan and I entered one of the barracks, where a number of American prisoners were already ensconced. There must have been about half a dozen two-tier bunks in the barrack and Stan and I occupied an

---

[73.] *Window was first used on 24 July 1943 over Hamburg and was extremely successful initially in confusing the enemy radar systems. As soon as the Germans discovered its existence however, they were forced to change night fighting tactics in favour of Wilde Sau – Wild Boar – fighters loitering over the target area.*

[74.] *See Appendix B for the circumstances leading up to becoming a POW.*

Lancaster Bale Out

empty one, one up one down. Some of the Americans were playing poker, but they seemed quite happy and well fed, compared with the miserable state that I was in. They must have been caught soon after they had been shot down, as they still had plenty of reserves of fat and energy. It was here that I became conversant with the term 'Red Cross Parcels'. I wondered what they were, as it appeared that each prisoner received one, although in this camp they were not issued individually, but were used for communal feeding. It was good to have a brew of tea or coffee handed to me, with sugar and powdered milk. Later, I had a dixie full of stew and corned beef, and was beginning to get my appetite back. I thought that life wouldn't be so bad after all if it was to continue like this.

One of the German guards came into our barrack and started talking to all and sundry. He spoke English, with an American accent
"If you guys could see the results of your bombing raids, you wouldn't do it."
He went on to describe the destruction of Hamburg
"People were running out of their burning homes" he told us
"Only to be burnt to death in a river of molten metal and tar flowing in the streets."
Somehow I had to agree with him. If we could see what we were doing we probably wouldn't have done it.

I can't remember how long I stayed at Dulag Luft, but it could not have been more than a couple of days and nights. On one of the nights we had to leave our barracks because of the air-raid siren. The RAF were bombing Frankfurt. It could not have been a major op however, because we only spent about half an hour in the trenches. These trenches had been dug in the compound outside the barracks, for just such an emergency. Before I left there, a small American airman asked me to swap my trousers in exchange for his. He had a pair of British Army trousers that were too big for him, and since my American trousers were too small for me, we swapped. My British Army uniform was now made complete. I was disappointed at having to leave Dulag Luft, but go we had to. Stan and I stuck together on our march back to the station, but when I saw the transport I think my mind went blank. It was a type of cattle truck, which must have been stolen from France. In huge letters on the side it had painted:

'40 HOMMES / 8 CHEVAUX'[75]

We were therefore loaded up, along with thirty-eight other chaps, and I must have gone into limbo crouched on the floor of that cattle truck. I can't remember how long that journey took or arriving at our destination - Mühlberg am Elbe.

[75.] *In 'With a machine gun to Cambrai', George Coppard, HMSO, 1969, the author mentions trains with the exact same markings being used during the First World War.*

22.
Prisoner of War - Stalag IVB

I don't remember walking the 3 miles from the station to Stalag 4B, but I have a fleeting memory of seeing what looked like a number of scarecrows wandering about on the road through the camp. All these scarecrows had close cropped or shaven heads. I seemed to come out of my trance when our guard - an army soldier - loaded Stan and I into the care of an RAF Warrant Officer. He wore a full RAF uniform, but he looked very scruffy and was very surly. No words of welcome or encouragement came from his lips.

Entrance to Stalag IVB (T. Hunt)

He led us to a kind of hut, and we were issued with a couple of dirty army-type blankets, an oval shaped aluminium dixie and a spoon. He then took us into our barrack, where he was apparently the barrack leader. On entering this barrack, I was filled with dismay at the sight in front of my eyes. I could scarcely see the other end of it, and it seemed so dark and smoky. Admittedly it was a late winter afternoon, which accentuated the dim interior, but to see the inmates of this hell-hole was a shattering experience.

Lancaster Bale Out

There seemed to be hundreds of scruffy individuals, all squatting or wandering about on some quest or other. They all seemed to have had their hair shaved off, and it was just starting to grow again. The WO told Stan and me to find ourselves a bunk each, and then he left us to our own devices. I had now become a POW, Kriegsgefangennummer 257.

Two men, lying in their bunks near the door, pointed and told us that there were two empty bottom bunks below them. Stan and I claimed our bed spaces. These bunks each had a mattress stuffed with wood shavings - which seemed to sag onto the floor. When we parked our bodies on these bunks we found out why. There was only half the required number of bed boards to support the mattress.

This barrack had three-tier bunks all along one side, to accommodate some two hundred prisoners. The bunks consisted of a high wooden framework, about 6 yards long and the space between the sides of the framework was filled with a number of wooden boards each about 2'6" long, 4" wide and about 1/2" thick. It took something like eighteen of these boards to make the bunk complete. Two of these frameworks were pushed together to make a block of bunks. A block of bunks then housed eighteen men, six men side by side head to feet with only a 4" high board separating each man. These were then in three tiers giving a block of eighteen bunks with a 2'6" walking space between. This was to be my home now until the end of the war, and I must confess that at the time I had a longing for my private cell in Fresnes again. At least I could lie on the bed by myself.

Stan and I arranged our boards in a number of ways, to try to find which was the most comfortable. The first night we ended up with all the boards at the head end, and we tried to sleep with our feet dangling on the floor. It was very cold and we kept our clothes on, boots and all. We never slept at all that night. Early next morning the barrack door was unlocked and in came a German soldier shouting
"Aufstehen! Appell! Heraus!," which translated meant, get up, roll call and come out. I was glad the night was over and we drifted outside into the compound, to stand in rows of five to be counted by

Inside the huts (T. Hunt)

the guards. Our WO leader conferred with the guard, and all was correct.

I noted that there were eight squads, standing in columns of five in the compound, so I correctly assumed that there were eight barracks in all, making a total of some sixteen hundred RAF and paratroop prisoners. We were a motley crowd. Some of us wrapped up in blankets, some standing with boot laces undone, just as if they had rolled out of their bunks, pulled on their boots and shuffled out to be counted. It was certainly not an RAF-type of parade at all. After the count we were allowed back in our barracks and left to our own devices. I walked the length of our barrack, gazing up the walking spaces between the bunks. Some people had quickly got back into their bunks, and covered their heads with blankets as if to shut out the noise and confusion. I didn't venture up the walking spaces, as I thought that I might be encroaching on the privacy of the occupants. Middle bunk men were standing with their arms and elbows on their beds. Some top bunk men sat with their legs and feet hanging over the edge, while those occupying the bottom bunks could scarcely be seen. Near the opposite end of the barrack from my bed space, there was a brick-built fire place with an iron hot-plate on the top. Numerous aluminium dixies were lined up on it and men stood round waiting for their water to boil. The fireplace had a horizontal brick chimney running along half the length of the barrack, before going vertically up through the ceiling. The horizontal section was occupied by a number of men sitting on it for a modicum of warmth. I was looking for someone that I might recognize, but other than Stan I knew no one else in this barrack.

Appell (T. Hunt)

Carrying on, I went through a door at the end, and entered a wash house, where it was bitterly cold. There were about half a dozen concrete troughs, with water taps and pipes - all cold. On from this I came to another door and entered into another barrack identical to mine. Swarms of RAF and paratroop prisoners were again milling about in the same manner. This then was the set up. Two barracks in tandem, separated by an icy cold wash house. There were four such complexes in what was known as the 'RAF compound'.

Returning to my own barrack, I noticed that the corner near the fireplace was curtained off with blankets, hanging on a wooden framework. Glancing into this I noticed that it only had one set of three tier bunks. Apparently this was the domain of our barrack leader, and two of his assistants, one of whom was the stoker who was responsible for keeping the fire going. When I got back to my own bunk I found that Stan had found some spare bed boards, so we set to and filled up the vacant spaces in our beds. Not quite complete, but an improvement on what we had tried to sleep on during the night. Stan was much chirpier than I was, but then he was in his full RAF uniform. He had been caught very soon after

Lancaster Bale Out

Sketch of Stalag 4B Camp (F. Smooker)

being shot down, and he still had reserves of fat and energy from home. He hadn't been in Fresnes prison for two months.

Shortly we heard the call,
"Kaffee up" and two lads arrived humping a huge iron bin, which seemed to be steaming hot. We went and filled our dixies with ersatz coffee. We had no milk or sugar, but at least it was hot, even though it tasted horrible. Twenty minutes later came the call
"Soup up"
"What sort of soup is it?" came the cry from various corners
"Turnip" was the answer. Only a few men had bothered with the coffee and the same applied to the bin of soup. Everyone except Stan and I had their own Red Cross parcels. We filled our dixies with the soup of the day. It didn't look very appetizing though. Golden-coloured liquid with large chunks of turnip floating about in it. When it was stirred with a long wooden stick, particles of minced meat could be seen floating in it - we were told that this was minced horse meat! However, we were both hungry, and although we didn't enjoy it we managed to get it down. Another prisoner came and spoke to us while we were eating, and informed us that we were in his 'combine' for rations. After the first course, another two men arrived lugging another bin full of potatoes, boiled in their skins. Our combine leader told us to get an empty Red Cross box, in which he gave us about half a dozen potatoes - none bigger than the size of a plum. The bin rapidly emptied as various combine leaders scooped out the spuds until the bottom of the bin was a mess of squashed potatoes and soil.

A good while later, loaves of bread arrived. The bread was rationed to one loaf between six men, and the combine leaders had their work cut out measuring each loaf fairly. If one man got one of the ends one day, he didn't get it the next, as these were slightly smaller than the middle portions. The bread was as hard as blocks of wood and had a slight sour taste. At least it was palatable. In addition to this, we got about a square inch of margarine and a dessert spoonful of jam. This then was the German rations. We had to survive on this for the first two or three days, until the great day arrived - parcel day. I don't know how the parcels were delivered to the barracks, but I believe they were brought by handcart from a central store

Red Cross Parcel (C. Smith)

in the camp. It appeared that each prisoner from a nation, which had subscribed to the Red Cross, received one parcel each week. The Germans - to give them credit - transported these parcels from Switzerland.

For Stan and I, Christmas had come a couple of weeks early in 1943, as it was actually about the 10th of December. I think the only nationals who didn't receive a Red Cross parcel were the Russians. The poor blighters had to survive on the German rations or whatever they could scavenge. Our combine leader called our names and we collected our cardboard boxes - a Canadian parcel. Each parcel contained a large tin of powdered milk called 'KLIM'[76], a tin of corned beef, and a tin of salmon or sardines, a bag of sugar, a bag of tea or coffee, a tin of butter, a packet of prunes or raisins and a large 6oz bar of chocolate. In addition to the parcel we each received fifty cigarettes. I didn't smoke at the time and my cigarettes were like gold, since they could be used as currency. For two cigarettes I bought a hand-made knife. For another two I bought a flat frying pan, which had been made from an empty Red Cross tin, hammered flat and turned up at the sides by some amateur tinsmith or other!

---

[76] *Someone at the Red-Cross must have had a sense of humour to come up with a brand name that is a palindrome of the word 'milk'!*

With this knife and the frying pan I could slice my spud ration into fritters and fry them on the stove hot plate using the grease that the Germans issued as margarine.

The turnip soup became much more palatable with a few cubes of corned beef or SPAM dropped in it. The lumps of floating turnip however, still turned the stomach. Soup rations over the months varied with the seasons. When the turnips had run out we were issued with barley soup or sometimes millet soup. Knowing that barley was apparently a healthy food, most men collected their ration, because when mixed with powdered milk and some sugar it was quite good. The millet however was horrible. Indeed, it was not soup at all, but it was a solid sticky white mass resembling blancmange. Without our Red Cross milk and sugar it was practically inedible. When Spring arrived we got cabbage soup, again with the minced horse meat. Later we got pumpkin soup, which also was not very pleasant; one could not add milk and sugar to pumpkin soup.

Outside the barrack door - which incidentally was always locked at night - there were two tea chests, into which our empty Red Cross tins were placed. These empty tins of soup, coffee, and the remains of our potato rations, attracted Russian prisoners like flies round a honey pot. They were so hungry and uncared for, that they took empty tin after empty tin and cleared any remains out with their fingers. The squashed mess left from the potato rations was scooped up until the tins were shining clean. After we'd peeled our potato ration we were met at the door with cries of "Comrade, Comrade" as we went to empty our peelings into the tea chests. They held up their long overcoats, like sacks in front of them, and invited us to empty our peelings into their coats. They were so hungry they actually ate them.

At first, when I was accosted by these hungry Russians, I was acutely embarrassed and refused to empty my peelings into their coats. How could I offer a hungry person my potato peelings, while I was in possession of a Canadian Red Cross parcel? Eventually though, I became hardened to such scenes as this and gave them the peelings. After all, it was not my fault that their Government did not contribute to the Red Cross. With regard to this situation, it was

Lancaster Bale Out

said that the Germans had contacted the Russian authorities and suggested that if German prisoners in Russia were allowed to write home to their families, they - the Germans - would allow the Russian prisoners to also write home. Apparently the answer the Germans received was that any prisoners that they had weren't Russians, how true it was I don't know.

One day I went to empty my spud peelings and noticed amongst the crowd of Russian beggars a very small man. He could not have been more that 4'6" tall. However, when I had a better view I saw that his legs had been amputated below the knees and he was actually standing on his knees, wearing leather knee pads. The Germans told barrack leaders that we must not encourage these Russian prisoners to congregate outside our barrack doors because they would spread typhus. One day I saw two German guards walk discretely up to these unsuspecting Russians, and when they came close up behind them, they started beating these fellows with sticks which they had hidden behind their backs. The Germans were armed of course, and the Russians scattered. There was no love lost between them.

As time went by, and the German rations were being augmented by some good grub from Red Cross parcels, I began to feel fitter. After a few weeks, during which Stan and I had only left our barrack to visit the latrine or go on parade, we returned to the camp proper. Apparently, before we'd arrived the RAF compound had been closed off by a barbed-wire gate and fastened with a lock and chain to prevent prisoners being able to enter the whole camp. It was said that so many locks and chains had been stolen from the gates and discarded into the latrine cesspit, that the Germans had finally allowed the RAF the freedom of the camp. We were still locked inside our barracks at night time, and there was a latrine just outside the door for night use only. Actually the freedom of the camp didn't mean a great deal, because we were still surrounded by double barbed-wire fences, with coils of wire in between. There was a low, wide, single fence about five yards from the main one which we were not allowed to cross, except with the permission of the guards in the watch-tower. If some lads were kicking a football about and the ball inadvertently rolled beyond this trip wire - as it was called - one had to catch the attention of the guard in the tower and motion towards the ball before retrieving it, or risk being shot. Permission was always granted, although the person collecting it always had a prickling sensation in the spine.

Football Newspaper (V. Stothard)

Lancaster Bale Out

It was very depressing wandering about the camp. There was a single concrete road about eight hundred yards long, running straight through the middle, from the main gate at the north to the gate at the south. On each side of this road were the dingy-looking wooden tandem barracks. The RAF compound was about half way along this road on the west with the Russian barracks being opposite on the east. Strangely, these two compounds were the only ones isolated by single barbed-wire fences. The barracks on either side of these seemed to continue on forever. The RAF and Russians must have been special. Running along the western side of the whole length of the camp was the German garden, which was cultivated by the prisoners, under the watchful eye of the guards in the towers. The towers were sited every one hundred and fifty yards around the whole perimeter. Because of this garden, which was also fenced off, the compounds to the west were smaller than those to the east. The wide open spaces of hard packed sand to the east was where the games of football and rugby were played, for those that had the energy. Here and there between barracks were buildings of special interest. The cookhouse, manned by fit looking British soldiers, the coal bunker, a large, locked brick building and the medical centre, without any special medicine. There was also a camp shop and the cooler, where unruly prisoners were confined for certain periods.

It was this camp shop where, for half a dozen cigarettes, I bought a safety razor and some re-sharpened razor blades. I also bought a tooth brush, with a wooden handle, and some unknown make of tooth powder. For another two cigarettes I also got a metal drinking mug with a handle, made out of Red Cross tins.

After our first tour of the camp, Stan and I had to return to our barracks so that we were in time to collect our rations for the day. In any case, I'd seen enough of the camp to realize that 'freedom of the camp' was no great shakes. We had seen a fair cross-section of the residents, Dutchmen in their operatic or music hall uniforms; Poles with their funny-shaped caps; and Frenchmen clattering about in wooden clogs. We'd also seen a teenage Yugoslav lad using one crutch, because he had had an arm and leg amputated on opposite sides of his body. We'd also seen half a dozen Russians coming along the road, pushing a huge wooden barrel on wheels. The stink from this was atrocious, as it contained the contents from one of the latrines. The Russian prisoners had to do this work using a hand pump to empty all the cess pits. They seemed to be immune from the smell, likewise the German guard who followed behind them, with his rifle on his shoulder. The contents of these barrels were emptied onto the fields outside of the camp. As time went by we became used to seeing these Russians with their offensive barrels on wheels. Sometimes there would be a solitary Russian with a horse-drawn barrel, and once in our compound one prisoner even arrived with a barrel pulled by a cow. I remember seeing one of the RAF POWs go over to the cow and try to milk it, but he got nothing because the poor beast was as dry as a bone. It was a good laugh though.

When Stan and I returned to our compound we were met by a lad called Dennis Morrison[77] who had been in the same squadron as Stan. After a few words of greetings, Dennis asked us which barrack we were in, and we told him 40B. He suggested that we should move into his barrack, 34B, which he claimed was the best one in the compound. First, we would have to see Pritchard, his barrack leader. After Stan and I had collected our own rations for the day we went along to have a look at 34B and to see Pritchard about moving. He said that he didn't mind at all, providing we could find two bed spaces. Our new friend Dennis took us in amongst the bunks, and although Stan and I were separated we moved in.

I found myself a middle bunk, right at the back wall and near a barbed-wire window. At night this window was blacked out with a wooden shutter. The barrack itself was identical to 40B and had the same number of occupants, but somehow it seemed more friendly. Dennis, suggested that as we hadn't had our hair shaved off, perhaps the occupants of the previous barrack had thought we were a couple of stooges. No one new us in there, but now as Stan was known to Dennis, and had met me in Dulag Luft, we were both accepted. Possibly correct, but who knows? Apparently, for some unknown reason, Stan and I were the first two prisoners that hadn't had their heads shaved.

[77.] *See Appendix B for the circumstances leading up to becoming a POW.*

Lancaster Bale Out

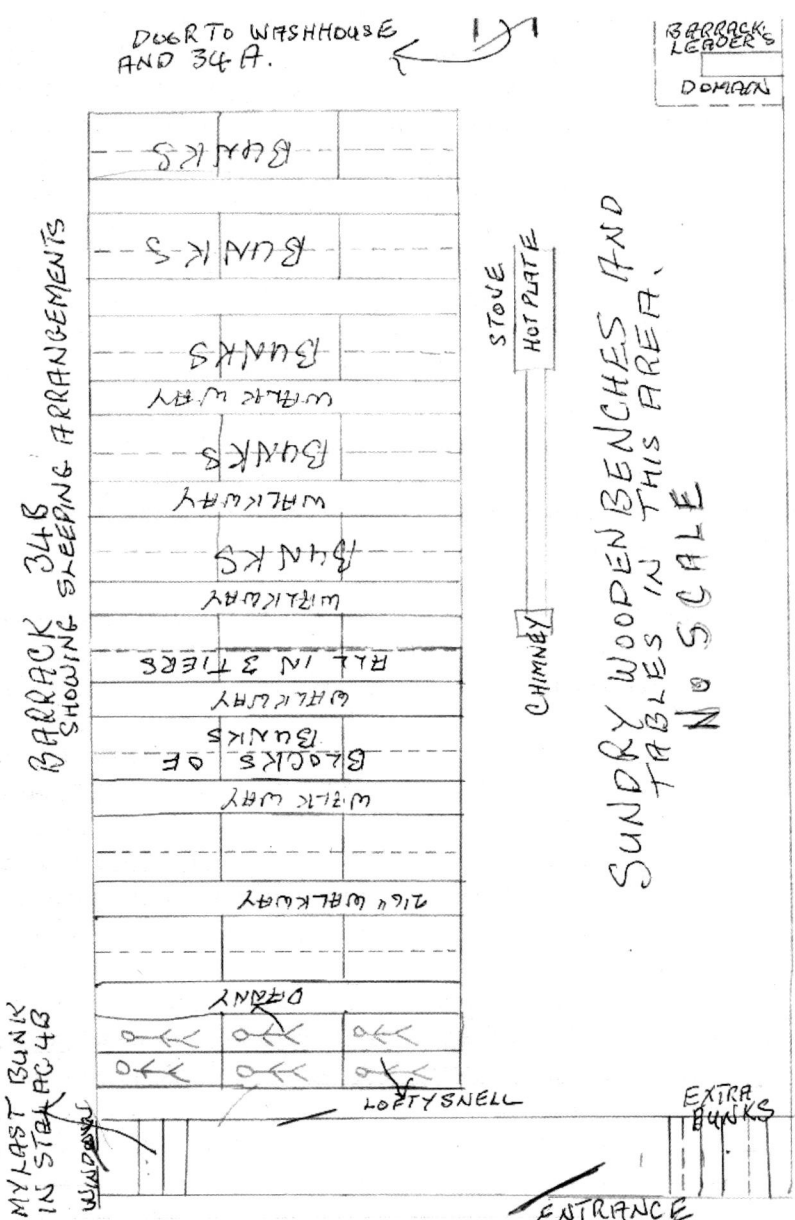

Sketch of Hut 34B (F. Smooker)

Lancaster Bale Out

I settled down into my new surroundings quite well. Immediately above me, on the top bunk, there was an American called Fisher. I think he was from Texas, quite tall and gangly, and he reminded me of a cowboy. I say he was tall, but I rarely saw him on his feet. The only time he put his boots on was to go to parade, use the latrine or collect his rations. Alongside him, also on the top was another American whose nickname was 'Igor'. He was just the opposite of Fisher, quite small and pixie-like, always pleasantly smiling. I think he got his nickname because of his hunched up posture, although not quite as bad as the Igor from the early Frankenstein films. At the feet of them, the two other bunks were occupied by two RCAF fellows, and these four used to spend most of their time on their bunks, playing cards, lying around or sleeping. They never seemed to use the hot-plate on the stove to boil water, for tea or coffee, but occasionally one could smell frying SPAM, or potatoes, wafting down from up high. I learned the reason why.

The ceilings of all the barracks were made of wood and the electric cables for our 60W lights were run along inside the roof cavity. Fisher had tapped into these cables with some wire that he had stolen. He had chiseled a channel into a house brick, and laid a coil of wire in it. Actually, he had told me that it was a guitar string that had been wound round a 6" nail, and so they had their own hot plate - ingenious really. I don't know where they obtained the bits from, but as I've mentioned, one could almost purchase one's freedom with cigarettes. The Americans and Canadians used to receive cigarettes by the hundred, from home in personal parcels.

The stoker in this barrack was called 'Darkie' Thacker. He was so called because of his swarthy complexion, besides which he was always dirty from his voluntary occupation. I think he was an ex-paratrooper. Before settling down in one's bunk at night, we would fill our dixies with water and line them up in a queue on the hot plate. The first one was placed in the hottest spot and the others followed up behind. Darkie Thacker used to rise early to get the fire going. As each dixie boiled, he would call out the name of each owner, who would come and collect it ready to brew some tea or coffee. He would then move all the remaining dixies up in turn - this job he did willingly all the time I was in that barrack!

Lancaster Bale Out

There was a brick-built coal store in the camp where tons of coal bricks were stored. Each barrack was rationed to an amount of pounds of coal bricks per day. Naturally the ration did not last long enough, but volunteers from each barrack would go daily and collect the coal using their kitbags to carry it in. The coal ration was issued under the supervision of the German guards. As it happened, the coal store was locked with a huge ordinary padlock, and one morning the German guard must have inadvertently left the key in the lock. Someone - I don't know who - had made an impression of this key on a bar of soap, and duplicate keys had been made by some ingenious prisoners. Almost every night, a coal thieving detail would leave most barracks to go to the coal store and collect extra rations. This happened despite the fact that the barracks were locked at night and searchlights constantly illuminated the compounds relentlessly. The people from our barrack who ventured out at night on this hazardous operation, started complaining about doing it all the time, so volunteers were called for. I volunteered to do it one night, just to show that I was willing to do my share.

Along with five other lads out we went into the dark compound one night, keeping an eye on the searchlight. We moved only while the searchlight was pointing away from us, then finding the nearest hiding place - usually flat on the ground - when the beam swept towards us. A hole had been cut in the single barbed-wire fence surrounding our compound, and we went through it one at a time, carrying our empty kit bags. No wonder those lads had complained about doing this job every night. I thought that if that searchlight picked us up, we could have been machine-gunned. When we finally arrived at the coal store I was amazed to find about a dozen people already there pinching coal. The door was already open and I wondered who would be locking up after us. We quickly filled our kitbags and headed off back to our barrack. It had been quite hair-raising going there with empty kitbags, but returning with a full kit bag of coal bricks was, to put it mildly, one of the most frightening experiences I'd had since operational flying.

Once back at the barrack the coal bricks were hidden beneath the floor. A channel had been made by removing a length of bricks. The coal was laid carefully in this channel and the bricks were placed

The Funeral of Taffy Jones[79] (T. Hunt)

back in position. Rather strangely, the loose floor bricks were never noticed during barrack inspections by the guards. Fortunately, this was the only time I was called on to make such a trip, although of course there were some people that never did it at all, even though everyone benefited.

A few weeks after I'd volunteered, another detail was called for. Amongst the volunteers there was a Welsh RAF lad called 'Taffy' Jones[78]. This detail was doomed for disaster. Of the six lads who went out, none returned to barracks that night. Five went to the cooler, and the unfortunate Taffy Jones went to the makeshift hospital. I well remember the next morning, when Pritchard, our barrack leader, called for silence in the barrack, before announcing that Taffy Jones had died that morning.

It appears that while the lads had been in that darkened coal store, busy filling their kitbags, two patrolling guards had arrived, and, on finding the coal store unlocked, one of them had opened the door and fired his Luger into the dark. Taffy Jones was unfortunately shot and killed. He was buried without military honours in the

---

[78]. See Appendix B for the circumstances leading up to becoming a POW.

[79]. Lofty Snell is 3rd from the left and Pritchard is 3rd from the right holding the bugle.

cemetery at Mühlberg. Only a limited number of his companions were allowed at his funeral.

Whenever I see the German golfer Bernard Langer I am always reminded of Unteroffizier Schroeder. He was the German corporal who was in charge of our RAF compound. He used to make a daily inspection of all the barracks in the compound, but spoke to no one, except the barrack leaders. He goose-stepped through the hut before entering the barrack leader's office in the corner, where he would sit for a while enjoying a Red Cross cigarette and perhaps a tin mug of good Canadian coffee. What they talked about I don't know. He was a tallish, fairly good-looking blond, who, it was said, had been wounded on the Russian front. He didn't seem to have any visible wounds but was now on light duties, inspecting our barracks. Brick floors had to be swept and clothes lines, nailed to the ceiling, had to be taken down. As he walked, or marched, slowly through the barrack, lads at the back lying on top or middle bunks would make cat-calls in seductive voices
"Blondie, Blondie" and make kissing noises with their lips. The Unteroffizier ignored it all and continued his slow march through the hut, and then had his cigarette and coffee when he had finished.

One morning he entered the barrack and just inside the door he spotted a string clothes line, still nailed to the ceiling. Hanging on the line - hopefully to dry - were obviously a number of items of underwear and shirts. Blondie walked the full length of the barrack to the stove, and, picking up a long coal rake, he returned to the offending clothes line. He reached up with the rake and pulled the whole lot down. Twisting it around, he carried on through the barrack, trailing the line and washing along the floor behind him.

The door at the end of the barrack was constantly being opened by people entering or leaving. Most times people forgot to close this door allowing a cold draught into the barrack. From those nearest to the door there was always the call of
"Door! door!" One inventive lad rigged up a pulley system - a weighted tin of sand attached to a pulley by a length of string automatically pulling the door closed. Blondie always left the door open deliberately, but the day the pulley system was put into use, he

got a surprise when he heard the door close behind him, apparently of its own volition. He stopped to find out the reason why and on seeing the pulley and line he pulled out his knife and cut the string, allowing the tin to fall to the floor. He then carried on his slow pace through the barrack.

We did acquire an ally, in the form of an elderly guard, who was given the name of 'Old Joe'. He was a soldier, maybe in his mid-sixties. I don't think he had done much fighting though; perhaps he had been recruited for the job he was doing, now guarding RAF prisoners. It was said that he had been a farmer in Southern Germany, and indeed that is what he resembled, with his splayed feet. He used to precede Blondie through the barracks and warn all and sundry
" Unteroffizier Schroeder kommt!" He became very popular with the lads, indeed, maybe too popular for his own comfort. One day a search of the barracks was organised by our captors. We were kept outside our huts for hours on end, while German guards, tore everything apart inside, searching, it was said, for a wireless receiver, or anything illicit. During one of these searches, while the German officers stood in the compound chatting together, Old Joe arrived on the scene and was given a rousing cheer from some six hundred voices to cries of "Good Old Joe!" The German officers looked in wonder at the object of our cheers, much to the discomfort of Old Joe!

There were radios in the camp, and we used to be given the news from the BBC each evening after it was dark. One man would run the gauntlet of the searchlights, from barrack to barrack, and read out the news. Locked barracks were no deterrent to certain people. It was said that someone had made a receiver and encased it in an army water bottle. There were other sets, made from parts paid for with cigarettes. Apparently, the main receiver was hidden under the wooden seat of the latrine.

The latrine in our compound was a forty-seater - four wooden benches each with ten holes cut out. It was very embarrassing really to be squatting there with trousers down below the knees. Due to

Lancaster Bale Out

the food we were having however, calls of nature were not too frequent. I remember one time I did go, I found myself sitting next to a six foot tall Australian, who was sitting and knitting himself a pair of socks. I gazed at him wondering where he had acquired the wool and knitting needles, but the latrine was no place to stay and ask questions.

After a few weeks or so, my original mate Stan and I, seemed to have drifted apart, and Dennis and I became mates, after a fashion. I was becoming very restless and bored stiff with the inactivity. I wandered about the camp staring out through the barbed-wire across the open German countryside. Dennis was always wanting to play a game called 'jenni quoits'. We had a net similar to a Badminton net but instead of racquets and shuttlecock we had a ring, about six inches in diameter, made of rope, which we threw at each other over the net. The rules were the same as badminton and Dennis was a master at this game - he always beat me - and eventually I got fed up with it.

It was due to Dennis that I met one of his crew, a lad from Birmingham named Cliff 'Danny' Daniels[80]. It was strange that members of the same crew who had shared untold dangers didn't seem to be very close. Most people seemed to mix with anyone who suited them. Danny looked quite fit, but he spent most of his time resting on his bunk. Personally, I seemed to have got over my starvation period and continually being on my bunk became abhorrent to me; except of course to sleep at night, amid a chorus of moans and groans, snores and various other noises from the other occupants of the barrack.

With my fifty cigarettes a week I used to buy extra grub from addicted smokers. For thirty cigarettes I bought a bar of Canadian chocolate. With the remaining twenty I bought extras, for instance, a tin of salmon or pilchards. I forget the prices in cigarettes but when I saw certain people emptying dust out their pockets to roll a cigarette about the thickness of a match-stick I was glad I was a non-smoker. Although I was restless and active, and Danny was

---

[80] See Appendix B for the circumstances leading up to becoming a POW.

a bunk-basher, we seemed to get on quite well together. One day when we were standing on parade waiting to be counted, I noticed a lad coming from another barrack who was dressed in pyjamas, carpet slippers, dressing gown with a white scarf around his neck. I said to Danny
"Who the hell is that?" Among us scruffy individuals he stuck out like a sore thumb!
"Oh," said Danny,
"that is Winston Barrington."
"Where on earth did he get all that clobber from?" I asked.
"His mother brings it" replied Danny. Later after roll-call I got the full story.

It appears that Barrington's father had died when he was a schoolboy, and his mother, Florence Barrington, had met a German army officer to whom she got re-married and moved to Germany with. As he grew older his step-father suggested that he move back to England to live with his aunt and uncle, otherwise he would have had to join the Hitler Youth Organisation. When the war started young Barrington was old enough to join the RAF, whilst his mother was living in Germany on her own again, her husband having been killed at the Russian front. Due to her second marriage she was now a German citizen, and therefore not interned.

Barrington became an RAF Pilot but was shot down in 1943 and became a POW in Stalag 4B so his mother moved to Mühlberg to be near him. She used to visit him at regular intervals, bringing him various items of comfort and so on. A bizarre story, but true. As it happened, Danny and I saw her once later on.

Volunteers had been called-for, to go out of the camp to a storage place to collect some bales of wood shavings to fill mattresses. I persuaded Danny to get off his back for a while and volunteer with me. So off we went, six of us, pushing a hand-cart out of the camp and down the road. It made a change to see the flat country-side without one's view being spoiled by the infernal barbed-wire.

As we proceeded down the road, with an armed guard walking behind, we noticed a lady approaching us going towards the camp.

Lancaster Bale Out

There were muted calls of
"Wow, look at her!" She was quite pretty actually and didn't look all that old but then to us, who hadn't seen a female for months, anything in a skirt looked pretty. We assumed she must be a German female employee who worked in the offices, but as we passed her she said, in English,
"Hello boys, where are you going, home?" We were so dumbfounded that nobody answered her. Danny said to me excitedly
"That is Mrs Barrington going to visit her son."

Many years ago the Barrington saga appeared in the Sunday Express. It appears that she had been smuggled into the camp to escape the marauding Russians, who had actually liberated us. It was said in the article that she had been given a British airman's uniform for her own protection and was nicknamed 'Pete'. This lady must have originally come from County Durham because at the time of the article, she was a resident of an old people's home at Leadgate, near Consett. At the time I thought of visiting her but I never got round to it. Apparently her son had emigrated to Canada.

There were other interesting people in hut 34B, such as Freddie Bamburger. His name sounds German, but he was not. He had broken his thigh when he baled out, and the Germans had set the bone improperly so that he had one short leg. To counteract this, he had been given a very thick soled boot for his short leg. He was a gentleman was Freddie, always pleasant and smiling. He was also our interpreter - being a linguist by trade. He spoke fluent German and French, and was now studying Russian.

Another lad told me his story. He also limped but not as badly as Freddie. He explained that he had been on a raid on Berlin, and all he remembered was a huge explosion then he blacked out. He didn't know how long he was unconscious, but when he came round he was lying on grass in a wood. He told me that it was a beautiful day, sun shining, birds singing; so much so, that he thought he had died and was now in heaven. After a while he realised he wanted to wee.
"I can't be in heaven" he thought, "otherwise I wouldn't want to wee." Doing the necessary to relieve himself he discovered that

Lancaster Bale Out

he was wounded in his groin because that was where the flow was coming from. He crawled on hands and knees out of the wood and lay down on a cart track. Eventually a German farmer arrived, with his horse and cart, and he was assisted or lifted on to the cart and taken to the nearest Police Station where he was given a pair of crutches and escorted to a hospital. The wound was stitched together, despite his protests that he felt that there was something in his groin. Later he arrived in Stalag 4B with his crutches. After numerous requests for medical treatment he was eventually operated upon and, from out of his groin, they produced the brass bead from the R1155[81] trailing aerial, together with one and a half inches of the aerial! He slowly recovered and although he still limped he was now quite fit.

It was not the same for one tall, young, man called Reg Dernam[82] - who had been shot down on his first operation. Reg must have been a fit young man to be accepted for aircrew, but now he was an epileptic. I saw him once standing beside his bunk one day, when suddenly he had a seizure. Gurgling in his throat, he fell backwards, banging his head on the brick floor, where he lay, uncontrollably shaking his whole body.

Then there was Bennie, a laconic Australian pilot. Poor Bennie seemed to be shrivelled up with the cold, and malnutrition. When the Germans told all and sundry to behave themselves they used the phrase,
"You play ball with us, and we'll play ball with you." Bennie, in his Australian drawl, commented,
"You play ball with Jerry and he'll stick the bat up your bottom."

Then there was the academic, Spud Murphy. He was a ghastly, pale, black, curly-haired Irish lad. I hardly ever saw Spud, but when I did he would always be carrying a book under his arm. Talking to him was just like talking to a University professor, and it made me feel very uneducated.

[81.] *The Marconi R1155 was the standard HF wireless receiver used in the heavy bombers.*
[82.] *See Appendix B for the circumstances leading up to becoming a POW.*

Lancaster Bale Out

Fights in the camp were rare, and I only ever witnessed one. A tall six foot New Zealander had an argument with a five foot five inch Canadian. I don't know why they fell out, but their bunks were adjacent to the same walking space. It was easy to lose ones temper in such a confined space, and I felt concern for the small Canadian as the New Zealander pounded his ribs with hammer blows. He was not hit in the face however, but his ribs must have been sore from the bare-fisted battering that they received.

When I mention about the Germans telling us to behave ourselves it was because occasionally the roll-call or "Appell" in the RAF compound was a miniature riot. After the count had been made, and those too sick to come out had been reported, there were always some two or three people missing. The guards then had to go into the barracks to check upon the missing bodies and enquire who was "krank" and who was not. It was sometimes amazing to see a tug of war in progress between a German guard and a shirking RAF airman. The guard would be trying to pull the filthy blanket off the man, and he would be pulling it back over himself. After a while, the game would end when the guard took his rifle from his shoulder and threaten to shoot the man. I have seen RAF men defy the guards and dare them to shoot. The guard would back down, but the dissident would end up in the cooler.

The Germans wanted us all to be on parade on time and behave ourselves or else they would keep the residents of the offending barracks standing outside for one or maybe two hours. It was a laugh one day, when one barrack was kept out on parade for a long period, and a lad from one of the well behaved barracks carried a makeshift chair - made out of Red Cross tea chests - into the compound for the guard to sit on while he watched over the offending barrack residents. Sometimes a football would be kicked-in amongst those on extended barrack parade. A proper mêlée would ensue and then the poor guard would have to give up and march off. Of course we had been told back home that if we were ever captured we were still on duty, and we had to cause the enemy as much trouble as possible.

23.
A New Identity - Escape

As winter gave way to spring the only thing that changed was the soup. Turnips gave way to cabbage. It is said that in springtime a young man's fancy turns to thoughts of love, but in my case my thoughts, and possibly others, turned to thoughts of escape. I wandered about the camp; it was called walking the wire, and I gazed longingly over the countryside. How could one get out of there? As far as I knew there was no escape organisation in this camp. Most men were quite happy to lie on their bunks and await liberation. Some did try an escape, because occasionally while slouching in the back row on parade, I would be aware of someone running behind in a crouched position. The runner had been counted at one end of the row and was now running to the other end to be counted again, obviously to cover up for a missing man. Information about who the missing airman was, or whether he had successfully escaped or not, seemed to be known only to those involved in the escape attempt.

I did hear of one man who hid himself under a pile of empty Red Cross tins to be taken out through the gates in a Russian hand-hauled cart. The empty Red Cross tins from hundreds of parcels were collected and taken out of the camp to be used for the German war effort. Apparently one man had had the idea of burying himself under the heap of tins and been transported out of the camp by the Russians. I don't know who it was, but he must have been caught later and returned to 4B where he must have confessed to his means of escape. From then all carts going out of the camp, except of course the stinking latrine cart, were viciously stabbed at the gate with a rifle and bayonet. Escape was constantly on the minds of certain people.

It was said that it was easier to escape from a working camp but at 4B only the Russians seemed to do any work at all. To the north of the RAF compound there was a large contingent of army NCOs who actually put the RAF NCOs to shame. They blancoed their gaiters,

Lancaster Bale Out

polished their boots and kept themselves clean and smart. Indeed they even had a bugler who we could hear in the mornings calling "Reveille."

To the south of us there were army privates, coming in and going out on working parties. I learned that, according to the Geneva Convention, only ranks below that of corporal could be forced to work. In this regard no RAF aircrew went out to work, because they were all made a minimum rank of Sergeant. There were a few LACs in our compound, also paratrooper privates, but none of these were forced to work. The Germans used to say that we weren't soldiers, we were civilians in uniform, we were "terrorfliegers" - terror flyers. They did, however, seem to have great respect for the army lads, and vice versa.

I heard a tale about some army lads who were POWs in the Berlin area and they marched through the streets to work so smartly that a German officer was heard to ask if it was an army of occupation. How true that was I don't know.

Occasionally the camp officers would organise a march past of all POWs in 4B. The German officers would arrange themselves to receive the salute and 'eyes right' as we marched past our barracks, with our barrack leaders ordering 'eyes right' and then giving the Germans the salute. The eight barrack leaders would confer together before this mock parade and discuss what could be done to spoil it. Usually it ended up with the RAF lads marching at our ninety steps per minute for a while but when we reached the saluting base we would be given the order,
"Augen links" or 'eyes left', instead of "Augen rechts." On the other hand we would break our smart marching order and start acting the fool, jumping on each other's backs or pushing each other out of line, in fact anything to show disrespect to our captors. The German officers took it all as being the actions of over grown schoolboys or 'English humour', as they were heard to mutter. I must confess that I sometimes felt embarrassed by our making such fools of ourselves, but I had to join in with everyone else, or risk being called a Jerry lover.

Lancaster Bale Out

From somewhere, I had acquired a second set of underwear, vest and underpants. I wore one set of undies as long as possible, until I began to have an unbearable itch under my armpits. The first time I felt this itching underarm I wondered if I'd got scabies or something, but on removing my shirt and vest, I found a little live creature with numerous legs moving about. I realised that I was lousy and shuddered with horror. The only means of washing my clothes was in the cold water troughs, between tandem huts, using Red Cross soap and then hanging them out to dry in the barrack. Apparently lice caused typhus and the Germans themselves were dead scared of an epidemic.

There was a bath house in the camp, and since I was not the only one who was itching, a visit to it was organised. This first visit, was after three months in the camp. We had to take all our clothes and belongings, including a towel and we sauntered down there. I found a huge room with about twelve sprays in the centre of the ceiling. Hot water at last, if you could get under it. We all stood naked under the sprays jostling for a position and soaping ourselves with our Red Cross soap. Our clothes were packed into a de-louser, towel included; so to get dry we stood in front of a huge fan blowing hot air at us. When our clothes came out they smelt nasty but at last we were clean, possibly not to be repeated for another three months. The workers in this bath-house were Russian officers, but it seemed that the only prisoners who didn't have access to it were the poor Russian peasants. No wonder the Germans warned us not to encourage them to congregate around our barracks; they must have been extremely lousy.

The Russian prisoners not only did the menial tasks in the camp, but one occasionally saw a group of about forty being marched down the road and out of the main gate. They would each usually be carrying a tool of some description, a shovel a rake or even a pitchfork, so I assumed they were kept busy working nearby at various gardens or farms. On their return, one or two could be seen carrying a turnip or perhaps a few potatoes to augment their rations. I once visited a Russian barracks just out of interest and, although it was similar to my own barrack in all respects, it seemed to be spotlessly clean. I noted that potato peelings which they had begged from 'capitalist barracks' had been rolled into a ball, and were heating on the hotplate of the stove. Because their western Allies all received a weekly Red Cross parcel we were called 'capitalists' such was their naivety of their own government.

I heard a couple of tales about the Russian prisoners, but I can't vouch for their truth. It appeared that one day they went on strike and wouldn't come out to go to work. The German guards in their wisdom sent in an Alsatian guard dog. The dog did not return, but the next day its skin was found hanging on the barbed-wire, outside the window. It was also said that if a Russian prisoner died his mates would keep his body and carry it out on parade between them. They would prop the body up to be counted and then collect his rations. How long they could do this for I don't know because a body wouldn't last for long - unless it was embalmed. From what I saw of Russian prisoners, I easily believe that these stories could be true.

There was another type of creepy-crawly, which one saw very little of, which only seemed to attack at night. When I moved into my middle bunk, beneath the American, Fisher, I used to have an unbearable itching on my hands, especially between my fingers. I eventually visited the makeshift medical centre one day, hoping to find some kind of skin ointment to rub on my hands. Nothing was available, and the RAMC attendant told me that I had chilblains, due to the cold weather at the time. Eventually after a few weeks the itching disappeared. Now, in mid spring, I noticed lads from various barracks, dragging their bunks out into the compound. They then proceeded to knock their bunks to pieces, and under control, set light to all the joints. I wondered why they were doing this and was told that they were burning out the bed bugs and their eggs which were hidden in the joints of the bunks. I realised then that I hadn't had chilblains earlier but, I had been attacked by these horrible little creatures. This set me to wonder why that bunk had been left vacant.

Danny told me one day that there was a middle bunk vacant near to him. When I went to investigate it was ideal - beside the door in the gable end of the barrack. It was three tiered but my head end was up

Lancaster Bale Out

against the gable and there was no other bunk at my feet, as it was situated at right angles to the normal arrangement. I was surprised that Danny hadn't claimed it for himself, but since he had a top bunk nearby, I think he could not be bothered to move. I decided to move again. I don't know where the previous occupant had gone, maybe he had escaped or just moved to another barrack more suited to his needs. I sincerely hoped that he had left no bed bugs behind!

Danny and I now became 'muckers' - that is two people sharing their Red Cross parcels. If one opened a tin of corned beef, salmon or pilchards, instead of scoffing the whole lot in one go, we shared it to prevent it going off.

Danny didn't smoke either, therefore we now had one hundred cigarettes between us with which to buy extras. Sometimes one could buy white bread from the guards. I remember I approached one guard, who was standing guarding some obscure building or other one night before lock up.
"Haben sie brot fur cigarretten?" I asked him, whereupon he produced a loaf of white bread from under his tunic! I can't remember how many cigarettes it cost, but I think he was gasping for a smoke. How he had got past the parade, before coming on duty with a loaf of bread under his tunic I don't know. It was a convenient arrangement for both parties. The German guards apparently were rationed to three cigarettes a day and white bread and Red Cross butter was a very tasty snack! One had to be discreet though; the guards also risked disciplinary action for bartering with prisoners.

At Danny's feet on the top bunk there resided one 'Lofty' Snell. His pilot, Ken Davie[83], was also in this barrack but one would not have thought they were from the same crew. Actually Ken was a Durham lad (indeed he came from Easington) but other than his Durham accent he seemed like a stranger to me. He was a pale, refined sort of lad, who looked as though he was suffering from malnutrition and he didn't seem to have the energy to do anything except lie on his bunk. Lofty was 6'4" tall and he had a fair moustache. He also

---

[83] *See Appendix B for the circumstances of Snell and Davie becoming POWs.*

Lancaster Bale Out

F/E Kevern 'Lofty' Snell (V. Stothard)

spent all his time sitting on his top bunk stroking his moustache; his unlaced boots and legs dangling over the side. He was the camp forger; resting the side of a tea chest on his knees and using a mapping pen and Indian ink, he would spend all his time forging German travel documents.

The original travel warrants which Lofty Snell was forging were borrowed from French POWs. He showed me a copy one day but I could not read it because it was in German. Some of the French prisoners were what were called 'trusties' in that they were allowed to work outside of the camp without being guarded. Indeed I believe that some of them used to get home leave.

I asked Lofty who the forgeries were for, but he wouldn't tell me. In any case they were of no use to me, because one would have to be fluent in German or French to use them, and I was fluent in neither.

I could not understand why Lofty didn't lace his boots up. When he had to get down from his bunk, he would have looked much smarter and presumably been able to walk better, instead of shuffling along. Personally I tried to keep myself smart like a soldier. I was already in khaki uniform and for half a dozen cigarettes I even purchased a pair of soldier's gaiters. At the time I preferred to be taken for a soldier, rather than a scruffy RAF NCO, even though I didn't have any tapes on my sleeve.

The weather in late spring became quite warm and pleasant and the RAF compound became like a nudist colony. Men who used to constantly lie on their bunks would now take a blanket into the compound, lay on it on the hard packed road surface, and lie stark naked in the sun, much to the disgust of the Presbyterian Padre. He commented on people lying about like 'hogs in the sun', instead of using their time at more creative pursuits. His remarks fell on stony ground!

There was a stagnant pond just north of the bath-house. I don't know where the water suddenly came from, but as the weather became warmer still we used to swim in it. I think that there must have

Lancaster Bale Out

German Ausweis forged by Lofty (V. Stothard)

been a burst water main leading to the bath-house. Wherever the water came from, we used it as a swimming pool - myself included. It's a wonder that we didn't all go down with typhoid or some such horrible affliction. As the water became shallower the bottom of the pond became thick with mud. Eventually the Germans themselves stopped this crazy caper.

June 6th 1944 - D.Day - raised our spirits somewhat. "Home by Christmas," was the cry on everyone's lips - how wrong we were. All thoughts of escape disappeared, as no one wanted to risk it with liberation being imminent. The Russians had halted the Germans at Stalingrad and were now on the offensive. Hundreds of Italian prisoners arrived in the camp, as Italy had capitulated.

We received the German version of the progress of the war from copies of the *Völkischer Beobachter* which were distributed to us freely. Someone had drawn a map of the continent with the lines of battle of both Russian and western Allies but the lines seemed to be hundreds of miles apart, which indeed they were. We hoped and prayed that the British and Americans would arrive here first. The lines of battle were altered on the map almost daily, as we were illegally read the BBC news. It seemed that the Russians were advancing rapidly and that they would be here first, because the second front in the west seemed to be bogged down. Unteroffizier Schroeder took a great interest in this map, which was pasted onto the vertical section of the chimney in our barrack - strangely he didn't even tear it down! Perhaps he also wanted the British and Americans here first, as did lots of his countrymen.

British soldiers were still coming into the camp, mainly from the war in Italy and since it seemed to take our western Allies so long to advance, I began to have thoughts of escape once more. Working parties from the batches of soldiers were still being sent out, and as the hot summer gave way to Autumn, I plucked up the courage to go to the soldiers' barracks to find someone to change identities with. Winter seemed to come early in 1944, and it was late October before I found a soldier willing to take on my identity. When the time came, I would become Private Marshall of the British Army. He didn't know where or when they would next be going out - I hoped that it wouldn't be to work in a coal mine, which happened quite often apparently.

I remember that there was snow on the ground when Marshall told me that they would be going out the next day. Danny thought that I was mad to be going out to work when I could spend my time in comparative comfort, lying on my bunk doing nothing until the liberation. I moved into Bob Marshall's bunk the night before we were due to go out. I met an army private and two Polish soldiers, who also wanted to try and escape - one of the Poles professed to speak German.

The next day we were lined up, and marched out of the camp and down to Mühlberg station where we boarded a cattle truck. This truck had a pot-bellied stove on the floor and a pipe out of the roof for a chimney. An elderly guard sat there with us. He had a rifle and sat smoking his pipe beside the stove, quite unperturbed. The other army soldier even picked up the rifle and examined it while discussing the merits of British and German rifles. Honestly, if we'd been so inclined we could have escaped there and then; but looking out across that dreary snow-covered landscape would have

Lancaster Bale Out

deterred even the most ardent escaper. We had no plan of action, and didn't even know where we were going at the time. From our Red Cross parcels we had a brew of tea, which we shared with the guard. He was so trusting; I would have felt very guilty getting him into trouble.

Our first train journey lasted about two or three hours, and we disembarked at a village station called Niederwiesa (5 miles NE of Chemnitz). We were met here by three guards, all carrying rifles on their shoulders. We were lined up, marched down to the village and into the village hall, situated on the sloping main street. There must have been village dances held there pre-war, as the floor was highly polished. In the centre of the hall stood familiar looking three tier bunks. I presumed that we were to be billeted here, much pleasanter living conditions than barrack 34B. I would say that there were at least 100 army privates billeted there. The place was even centrally heated by a coke boiler down below in the cellar. Niederwiesa resembled a ghost village though; other than the guards and railway workers at the station I didn't see any other adult civilians. The next day after we'd arrived, we were told that we had to be out of our bunks at 4:30 am the next morning, to go to work. The other prisoners told me to make some black bread sandwiches the night before, because all we would get to eat at work would be soup and ersatz kaffee.

We were marched out of the door and lined up in fives on the village main street. I noticed that no count was made - anyone could have slipped away in the dark, frosty morning. The barrack gates were slammed closed behind us and we were marched off to the village station. I was glad that I had my army greatcoat, on the very cold train journey to Chemnitz railway yard. It was a massive complex with railway wagons parked all over the place. I was issued with a long-handled shovel and taken by a guard to a line of trucks where he showed me my work. The bottom doors of those trucks had been opened and the contents of clinker or ashes from them had been dropped on to the rails. There was a line of trucks like this and there must have been tons of the stuff to be thrown back to clear the lines so the trucks could be moved. The guard left me on my own to get on with it. He told me to come over to his hut for coffee and soup later.

I was not used to this long-handled shovel; the only type of shovel I had ever used had a shorter handle, as space down a coal mine is much more restricted. I tried to shift some of the clinker, but it was a meagre amount that I actually moved. Coffee break arrived and later the soup ration, but I was pleased that I had brought my black bread, beef sandwiches.

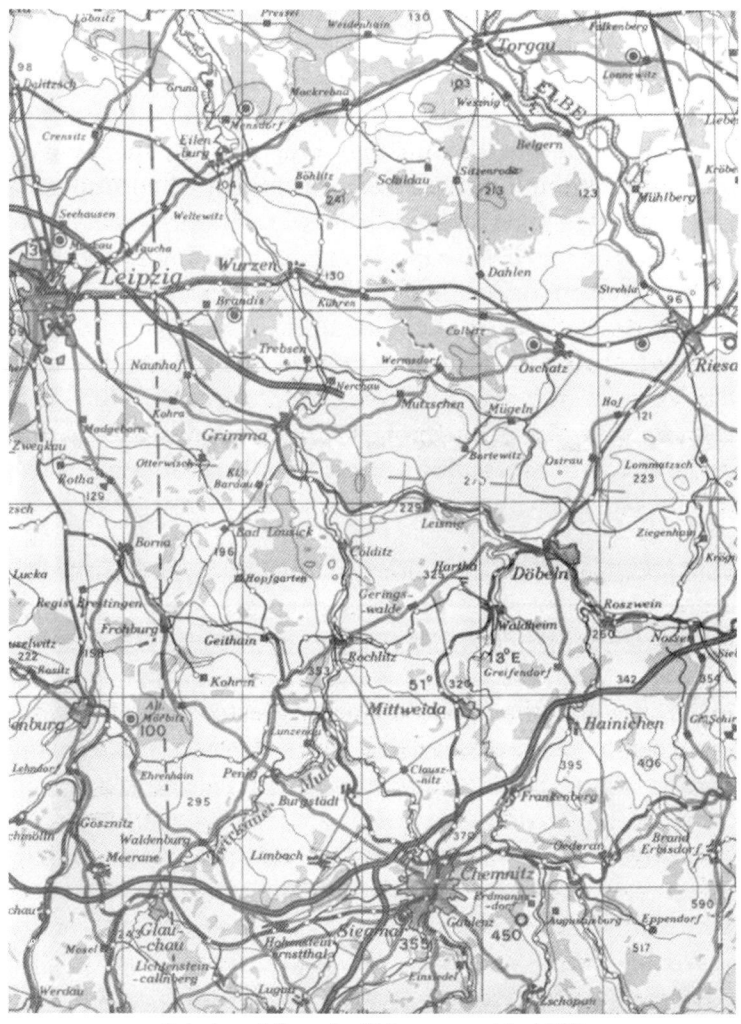

Leipzig and Chemnitz (© Crown copyright 1943)

Lancaster Bale Out

What a boring job! No one checked to see what I had done and I was on my own all day. I could have just walked away, but where could I go to in this weather? In any event, I felt too exhausted to try to escape. At about 4:00 pm we were assembled at the guard's hut and marched off to the station to catch the train back to Niederwiesa. Back at the barrack we received our rations of black bread and potatoes, and then off to bed to be ready for 4.30 am again next morning. I was beginning to regret my decision to volunteer for this. We worked for eleven hours a day, six days a week. If this went on for long I would be too weak and exhausted to attempt an escape.

Sunday was the only day we had off. The door to our barrack was unlocked and we could go outside. We discovered three or four concrete steps into an area some thirty yards in length, surrounded by barbed-wire with a gate leading out onto the deserted village street. It was really boring; we were more confined here than we were at Stalag 4B. One Sunday a load of coke arrived for the central heating boiler in the basement, and a volunteer was called for to shovel it from the footpath and down a grid into the cellar. My soldier friend volunteered; he was much fitter than I was. I can't remember his name, so I will call him Tommy. I went out of the barrack as far as the gate to watch him. When I got there, I found that some children were sledging down the main street and Tommy had downed tools and was playing with them. The kids were really enjoying themselves with their British enemy. One of our guards soon came out though and put a stop to it. Tommy was told to get back to shoveling the coke.

It was then that I found our means of escape. When we left our barrack in the mornings to go to work, we always came out of the main door and turned left and descended three or four steps before lining up on the road to march to the station. That Sunday morning I went to the right of the steps and discovered an empty garage, underground. The door was open so I went in and found that at the back there were two small windows without any barbed-wire over them. I tried one and sure enough it opened outwards at ground level. I went back and told Tommy and the two Poles what I had discovered. They decided that we would go in the morning. We would hide in the garage until all was quiet, and then with our stored up Red Cross chocolate and food we'd make our escape attempt. Personally I would have preferred to have waited until the weather became warmer, but everyone else vetoed the idea. They were, like me, fed up with working the long hours, and wanted to be off.

The next morning the escape plan was put into operation and, with our haversacks, we scrambled, one at a time, through the small garage window. We walked out of the blacked-out village and set off for Czechoslovakia, more or less due south we assumed. We had no real plan at all. We didn't even have a map, and were all in army uniform - we must have been mad.

After leaving the village of Niederwiesa we decided that we'd better get off the main road before daylight. We jumped over a fence and into some fields, ending up almost knee deep in snow. We struggled through the snow and entered a wood where we had to rest. Although it was cold I was soaked in sweat, so like a fool I discarded my warm army greatcoat, burying it in the snow. In the distance we could hear a dog barking so we changed direction. We ate some of our chocolate and washed it down with melted snow. What a foolhardy escape attempt this was!

After struggling all day from 4:30 am we were becoming exhausted, and by late afternoon it was decided that we'd return to the main road - wherever that led us. When we finally stepped onto the fairly clear road a sigh of relief was breathed by all four of us, and we were pleased to be back on firmer ground. Tommy and I led at the front and the two Poles followed. We met no one, until it was almost dusk, and coming to a bend in the road we looked down a hill and saw a small town nestling at the bottom. Smoke was rising from chimneys - straight up into the frosty air.

We set off down the hill and saw on the opposite side of the road a woman pushing a pram, accompanied by a German policeman. Seeing us, the policeman crossed over and stopped us. He said something like,
"Von wo kommen Sie?" or "Where have you come from?"

The Pole who professed to speak German remained silent, but

Lancaster Bale Out

Tommy took on the conversation. I think that he told the policeman we were going to Czechoslovakia. The policeman drew out his revolver and said,
"Kommen Sie mit."

We followed him like four sheep down into the town which I believe was called Zschopau (8 miles SE of Chemnitz). We were escorted to the police station and taken to the head man's office. It was lovely and warm and the elderly police officer could not have been nicer. He had white hair and a white moustache, like Bernard Hepton in the Colditz series. I think we'd made his day!

"Where have you come from?" he asked.
"Niederwiesa," we said.
"Where were you going?"
"Wir wollten in die Tschechoslowakei gehen," we answered. The officer spoke no English but he could have been anyone's favourite uncle.

He spoke by telephone to Niederwiesa and then he told us that we'd have to stay there for the night, in the cells. There were only three bunks in the cell and so we asked if we could have one with four in. He agreed and allowed us to drag a spare bunk into our cell so that we could all be together.

We then asked him if we could light a fire and make some coffee.
"Haben Sie Kaffee?" he asked.
"Ja, ja," we answered. He allowed us to collect some coal bricks from a store and light a fire in the stove in the cell.
"Wo ist der Kaffee?" he asked. We gave him a packet of Red Cross Canadian coffee and later a large tin bowl of coffee was produced. He kept the remainder of the packet of coffee.

So we lay there in our bunks in that nice warm cell, drinking steaming, hot coffee and singing patriotic songs like, "There'll always be an England," and occasionally exchanging Poland for England in the song. Due to our freezing exertions that day, we soon fell asleep. I thought to myself how glad I was that we'd been caught and I also thought that not all Germans were bad.

Next morning we were awakened by a hammering on the door of our cell and a raucous voice yelling,
"Heraus." One of our guards from Niederwiesa had arrived to pick us up. He escorted us to the railway station, yelling and shouting at us until we were alone with him in the compartment of the train when he changed completely. It was all an act of toughness for all who were there to listen. When we were alone with him his apparent anger subsided and he became more reasonable.
"What was wrong with Niederwiesa?" he wanted to know. I'm afraid that his reasonableness fell on deaf ears.

When we arrived at our village hall we were taken in front of the guard in charge to be judged and punished. I think he was only a corporal but he sentenced us to "Drei Tage, Brot und Wasser." We were taken to the village jail - Tommy and I in one cell and the Poles in another. We spent the three days lying on our beds, again singing our heads off. The village children used to come to the iron-barred window and look in at us, just as children will. We were issued with a hunk of black bread and a jug of water daily. No hot coffee here, and no fire in the stove.

We were released after the three days were up, and told to be ready for work again the next morning. The next day was awful. After my punishment of bread and water for the last few days I had become totally lethargic and by the end of a days work I was completely exhausted. I was so weak that my legs nearly folded under me as we walked back to the village hall. I was light-headed and nearly fainting with hunger. For my own well being I told the German corporal that I was really a RAF Sergeant and that I shouldn't have to work.

He was so astounded, that he gave me a day off work, while he sought advice as to what should be done. I felt awfully guilty but my own health had to come first. In any case, I had come here to attempt to escape not to be working. I had given Bob Marshall some three weeks rest, while I worked in his place. Our escape attempt, which had been doomed from the beginning, was now foiled. I thought it better to go back to Stalag 4B to recover, before trying again.

Lancaster Bale Out

Those three days on bread and water had taken what little energy I had left, and once again, I could not remember the walk from Mühlberg station to the camp. On arrival I was sentenced to ten days in the cooler, on German rations only. No Red Cross parcels. The cooler was a brick building with about ten or twelve cells on the left side of a concrete corridor. Each cell had a wooden bed without a mattress and only a blanket on which to rest one's weary bones. The bed had a raised wooden portion at one end for a pillow. Each cell also had a chamber pot. The back wall of the cell had two small windows which were too high to stand and gaze out of. The first cell near the entrance was the warder's office, and the warder of course was a small middle-aged soldier. He had a terrible bad temper.

We were allowed out of our cells only once per day in order to empty out the chamber pots and have a cold water wash in a tin bowl. These ablutions were performed in a sunken place off the corridor, and we used to have quite a friendly get together with our fellow inmates of the cooler. Sometimes, if we spent too long over our ablutions, the bad tempered little warder would come out of his office, shouting and bawling obscenities at us. He would run along the corridor in his hob nailed jack boots and take flying kicks at our tin bowls resting on the floor of the corridor. We all used to retreat hurriedly into our cells laughing our socks off at his insane antics. Actually I became attached to my private cell. Although all we got to eat was the German rations for the day, with nothing to do but lie on my wooden bed all day, it did not affect me unduly. I found that if I dragged my bed near to the back wall, I could easily reach the small windows which would open by a gap of about two inches, where I could stand and gaze out upon the German barracks just outside the barbed-wire fence.

After my ten days were over I was released and it was with some trepidation that I returned to my barrack 34B. What sort of a reception would I get I wondered. Actually it was non-committal. I think all the condemnation for disclosing my means of escape was self-inflicted. My bed space was still available, I had a Red Cross parcel, still unopened and rather strangely, it was only my 'mucker' Danny who chided me. I thought then "How dare anyone who did nothing but lie on their backs awaiting liberation criticise someone who at least caused some trouble to our captors?" - I hadn't actually escaped, but at least I'd had a go. I held my head high, and Danny soon relented and we were still muckers. After a week or so of the old boring routine, when liberation still seemed to be as far off as ever, I thought I'd try again. It was said that the Germans were now attaching photographs onto the records of private soldiers who were to go out on a working party, so now I had to find myself a soldier who looked like me. Actually it was difficult because all the soldiers, newly taken prisoner, were fit and well-fed individuals, whereas I was beginning to look what I was - a skinny, underfed POW of many months duration.

I found another soldier again who was willing to change identities with me. We knew that we didn't resemble each other feature-wise, but we thought that perhaps the passport-like photos on our record cards would not be too good. As he dreaded going out to work, he eagerly agreed to give it a go.

The same procedure was carried out again as before. I marched with the working party as far as the German offices. We were called out one by one - I forget my new soldier's name now - but I was scrutinized and compared with his photograph. The likeness must have been worse than we had thought. I failed the test, and was told to stand aside, with my Red Cross parcel under my arm, my tin mug, knife and frying pan.

This time I was sentenced to ten days in the punishment block. This was not as bad as it may sound. The punishment block, or Strafe Lager, was an ordinary barrack, separately barbed-wired off and locked at all times. Fortunately, we did keep our Red Cross parcels. The barrack was only half full, I think the cooler must have been full to capacity. The residents of the Strafe Lager were a mixed lot and I was the only RAF chap, even though I looked like a soldier in my khaki uniform. There were soldiers of various nationalities, even one paratrooper from my own barrack 34B. I never acknowledged him however because he had a brutal look about him. He was only slightly taller than me but he was built like a brick wall. Indeed his nickname in our barrack was 'Muscles'.

Lancaster Bale Out

There was a skinny, little Italian soldier in this Strafe Lager and one day someone had caught him stealing from somebody's Red Cross parcel, or so it was alleged. I witnessed a scene here of horrible brutality. The little, skinny Italian was stripped to the waist and held face down by 'Muscles' and his cronies. Muscles himself removed his own leather belt, about two and half inches broad, and beat the Italian about his back and buttocks, until he was bleeding. His screams of "Mama mia" were terrible to hear, but I could do nothing; if I'd complained or told them to stop I might have received the same myself.

It was a tense 10 days which I spent there and since the barrack was only half full, I found myself a bunk more or less isolated from the others. I was pleased when my time was up and I could return to my own barrack where I was among mostly RAF personnel. I told myself to settle down and await liberation. It could not be long now. We even heard Allied war planes in the distance. The RAF were still carrying out massive raids on Germany, during which even the searchlights in the watch towers were switched off and we used to lie in our bunks in total darkness. During these blackouts guards with dogs were let loose in the compound and, if anyone as much as struck a match to light a cigarette, a raucous cry of "Licht aus!" would be heard from the patrolling guards.

It was late November 1944 and we had an influx of 3,000 American GIs who had been taken prisoner during the 'Battle of the Bulge', when the Germans made a last desperate offensive to reach the port of Antwerp in Belgium. I'm afraid these GIs were given a poor welcome from the inmates at the camp. We were requested by the barrack leaders to remove the four-inch wooden board between bunks, in order to accommodate an extra person. Instead of two men lying side by side there would now be three. This request was refused by all and sundry, and so the poor Yanks had to sleep on mattresses on the brick floor. One Yank in our barrack later told me how he had left the USA in November 1944 and by Christmas 1944 he had been taken prisoner. These Yanks were very disillusioned men, who I think had expected the Germans to run away when they arrived. He told me that when they were captured, they had been made to kneel while being relieved of their cigarettes and chocolate bars. They were then transported east to Mühlberg.

After a while seeing the Yanks in our barrack sleeping on the cold brick floor, I felt sorry for one poor chap who seemed to be suffering with bronchitis. I took him to my bunk and told him that he could sleep there during the daytime, but I wanted it back at night. He agreed to this arrangement, and while I was out walking the wire during the day, or talking to acquaintances elsewhere, he would sleep in my bunk. I never bothered him for a couple of days, but then I returned to find him in my bunk with all his clothes on, even his boots and woolly hat. He also had a small cigarette tin which he was using as a spittoon. He coughed quite a lot due to his bronchitis.

I told him that if he wished to continue to sleep in my bunk during the day he must remove his outer clothes.
"Well" he remarked in his southern State drawl,
"I'll take my boots off." I then told him that it was all or nothing - I'd been lousy once and I didn't want it to happen again. Rather than remove his outer clothes he chose his mattress back on the floor.

Christmas 1944 was a dull occasion. No tinsel or glitter, although one or two of the lads used to start a carol going as we lay in our bunks at night. The situation was made worse due to the fact that our Red Cross parcels were running out and we were now reduced to one every two weeks instead of our weekly issue. Our captors explained that they could not now afford to transport supplies from Switzerland. Apparently the only railway line between Berlin and Southern Germany was the one which passed about a mile to the west of our camp, and it was occasionally under attack from Allied war planes. A rumour started going round that Hitler had decided to execute all RAF personnel, but he was persuaded not to by his generals. Another one a bit later suggested that American forward units had reached the River Elbe, but they had been withdrawn to Leipzig, which was thirty miles or so to the west of us. " What was going on" we wondered? "Were we being abandoned?"

Around about February 1945, I was standing moping outside the door of our barrack one day, when I noticed an RAF chap emerge from another hut in our compound carrying a number of bed boards

Lancaster Bale Out

under his arm. I watched him walk over to the hut, which we called the recreation hut, about thirty yards or so from where I was standing. After about fifteen minutes this fellow returned empty-handed. I approached him and asked discretely,
"Are you digging a tunnel over there?"
"Yes," he replied,
"but keep it quiet."
I explained to him that I was an ex-coal miner and said to him,
"Could I get in on it?" He was delighted and took me into his confidence. I felt as though I'd just been employed, and the next morning I went to the recreation hut to do my first shift at the 'coal-face'.

This hut had nothing much to do with recreation really. It was used more as a store room, where footballs and nets were kept, but some of the lads preferred playing cards in there. The hut was on stilts, about eighteen inches high, and during football games, the ball would occasionally get kicked underneath. Someone had asked one of the guards if they could pack sand around the sides to prevent this happening, and he had agreed.

When this was done, part of the wooden floor had been removed, and a shaft had been sunk about six foot deep. The sand from the shaft had been packed under the hut, unseen now by prying eyes. I was amazed on my first shift down there. An electric cable had been laid and bulbs illuminated the tunnel which had progressed about 20 yards, leading west, towards the German garden. For ventilation, someone had fitted a coil spring inside an ordinary kitbag, to keep it expanded, and a garden hose fed a certain amount of fresh air to the face of the tunnel. One man sat at the bottom of the shaft compressing the coiled spring. The roof and sides of the two foot six inch square tunnel were supported by bed boards.

I crawled along the tunnel until I reached the face, where I found a bricklayer's hammer, with which to dig. It was much easier than digging coal. Behind me there was a blanket with a rope fastened at each end. When I had dug enough sand, I raked it onto the blanket by hand, gave a tug on the outgoing rope and the blanket was hauled along the tunnel by a man at the shaft. At the shaft, the sand I had dug was filled into empty Red Cross boxes and passed up the shaft where other men lying under the hut packed it solid. Ingenious really. I don't know how long the tunnel had been in existence but I wondered, "why was anyone trying to escape now?" For months (or even years), these men had probably been doing nothing except lie on their bunks, and now with the Russians approaching from the east and the Allies from the west they had decided to start tunneling. It kept me occupied anyway, so I kept going into this tunnel every day for about two weeks. I had been given a boiler suit to wear while I was underground and now the tunnel had advanced under the German garden. I knew this because I could hear footsteps passing overhead, presumably the workers in the garden. There was no survey carried out and I think the tunnel was rising slightly because, one day, water started to seep through the roof, as though someone was watering a garden. We had a system of signals. If a guard came near the hut the light was switched off, and, as he went away the light came on again. I think the tunnel was about sixty yards long and breathing sometimes became difficult. When that happened one had to insert the hose-pipe into one's mouth to receive a breath of fresh air from the makeshift kitbag- bellows.

One day, while I was digging at the face, the light went off. "Ah," I thought, "Jerry is about." After a few seconds the light came on again, and I had just started digging when it went off again. The light was off for a good while and then it started going on and off in quick succession. Finally, it stayed off. I was left completely in the dark.

I stretched myself out on my back with the hose pipe in my mouth, but I realised that no fresh air was coming through, and therefore no one was working the bellows. I got onto my knees and started crawling backwards out of the tunnel afraid to turn around in the dark in case I dislodged the bed board supports. Eventually I arrived at the bottom of the shaft to find that I was alone, everyone had scarpered. Looking up through a gap in the floorboards of the hut, I could see a German NCO guard. He had a shovel and was banging it onto the floorboards exclaiming excitedly,
"Ach, sie graben einen Tunnel!"

Lancaster Bale Out

I scrambled up the six foot shaft and scratched my way through the loose sand which had been packed under the hut until my head emerged into daylight at the side away from the hut door. Looking over towards my hut 34B all the occupants were outside the door and when they saw me they motioned me to come out. I crawled out, stood up and sauntered towards my barrack, forgetting that I still wore my boiler suit. The lads at the door indicated to me to remove it, so I quickly did, throwing it under the hut from which I had just emerged.

I felt quite the hero as I carried on slowly walking towards my barrack. When the guards had arrived at the hut there had been about four or five bodies under it, with 'yours truly' at the face of the tunnel. No one had been caught and the Germans were still banging about in there - they seemed to be having difficulty in finding the entrance to the shaft. I mingled with the crowd around the door of our barrack, watching the proceedings. After a while one of the guards emerged from the door, crossed the compound and into the camp proper. He returned later with some Russians pushing their stinking latrine barrel on wheels. The contents were then pumped into the hut and down the shaft of our tunnel. The smell in the compound was atrocious, and more barrels arrived later in the day. Our captors certainly ensured that no one else would enter that tunnel. Indeed I don't think anyone else would enter the recreation hut!

Another means of escape had been foiled, but in our case, I think it was bound to fail. The people carrying bed boards across the compound for shoring-up our tunnel, were always in full view of the guards in the watch towers, and they must have become suspicious.

At least it had been entertaining or, at least, a relief from the utter boredom of life. Over the next month one parcel every two weeks was now not enough to keep us active and even I resorted to lying on my bunk all day. Things got worse, however, at the end of March. Parcels stopped altogether. We were now back on German rations. One became so weak that when we got off our bunk for any reason we had to hang on to the wooden framework for a while until our head stopped spinning. The Russian prisoners did not now find the mess of squashed potatoes and soil which they used to clean out of the bins, because these were now cleaned by hungry RAF people. Although I was hungry myself I could never stoop to this, not yet anyhow.

Air activity north, south and west of the camp became frequent. A goods train on the remaining line between Berlin and the south of Germany was attacked and set alight by Allied planes. There were huge explosions and truck wheels came hurtling through the air to land nearby. Whatever bricks or stones could be found were collected and a huge sign was laid in our compound proclaiming 'POW' just in case the camp was thought to be a German barracks by some gung-ho Yankee pilot.

24.
Victory in Europe - Liberation

It was April 23rd 1945, when I awakened in the morning expecting to hear the guard's usual "wakey, wakey" call, "Aufstehen! heraus! appell!"; but all was quiet. I got dressed and strolled out of the barrack into the compound - dead silence - "where's everyone gone?" I wondered, no guards. It was then that I heard a burst of machine gun fire down the road towards the main gate. I hurried along the sides of the barracks, 34B and 34A, towards the main road through the camp hoping to see an American or British soldier. Instead I saw a Russian Cossack on his horse, galloping up the road, waving his machine gun in the air.

Russian prisoners were running towards him to greet their liberator, but he was knocking them aside with his gun as he galloped past me and up to the other end of the camp. I was rather perturbed really and not a little disappointed. If this was how he greeted his fellow countrymen what would our chances be? I think now that this Cossack was mainly searching for Germans to shoot. He disappeared towards the other end of the camp. It appeared that all the Germans had fled and we were now in the hands of our Russian Allies.

Our barrack leaders conferred together and went down to the main gate for a meeting with whoever was in charge. I don't know with whom they met but when Pritchard, our barrack leader, returned he told us that our orders were to stay in the camp because there were still pockets of German resistance outside in the woods.

Most of us obeyed these instructions but some of the lads, rather than attempt to leave the camp by the main gate, pushed the barbed-wire fences down and wandered off across the countryside in search of what could be found to eat. The German garden was plundered of everything edible.

Lancaster Bale Out

Some of the wanderers returned with harrowing tales of suicides in the town of Mühlberg. The local doctor and his wife had hanged themselves after killing their children. Furniture in houses had been smashed to pieces by marauding Russian troops. An elderly farmer and his wife were found weeping bitterly because the whole of their livestock had been confiscated by the Russians. Actually I'd never seen any Russian soldiers, except the one on horseback riding triumphantly through the camp.

Our rations remained more or less the same as with the Germans, except for our soup which was now made from peas. This had disastrous effects on our bowels and the latrine was quite busy. Some German soldiers had been made prisoner, and it was ironic to see them now employed pushing the stinking latrine barrel through the camp instead of the Russians. How the mighty had fallen! I actually felt sorry for those Germans even though I'd never felt sorry for the Russians. They seemed to accept this demeaning chore quite unperturbed, as if it was expected. The Russian prisoners had been told to pick up a rifle and join in the continuing fight, or walk home, so I heard. I also heard of one Russian ex-prisoner who had died, eating an uncooked, tame rabbit. Apparently, not all our previous guards had escaped. It was said that one nasty little piece of work had been captured by Russian prisoners and had had both his hands chopped off.

Danny and I left the camp once when we wandered in the German countryside. We came across some British soldiers in a farmyard where they had butchered a pig, and they were busy carving it up into pieces. We asked them for some bacon, so they gave us a couple of slices each. When we returned to the camp we fried our uncured bacon on the stove. The smell was mouth watering. I seemed to know we shouldn't eat it but we could not resist - the smell was so tempting. Needless to say we were both violently sick afterwards. Our stomachs were in no fit state for luxuries!

We were a week at Stalag 4B, under the control of the Russians, before we received orders to leave Mühlberg for a place called Riesa. No one had heard of this town, but it was situated to the western side of the River Elbe. We set off one morning carrying our meagre

Lancaster Bale Out

belongings on our 15 mile hike, hoping that the route would take us nearer to the American (or preferably British) lines. We were strung out along the roads for miles and no one seemed to be in charge of us.

We sauntered along following our fellows in front like the evacuation of the Israelites from Egypt. We passed a number of villages where white flags of surrender hung from numerous upstairs windows. It was a very warm day and German villagers came out with jugs of cold water to quench our thirst. The only food we had, however, was what we had saved from our rations. I believe Mrs Barrington was on this trek to Riesa dressed in an army uniform. I also believe there were a number of German guards similarly dressed. Apparently we were welcome to stay in any German household since it was said that if any Russian soldiers arrived and found British or Allied personnel in residence, they would leave the Germans alone. We were made very welcome, but I don't know of anyone who took up this offer.

Later in the day I remember crossing a wooden bridge which would have been over the River Elbe, before we entered the town of Riesa. By the time we arrived it was late afternoon and we were told to find some place to lodge ourselves. Actually the town was bursting at the seams with British Tommies hanging out of all the windows of the houses. Flags of the Allied nations were much in evidence and my eyes filled with tears when I heard the voice of Webster Booth singing "The Perfect English Rose" on someone's radio.

We eventually received some rations, more pea soup and black bread, but we didn't know where we going to sleep amid all this throng. We heard rumours that the Russians were not going to let us go until we'd all been interrogated. They were obviously looking for Germans in British uniforms. Danny and I left the centre of Riesa and wandered out of the crowded streets in search of a place to stay. We came to a street of terraced houses with long back gardens. I never knew if these houses were occupied or not, but we spotted a garden shed and found that it was unlocked. We made this our home for the time being. There was a wooden bench at one side of

Lancaster Bale Out

the hut and we agreed that one of us would sleep on the floor and one on the bench alternately.

The first night we were there however we were both crouching on the floor! It was apparently May 1st and drunken Russians were making merry, firing machine guns into the air, and not always into the air. We thought the war had started again as we crouched as low as possible to avoid being accidentally killed by Russian bullets.

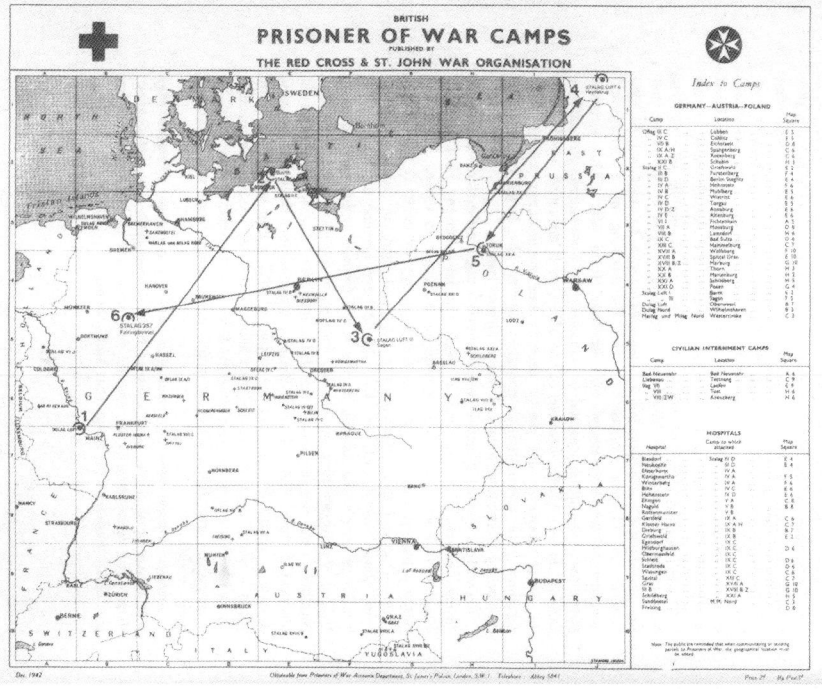

Map of POW Camps[84] (Red Cross)

We lived in this hut for three days and nights going to the town centre to collect our rations daily. We asked who was organising the interrogation but no one seemed to know. We eventually presented ourselves to the interrogating body, who were living in the houses. We wanted to find out what our chances were of being moved to the west. The interrogating body consisted of two Poles and one

---

[84]. *Stalag 4B was luckily not too far from the American lines at liberation. A lot of the camps much deeper into Eastern Germany were not so fortunate though.*

235

Lancaster Bale Out

Russian officer. One of the Poles questioned us in English asking for number, name and rank etc. He then informed the second Pole in Polish of our details and the latter Pole informed the Russian Officer in Russian. Quite complicated actually! We did however pass muster and they were convinced that we were not Germans.

That night Danny and I agreed that we would make our own way to the west. Our decision was reinforced the next day as we left our garden hut to go into town for our rations. On the way we met a Russian who was quite drunk and was staggering all over the road. He was one of the few Russian soldiers we'd met up to now. He was quite smart really with shiny jack boots and short brown tunic. He shouted something at us as we drew near and pulled our his revolver. We stopped in our tracks as he asked us in German why hadn't we saluted him, all the while trying to stand up straight. We saluted him with alacrity and said
"Wir wissen nicht dass Sie Offizier sind." Our salutes had satisfied him and off he went continuing his drunken way down the road.
"That does it Danny," I said.
"Let's get out of here or we'll probably end up in Siberia."

We collected our rations and our belongings from the hut and set off for the railway line, which we'd seen on the way there. The straightest path west, we thought, would be to walk along the railway. We set off walking along the sleepers towards home. There were no trains running. Apparently the German railways had a rail man's house every mile and it was that man's job to look after his stretch of railway.

We reached the railway and set off westwards hoping that eventually we'd reach Leipzig, where we had last heard the Americans had pulled back to. Fortunately the weather was kind to us as we trod the sleepers. We met very few people and those we did meet either ignored us or glanced at us suspiciously. We met no Russians as we walked all day, occasionally stopping to rest and nibble our ration of black bread or quench our thirst at an outside water tap nearby the railway men's houses.

Lancaster Bale Out

Towards evening on the first day we were worn out, and so we stopped at one of the houses. A railway man emerged and we asked him if we could stay there for the night. He agreed and motioned us to follow him into his house. I got the impression that he thought we were French as he addressed us as, "Monsieur." It was almost dark and he told us we could sleep on the floor of his downstairs room. Before he retired upstairs to bed himself he said to us,
"Monsieur nix comme si comme sa" which we took to mean, "Don't steal anything."
"Nein, nein," we assured him.
"Wir sind Engländer" hoping that he wouldn't hold any grudges against his enemies.

Danny and I slept soundly on the floor. Next morning we were awake early and we went outside to have a wash in a trough. We still had a bar of Red Cross soap and when our host saw it he asked if he could have it. We gladly gave it to him because we had nothing else to give, whereupon he presented us with a dozen fresh eggs.

Raw eggs are not much use on an empty stomach. Therefore, our German host boiled them hard for us before we left and began our journey again, eating them on the way. This German told us that we had been spotted walking along the railway and his women-folk, thinking we might be Russians, had run away to hide in the woods and fields. We could well believe this; the tales we'd heard of rape and pillage by Russians are too horrific to mention.

About mid day on the second day of our trek to the west, we reached a tributary of the river Elbe, called the Mulde. There had been a railway bridge over the river, but unfortunately, it was now about twenty or thirty feet below us in the water, and quite impassable. About one hundred yards to the left of the railway embankment, across an open field, we noticed a group of women and children. They seemed to be talking to a Russian soldier who was standing guard at the end of a road bridge. This bridge was also lying in the water but one by one the women and children were being allowed to crawl over the collapsed girders.

Lancaster Bale Out

Danny and I ran down the embankment of the railway and crossed the field to where the Russian was guarding the bridge. I think he was being bribed by the women to allow them to crawl over, because he had wrist watches up to his elbows on both arms. The guard looked very sheepish when he saw us but started to smile!
"English, American?" he queried.
"English," we answered, whereupon he motioned us over the bridge.

Danny and I joined the women and children in crawling over the girders of the collapsed bridge. It was not difficult crossing really, but we breathed a sigh of relief when we reached the western bank.

In any event Danny and I now made our way along the western bank towards our railway. After climbing back up the embankment we sat down to rest a while on the ends of the sleepers. Unknown to us, about 100 yards to the west, there was a road tunnel which passed under the embankment and, while we sat there resting, two army lorries passed under this tunnel and drove down to the collapsed bridge which we had just crossed. I'm not sure now but I did think that these lorries had the American white star on their sides.

The lorries stopped at the end of the bridge which we'd crawled over and, as we sat and stared in astonishment, numerous ragged looking people disgorged from these lorries and headed towards the river crossing. We now had enough experience to know that these were ex-Russian prisoners and - what luck - our friends, the Americans, were sending them to the east.

In our excitement, Danny and I ran down the embankment to these lorries before they drove off. Self-consciously and not without fear of a rebuff we asked the American driver
"Any chance of a lift, pal?"
He looked down at us with pity,
"Sure," he said.
"What are you, English?"
"Ex-POWs," we explained.
"Climb aboard, boys," he said and we joined him in his cab.

Lancaster Bale Out

I don't know how Danny felt but I could have cried at hearing such a friendly welcome.

"Have some gum, or a candy bar," he said, as we turned around and headed for the tunnel under the railway. I think that Danny and I had become so obsessed with our railway line that we had forgotten that there were roads. We were now headed westwards but in comfort and on a road. Our friendly American driver tried to get us into conversation but other than to confirm that we were shot down aircrew, we were somewhat tongue tied and eventually our driver seemed to give up the effort to get us to talk.

After about a twenty minute drive we arrived at an ex-Luftwaffe airfield near Halle, and our driver pointed us towards the offices.

Rather strangely, the only thing that I can remember about this place was a clean single bed with white sheets. We must have been fed, but I can't remember what we were given to eat. Next morning we were lined up out on the airfield with a lot of other ex-prisoners.

After a few minutes a Dakota landed and twenty to twenty-five men climbed aboard, and it took off again. Dakotas were circling overhead - I don't know how many - but as one landed and loaded up and took off again, another one landed. It was a really efficient shuttle service.

Our turn came at last, and once more I was flying - not without some trepidation. Danny had a POW mark note in his pocket and he pencilled his address around one half of the border of the note, and I did the same on the other half. Danny tore the note in two and gave me his address which, if I remember rightly, was something like Chapel Town, Birmingham. I've never seen or heard of him since.

I don't know how long the flight took, but I remember at one time I glanced down below out of the window and saw the destroyed city of Cologne. I knew it was Cologne, because towering up, as if in defiance, amid the devastation was the famous Cathedral.

Lancaster Bale Out

Cologne Cathedral - defiant amid the destruction (Popperfoto)

Eventually we landed in Brussels and again my memory is somewhat sketchy. We were billeted in a huge hanger with beds with white sheets and what seemed to me like spotlessly clean, Red Cross nurses.

After a night in Brussels, (where some of our colleagues went 'out-on-the-town') we were loaded, amazingly, back onto a Lancaster, flown for a short while across the North Sea and we landed at an RAF station near Guildford in Surrey.

25.
Back in England - Welcome Home

We were once again in the care of the RAF. We were showered, deloused, medically examined and given new uniforms. I had been promoted; I was now a Warrant Officer. We were given some pay, double rations for home, travel warrants from Guildford to the station of our choice and we were off home at last.

POW Airlift[85] (F.D. Wolfson)

The speed of our return and reception had left me somewhat stunned and I felt awfully lonely as I waited on Kings Cross station for my train to Darlington. I had been at Kings Cross some years previously, but seemed to have forgotten from which platform the Darlington train departed. I self-consciously approached a porter to make enquiries. Amid all the throng of people 'toing and froing' I seemed to have lost all my self-confidence.
"What had some twenty months of imprisonment done to me?" I wondered. I felt very conspicuous - as if I had POW etched on my forehead.

---

[85] *The repatriation of POWs, Operation 'Exodus', was well under way by VE Day and each Lanc carried twenty five passengers, dressed in whatever motley clothes they stood up in.*

Lancaster Bale Out

Arriving at the platform, for Darlington I spotted another RAF uniform, also brand new. The man turned towards me as I approached and I immediately recognised the gaunt white face of Ken Davie. "Of course," I thought, he is from Easington and will be traveling to Darlington too. We stuck together as we boarded the train, and huddled side by side in the same compartment. As the train traveled north, Ken confided in me that he was in turmoil. He was married and his wife was living in Chester, yet here he was going on a train up to Durham. He had been torn. Should he go first north to see his parents or should he get on a train to Chester and his wife. He asked my advice and, coward-like and not wanting to be left alone in the compartment with all these strangers, I encouraged him to go to Durham first. Such was our state of mind as returning POWs. However, Ken left the train at Grantham, his duty to his wife coming first. I was not married, so fortunately had no such decision to make. For the rest of the journey I felt lonely, yet not alone, for the compartment was full.

I left the train at Darlington and went in search of a train to Crook. I was told by a porter that I may not get to Crook that night because the train terminated at Bishop Auckland. This information turned out to be correct and I found myself stranded for the night on the station at Bishop Auckland. The next train for Crook was at 6:00am the next morning - it was called either the mail or the milk train. It was eight miles to Crook and I had no intention of walking that distance in my worn out condition so I bedded down on a seat on the platform. Fortunately the weather was kind to me and I made myself as comfortable as possible. After a while I heard a door open nearby and a railwayman emerged from one of the offices. He didn't notice me at first and, rather laughably, he proceeded to urinate over the edge of the platform onto the rails. When he turned round to go back into the office he spotted me stretched out on my seat.
"What train are you waiting for?" he asked.
"The Crook train," I replied.
"The next one is not until six o'clock in the morning," he said, "You'd better come in here."
I followed him into the office where, lo and behold, there were two single beds.

Lancaster Bale Out

"Get yourself stretched out there," he said, "I'll wake you in the morning."

True to his word he woke me in time to catch the Crook train next morning.

I arrived home early in the morning after walking the familiar mile route to Roddymor. I had been gone for nearly two years, since my last leave before the fateful last op to Cologne. My sister Gladys was at home at the time, since she was expecting her first baby. She had been a nurse and had married one of her patients, Arthur. He was a Marine Commando who had been sent to her hospital in Cumbria for some minor ailment or other. She had been looking out of the bedroom window and had seen me walking up the road past the local farm, and with a cry of excitement, she ran down the stairs calling out,

"Here's our Fred".

My youngest sister Elsie was already up preparing breakfast. I was met at the front door by my two excited sisters, who moments later were hanging around my neck. My poor old mother tottered downstairs in her night dress with tears of joy streaming down her cheeks.

We had never been a family who showed much emotion or affection and I was actually somewhat embarrassed by this scene. Our living room seemed to have shrunk in size since I last saw it. It was still shining clean however, with a huge coal fire burning in the grate and the kettle boiling on the hob. Some of our neighbours must also have seen me arrive because someone had hung out a huge banner saying 'Welcome Home Fred'. It was of course a time of strict rationing of food, but from somewhere, my sister Elsie produced bacon and eggs for me. The RAF provided returning POWs with double rations for a while, so I was soon able to replace the foodstuff.

It was after 11.00am when my father returned from the mine. He always worked the unearthly hours of 3.30am until 11.00am. He was of course black with coal dust but he stuck out his pit-dirty hand and shook mine.

"I'm pleased you're safe and sound, lad," he said, hiding his face in case I saw his eyes full of tears. He was a hard little man my father.

Lancaster Bale Out

He had been - as one would say - 'dragged up' in his childhood. His mother had died when he was four years old and his father - my grandfather - showed him no mercy. His father died when he was about ten years old, and my dad told me once, that he never shed a tear. From then on he was brought up by his grandparents. I think he did not know how to cry, I never knew my dad show any emotion at all, but I knew then how glad he was to see me.

I never went out of the house for about four days, and it was my dad who finally said to me,
"Are you not going to go out lad?"
I didn't want to go out but he persuaded me to go for a walk around the surrounding countryside with him. Unknown to me, at the time I was suffering with depression. Letters were arriving from the families of my crew asking me for confirmation that their sons had been killed. What could one say? I'm alive but your son or brother is dead. I must say that this had an awful effect on me. Rosner's brother Milton said that he thought that he had seen Gene in a photograph taken in a POW camp. I felt extremely guilty that I was the only one out of a crew of eight that had survived, and for more than fifty years I have lived with the question, "Why me?" I also had a letter from an RAF Group Captain[86] in the form of a reprimand for not answering a letter that Madame Janssoone had written to me. I wrote a testy reply stating that I had only just returned from POW camp and had not even received a letter from her. I heard no more from him.

Later on, I received an invitation, rimmed in black, from Madame Janssoone, inviting me to her husband's funeral in France. I didn't even know that he had been arrested and shot. You can imagine the stress I was under. "Had he been shot because of me?" I wondered. I replied to Madame Janssoone and asked her about the circumstances of Lucien Janssoone's arrest and whether it was my fault. She wrote back and said that it was believed to be Mrs Mouse[87] who had betrayed them, and said that Ritchez and Thuru had also been arrested and shot.

---

[86] This was likely to have been Squadron Leader (later Group Captain) Bufton, one of the other airmen that the Janssoones had harboured.
[87] It is difficult to believe that Mrs Mouse would have deliberately betrayed Janssoone, Thuru and Boyer as there had been numerous previous occasions when she could have done so.

1048639 W/O SMOOKER. F.H.
24, High Terrace,
Roddymoor, Crook.
Durham. England.
18-5-45.

Dear Mr & Mrs Calder,

Since you have been corresponding with my people, my task is somewhat lightened in writing to you. I guess by now you have consoled yourselves to the grievous loss of Jim your son, and my mid upper gunner, although I realize you will never wholly forget.

I think you would gather from his letters, what good friends we all were, and as for me, having trained in Canada, Jim and Arnie were my special favourites.

I have often wondered, during my confinement in Germany, why I was chosen out of 8 lads to be the only one saved. I guess it was my fate in being a bomb aimer and my position in the nose of the aircraft being directly over the escape hatch.

At the moment I am on a month's leave, having returned to England a few days ago, so if there is anything you would like to know, please write and I'll try to enlighten you.

Yours sincerely,
Fred Smooker.

Fred Smooker's letter to Mr and Mrs Calder (F Smooker)

Lancaster Bale Out

My only brother Ernest, who was eight years younger than me, had joined the RAF in 1943 as an aircrew trainee. I think he was stationed at Blackpool. He was granted a few days leave to come home and visit me, on compassionate grounds. It was him who finally got me going out. I remember one time we journeyed to Bishop Auckland to the cinema, and afterwards we had a fish and chip supper at a cafe. He could not help but stare at me as I wolfed down this tasty meal. I had unconsciously cleared my plate of chips with my fingers, since months as a POW, in a constant state of hunger, had made me grateful for any food.

It was shortly after my brother returned to the RAF that I received a letter from the Air Ministry asking me to report to them in London. I remember that I did the return journey in one day. I cannot remember all that they asked me except, who had helped me in France, had I tried to escape, etc. I remember wondering whether they thought I was a German because they were very supercilious. After I left there I journeyed straight back to Kings Cross. En-route I noticed a crowd congregating to watch someone dismount from a huge limousine. A red carpet was also laid on the pavement. It was the King and Queen and Princess Margaret. I was astounded to note that the King was highly made up with face powder and lipstick. I was that close to him.

After I arrived home from London I started going out by myself but I must have still been in a distressed state. If I went to the cinema and children were shown on the screen I used to cry. How many innocent children had I killed by our bombing, I wondered? Another time at the cinema I started to sweat and feel faint. I had to leave and I remember I went into a back street and bent down with my head to my knees, as sweat was dripping from my face.

I reported to a doctor's surgery the next day and he told me I was suffering with my nerves. He said he could give me a bottle of medicine but I could only cure myself. So much for counselling in 1945!

The buses to Durham and Newcastle were double-deckers and I used to force myself to ride on the top deck. When the bus was negotiating corners and the bus heaved over, I used to cling to my seat until it straightened up. I talked to my brother-in-law about this. As he had been in the Commandos, he confessed to the same reaction. He had taken part in many daring exercises during the war, and had now returned from Normandy. He told me that he was also a nervous wreck when travelling on trains and always debated to himself where the safest position to be was. If he sat at the rear he imagined another train would run into the back, or if he sat near the front he thought another train would crash head on.

After I had been home for about four months, boredom became the enemy and I began to worry about my future. Should I stay in the RAF or should I leave. The RAF had left me alone all this time, as I suppose my leave had accrued from July 1943 until May 1945 (some 22 months). I couldn't be like my dad, I thought, who was always content with his lot. I saw him daily coming home from the pit after having hewed and filled some four or five tons of coal into 10 cwt tubs or trucks. He would get washed in the tin bath in front of the fire, have a huge dinner and then go to bed. He would get up again at about 5:00 pm, have some tea and then shoulder his garden tools and go to work in his allotment, which was half a mile away. He grew all kinds of vegetables. On his return at about 9:00 pm he would have supper and go back to bed until 2:30am and then return to the pit at about 3:30 am. That was my life, I thought until I joined the RAF in 1941. Could I return to such a life again? I shuddered at the prospect.

My uncle, Ned Ramsay, had studied at night classes before the war, and he was now an Under Manager at a neighbouring coal mine. When visiting him as children, we were in awe of his semi-detached dwelling with its three bedrooms and numerous other rooms downstairs. He had a large garden and even a gardener, provided by the coal company, who also carried out many household chores. Uncle Ned went to the pit at 9:00am, came home for lunch and spent the afternoon at his office, which was part of the house, conferring with or reprimanding his underlings, or inducing them to get more coal out of the mine. His lifestyle seemed eminently preferable to my dad's.

Lancaster Bale Out

I was at home in September 1945 and still to make a decision about my future. I was an Aircrew Warrant Officer Air Bomber, earning almost £7 per week. The RAF would not keep me on leave forever though. If I decided to stay in the RAF I knew my rank and pay would be down graded, and besides, I had no desire to fly again. I decided to go to Sunderland Technical College and enrolled for a course in coal mining. Sunderland was about 20 miles from where I was living so I booked myself into the YMCA Hostel there. Actually I only attended this course for about a week because I heard from home that I had been summoned back to the RAF. My mining studies were interrupted again.

RAF Cosford was near Wolverhampton and I think some of us spent more time in the pubs and dance halls there, than on the camp. We were there to be interviewed about our futures, but there were so many of us that the procedure was very slow. I was eventually interviewed by a Flight Lieutenant. He asked me if I wished to stay in the RAF or return to civvy street? As there was no requirement for bomb aimers in peace time, if I wished to stay in the RAF I could have become a Wireless Operator, as I had done a signals course at Cranwell. I told him though I was not keen on flying again and so he suggested that I could be a W/Op on the ground staff, but I would have to be assessed as to my capabilities before a decision was made about my rank. I was very undecided so he sent me on leave again to make up my mind.

I went to Stamford and booked into the George Hotel, because I had become engaged to a girl that I had met at a dance there. She was from Nottingham but worked locally as a nurse. The George was very expensive so my new fiancée found me some private lodgings, which were much cheaper. This situation didn't last very long however, and within a couple of weeks we had called the engagement off and I went back home.

In November 1945, I was recalled to Cosford and interviewed again by the same Flight Lieutenant. He found me very indecisive and finally lost his temper and shouted at me,
"Make your bloody mind up, Smooker!"

Eventually he told me he was going to arrange for me to go to a resettlement centre at Chorley, in Lancashire, where I would have three months in which to study for a new career. I knew that Chorley was not far from Wigan and I remembered that Wigan Mining College was a centre of excellence as far as mining was concerned. It was one of only six centres in Britain where examinations were held for second and first class mining certificates of competency. Indeed one could study for a BSc in Mining there.
"Thank you very much, Sir," I replied. "I will willingly go there."
"You can't go yet though," he answered. "The place is full of Yanks. You'll have to go on leave until they've gone."

With that I was sent on leave again until January 1946, when I was told by letter to report to Washington Hall, near Chorley, Lancs. The residents there were all aircrew ex-POWs, who were no longer needed. I knew none of them but it didn't matter. I was there to study for my second class certificate of competency, which I hoped to prepare for and then sit the exam at Wigan in May 1946. We all had separate rooms, but the dining hall was communal. I accompanied a Squadron Leader to Wigan the next day and I was booked in as a student by the head of the Mining Dept, who was a Scot called Mr Bryson. He was also the editor of a mining publication called *The Science and Art of Mining*. I used to be a reader of this publication before the war and I knew of Mr Bryson and was quite thrilled to meet him. The offices of this publication were at Rowbottom Square, Wigan. I had sent one of my previous post cards to the Editor from Stalag 4B asking for information about training courses after the war. "How strange," I thought, "here I was talking to the man himself!" I started the course the following day and Mr Bryson was our lecturer. I was the only person there in uniform. Before the lecture started, Mr Bryson addressed me.
"Sergeant Smooker" he said.
"Warrant Officer, Sir," I quickly responded.
"Yes," he said "but in April 1944 you were a Sergeant and you sent a postcard to the Editor of *The Science and Art of Mining* asking about prospects for mining students after the war. I met you yesterday," he continued, "and I received your postcard the same morning!"
What a coincidence. It had taken from April 1944 to January 1946 for my postcard from Germany to reach him and now here I was in

Lancaster Bale Out

the flesh on the exact same day. Mr Bryson was so amazed by this that he wrote an article about it and had it published in the local newspaper, *The Wigan Observer*.

I really set my mind on my studies, going to college by bus every day and then studying in my room at night. I only had three months to prepare for my second class or under managers certificate, although I learned that if an exam was due an extension of one month was allowed. I therefore prepared to take my exam in May 1946. I received a letter forwarded from home from my ex-fiancée in Stamford returning my engagement ring. I really couldn't have cared less. I was walking through the camp back to my billet and I threw the ring into the static water tank.

That night while I was in my room studying, a lad called Ted Waughman barged in. "Fancy going down to Smokey Joe's pub?" he asked.
"No," I replied, "I've got to study for my exam."
After he'd been gone for a few minutes though, I thought about it and went and called out,
"Ted, have you gone yet?"
He hadn't luckily, so I tagged along with him and some others to Smokey Joe's, about 100 yards along the road from the camp. The group consisted of myself, Ted, a cockney from Wood Green, and four scots; Rusty Highlands, Jimmy Pride, Henry Hamilton and an ex-pilot called Andy Clyde.

Smokey Joe's was well named. We sat in a small room drinking whisky and chasers. Rusty was a good pianist and he sat and played the piano while the rest of us sang ourselves hoarse singing stupid RAF songs, such as,

There was flak, flak
Lots of Jerry flak
In the Ruhr, in the Ruhr
There was flak, flak
Lots of Jerry flak
In the valley of the Ruhr.

Lancaster Bale Out

My eyes are dim, I cannot see
The searchlights they are blinding me
The searchlights they are blinding me.

The second verse from what I remember was about fighters, fighters, lots of Jerry fighters etc. What a time we had, and what a head I had next day, but somehow I still managed to get in to mining college.

This started to become a regular trip for us, and some nights, after we had been to Smokey Joe's, we used to wander along to the Highways Hostel nearby, to dances, or maybe to have a coffee and sandwich in the canteen. This place was full of young women who worked on munitions at a factory near Leyland. It was here that I met a lass called Evelyn Wood, from Ashington, Northumberland. She had been working on munitions for about five years and used to fill bombs and detonators with all kinds of nasty explosives. She told me that she used to get danger money for some of the products that she was handling.

I sat my second class exam in May 1946 and passed with flying colours.

26.
Demob - Post War

I was de-mobbed in June 1946, and I was given my demob suit at Hednesford, in Staffordshire. Evelyn and I got married in August 1946 and we lived in a place called the Woodlands Hostel for a while, 100 yards from Washington Hall. Unfortunately, the rules for living at Woodlands were that one had to be working. I was accepted because of my status as a mining student, but Evelyn, who had just been made redundant at the factory had to find a job, so she went to work in a cotton mill at Coppull. In the meantime I had put in a claim to the Ministry of Education to the effect that my studies had been interrupted due to my war service. I therefore received a grant so that I could continue studying at Wigan Mining College for my first class or colliery managers exam.

Fred Smooker, 1946 (F.Smooker)

Lancaster Bale Out

It was a very rough time, especially for Evelyn. The noise of the cotton mill was affecting her badly, so we moved from Woodlands and went to live in a boarding house at Southport. After the war, living accommodation was very difficult to find.

I sat my first class exam in May 1947 and after having moved from Southport to Wigan I went to the local colliery and presented myself to the colliery manager at Chisnall Hall Colliery, near Coppull. It was here that my Uncle Ned had been the Under Manager.

I was accepted as a shot-firer, starting on the 6:00am shift every morning. It was down to the manager to interpret the legal requirements as to how many detonators a man could carry per shift. There were five of us shot-firers on one coal face and we all carried 10lbs of explosive and forty detonators, and had an oil lamp gas detector for safety.

In August 1948 we moved back to Durham and lived in with my parents at Roddymoor because Evelyn was expecting our first baby. Our first son, was born in September 1948 at Bishop Auckland.

I was promoted from shot-firer to deputy and then overman at the colliery. In 1949 I applied for an afternoon shift under-managers position at the William Pit, Whitehaven. There had been a terrible explosion at this pit in Cumbria in August 1947, and experienced people I knew advised me against accepting the job because of the poor safety reputation at this pit. The death toll after the explosion had been one hundred and twenty four men and boys. I was offered the position after being interviewed and on ascertaining that a house was available, we moved there in August 1949.

At last we had our own house, but at what a cost I thought. The pit was in a terrible state. It was so gassy that no electricity was allowed at the coal-face and explosives were banned. Everything was powered by compressed air. I later applied for numerous other positions, but it seemed to me that no one from the Cumbrian coalfields was wanted.

After almost two years at Whitehaven, I noticed in *The Colliery*

Lancaster Bale Out

Guardian - a weekly mining magazine - that the Assam Railways and Trading Co. were looking for mining engineers to work in North East India. I wrote to their offices in London, had an interview and a medical examination at Harley Street and was offered a position as assistant manager in little more than a week.

We left for India in June 1951 on the good ship Caledonia and stayed there for nearly six years, during which time my other son, was born. I returned to England and started work at Easington Colliery as an under manager on 1st June 1957. After working there for nine years I was transferred to the colliery at South Hetton and then finally finished my mining career in 1972 on health grounds. After a couple of unhappy years in the civil service I then became a factory warehouse assistant until March 1985, retiring at the age of sixty-nine.

Ken Davie is the only ex-resident of Stalag 4B that I have ever seen since my POW days. Soon after starting at Easington Colliery I met a workman down the mine who was named Davie. I mentioned to him about an RAF airman with the same name who I had met in a POW camp.
"Oh," he told me, "that would be our Kenny."
This workman it turned out was Ken's uncle. Ken had become an accountant and still lived in Chester when he made a visit to Easington in about 1961, his uncle brought him to my house and we had a good talk about our experiences.

What a charmed life I have had. I had escaped from my burning Lancaster in 1943, and I had missed explosions at two pits that I worked at. The Cathedral (Cologne) and I survived.

27.
Epitaph -
Here are the Young Men

Year - 1939
The call to war stirred the adventurous hearts of many young men
Including him.
Soaring the skies on the wings of a steel bird
Proved more romantic
Than being swallowed up by the dark, hungry earth.
He carefully packed his meagre possessions
And kissed his Dear Mom goodbye.

There were 8.
Night after night they ravaged large capital cities.
Lights,
Like tiny twinkling stars, dying in their wake.
With Apollo's arrival they would put the chaos behind them
And raise a glass to their victories.

He was 22.
Still her little boy.
At home, Dear Mom waited patiently for his faithful scrawls.
He spoke of trivialities
Of friends and the weather.
Never of those unseen
Who haunted his thoughts and dreams.
One dark day, a letter with a shiny crimson seal broke her heart
And dear Mom stood by the mailbox no more.

60 years later
His smiling face immortalised in sepia
Resides above our mantle
Not as a reminder of the life he lost
But of the one he gave to us.

Poem by Jennifer Calder[88]

---

[88]. *James Reginald Calder's Great Niece*

28.
Crash Site - Quiévy Wheatfield

Lancaster ED720 crashed in an area called Fontaine Au Tertre, near to Quiévy Railway station as detailed in the following Gendarme reports from the Archives in Lille (See Appendix E):

Report 1 - "On the 9th July 1943 at 02:30 AM a British plane crashed in flames into a wheat field north east of the locality of Quiévy. There were no victims from the French population. The German Authorities advised putting in place the necessary security measures. The damage caused to crops was perhaps two thousand Francs."

Report 2 - "Last night at 02:45 AM, a plane on fire, assumed to be British, crashed next to Quiévy Railway Station. There were no victims or damage to buildings. The airmen, except one or two who took flight, were burnt."

In the words of Madame Denise Lorriaux (Marie Adjoint in Quiévy) who was 14 at the time:

"I remember going against the wishes of my parents to the spot where the plane had crashed with a friend of mine, but the Germans were already there, shooting at the curious crowd. We quickly left crawling along a wheat field.

My cousin was responsible for maintaining the peace at Quiévy and he told me that 3 bodies had been buried very quickly before the arrival of the Germans, but I do not know where. These were hard times believe me! It had always been said that only one airman escaped to another village at Béthencourt."

Quiévy station was part of the Cambrésis Railway system, first opened in the 1880's and was on the Caudry to Denain line. There was also a branch line from Quiévy to Solesmes. The railway served

Lancaster Bale Out

to carry workers commuting back and forth to the lace making and sugar factories in the vicinity and for transporting goods such as sugar and coal. The railway line is disused now having been closed in the 1960's, but the station building still exists as a private dwelling.

Today the field is a meadow, and there is a solitary tree which appears to have been planted in remembrance to the crash and the airmen who died.

Lancaster ED720 wreckage. One propeller just visible (A Verriez)

29.
Ephemera - Will and Letter

The loss of a family member not only affected the parents, but brothers, sisters and other family members too.

In the words of my cousin Carole Hawkins:
"When Aunt Ada and Uncle Jack died, I was about 12. My mum went to help clear out their house and I was left to my own devices. I remember finding in Uncle Jack's workshop, clipped together with rusting paper clips, press cuttings about the crash from the Kent local newspaper, but more importantly a letter from Ottowa. I knew there was a survivor who was English and had been a POW. There was also a picture of one of the crew by a plane.

GUILTON SERGEANT BURIED IN FRANCE

Sergeant J. Hougham, R.A.F.V.R., son of Mr. and Mrs. J. E. Hougham, Guilton, Ash. Canterbury, has been reported killed on July 9, 1943. His parents were first informed that he was missing, now they have heard that while returning from bombing Cologne the aircraft developed engine trouble and when 120 miles from the English coast was attacked by an enemy fighter and shot down. This tragic news came through W.O.I. F. H Smoker, the only surviving member of the crew. They are buried at Cambrai, France. Sgt. Hougham was on his 19th operational flight and was a wireless operator in 106 Squadron. He was employed at Betteshanger Colliery for 6 years.

I didn't say anything at the time because I thought everyone knew all this. Uncle Jack had probably hidden all the cuttings away so that Aunt Ada wouldn't be upset. I remember the house too being a shrine to Jack and his room was exactly as he had left it. I seem to remember his will told them to sell his possessions, but they never did. Everything was still there down to rusting compasses and pencil sharpeners."

> Sunday 14/2/43
>
> To the one who opens this letter,
> In the event of anything happening to me Sgt. J Hougham 1271588 RAF I leave all my worldly belongings to my Father and Mother
> Mr & Mrs J E Hougham
> Bank Cottage
> Guilton
> Ash
> Nr Canterbury
> Kent
>
> They are to keep anything they want of mine. My father can have my bikes & one for work and one for occasions. They are to sell all my other things and put the money with that which is already in the Post Office in my name. It is to be drawn out as they require it for anything they may want in their older life. If possible, I should like to be buried in "Ash Church Yard."
> Signed:— Sgt J Hougham 1271588.

Jack Hougham Will[89] (C. Smith)

[89] Note that the handwriting is different between the two parts

Lancaster Bale Out

The following letter written 4 months after they were posted missing, shows that the families still had no further news as to what had happened:

> Ivydene
> Moira Road
> Donisthorpe.
> Burton-on-Trent
> Staffs Eng
>
> Nov 17th
>
> Dear Mr-Mrs Calder
>
> We recieved your most welcome letter this morning, and we are more than pleased with the enclosed picture of Jimmy, he looks a fine lad, but I agree with you when you say the air force takes the best, it needs the best. Do you know our Bill got on well with all the crew, but Jimmy and Arnie were his best pals, and next to them Jean Rosner. He also thought a lot of Jean as a pilot, I must write to Mrs Rosner, I have both recieved and answered Mrs Turners letter.
>
> You say I was luckier than you as I could see Bill oftener than you could your Jimmy, I have said that too Dad myself many a time. Bill came home on the Wednesday tea time, to see his brother, who was home on leave from his gun boat in the Navy, he returned

Lancaster Bale Out

(2)

to his station on the Thursday morning, going on the raid to Cologne the same night, I recieved my telegram posting him missing on the Friday afternoon at ten to three, ten minutes before his Dad came home, from the colliery, where he works on the coal face I have had no further news

You ask about Bills little sister Dorothy (Dot) she was in hospital for eleven months altogether, and she had lots of tasty bits from both Jimmys and Arnie's parcels. I once got two tins of coffee, milk and sugar, from them along with a parcel of washing, which Bill said it took all three of them to pack, and then the postman could tell it was washing, for when he brought it to the door, he said a bit of washing for you, Mrs Bailey, you see there was a leg of a pair of dirty pants hanging out of the parcel, so much for their packing. Dot has been at home for a year now but after Xmas she has to go into hospital again, she has a slight deformity of the shoulder, and this can

Lancaster Bale Out

only be cured whilst she is still quite young (3)
(9) The Doctor knowing our trouble said he would leave her at home with me for Xmas, as he didn't like to take another of my children away at this season.

It was Fred Smooker who was to have been married at Xmas. Mind you if our Bills girls father would have agreed, I don't think Bill would have been long after him, but you see Nora was then only eighteen and Bill twenty one. his birthday is on December the eighth. I dread it coming, we had such a good time together last year, and he was here for Xmas, I sent the lads what was left of his birthday cake. His girl Nora has been a great comfort to me in my trouble, she lives thirty two miles away, but she comes to stay with me every week end since it happened

Do not I beg of you speak of returning my kindness to your boy. I wish he was still here for me to do it again, it was a pleasure, believe me nothing was too much trouble.

(4) glad you liked the snap of Bill

You will I am sure forgive me for rambling on like this but, Oh how I wish that I could see you and talk with you, it would be just grand but we will do our best by corresponding as often as we can.

It would indeed be a lovely Xmas present if we could hear that they were prisoners of war, or just a little line from them themselves. I know just how you feel about not being able to send a parcel to him, and it is only we mothers who are in this together who really do understand. When you write again tell me how old Jimmy was and his birthday date and has he any more sisters and brothers, Bill had two brothers and two sisters besides himself, Eric twenty Gerald fine. Marjorie fifteen Dorothy nine. Well Dear Mrs Calder we must have patience for a while longer, and trust in Him who watches over us all, whenever they maybe our boys are together

Yours Sincerely Mrs Ada Bailey X

write soon.

Lancaster Bale Out

> I forgot to tell you in my letter, so am writing a postscript. The girl who used to take our boys out to their bomber in the motor transport lives in the next village, and she says they were the best and by far the nicest crew on the Station, and she says Rosmer was the finest pilot ever, she didn't take them on the night of the catastrophe as she was on leave at the time, and she said she could not have bourne it if she had have done as she was so very fond of them all. When she took them out she used to get up at the most unearthly hours in the morning to see if they were back OK she knew them all.
>
> Good night
> God Bless you
>
> The bombers are roaring over our house now as I write, the very sound upsets me and gives me no rest.

Ada Bailey's letter to Mr & Mrs Calder

30.
Post War - The Missing

By the end of the war in August 1945 there were around 41,881[90] airmen listed as missing. During the early years of the war it soon became apparent that the system for tracing the whereabouts of these airmen was totally inadequate. The Missing Research Section (MRS) of the Air Ministry was set up in late 1941 to deal with this increasing problem. It collected and collated intelligence reports from a wide variety of official, unofficial and covert sources in an attempt to establish the fate of missing aircrew.

Cambrai Cemetery, Joint Grave Disbury[91] / Hougham[92] (C. Smith)

---

[90] 'Missing Believed Killed', Stuart Hadaway.
[91] P/O Disbury was killed just 3 weeks after his 21st Birthday
[92] Note that 'Hougham' has been incorrectly spelled as 'Houghman'.

Lancaster Bale Out

In December 1944 the MRS was expanded and a small team of 14 men, who were ex-aircrew officers, named the Missing Research and Enquiry Service (MRES) were sent to France to seek the missing men on the ground. With thousands of aircrew unaccounted for though there was still a limit to what such a small group could achieve so it was realised in August 1945 that there was a need to expand the MRES even more. It was decided therefore to increase its size by over twenty five times, with set geographical areas of responsibility.

The work undertaken by the MRES involved long hours and at times often gruesome excavation of graves to identify bodies, working with local population who ranged from generally friendly in France, Belgium and Holland to the more openly hostile in Germany, who had been on the receiving end of the bombing offensive.

MRES Officers Exhuming a Grave (A. Archer)

Lancaster Bale Out

In the case of Fred Smooker's Lancaster the whole identification process must have been difficult because of the six bodies pulled from the badly burnt wreckage, only Ted Amor was identifiable. Jack Hougham and Geoff Disbury were initially given a joint grave, as the photo above illustrates. Various effects and clothing were used in the identification process. The Bomber Loss Card narrative (See Appendix D) gives some details:

168/63-68 - Amor C of E? 752196; Seylos (N/T)? Unknown with WB on ring (?Bailey) + 3 Unknown;

181/3 - Turner DA (belonging 168/63-68 R111537)

Ted Amor's tags with 'C of E' (Church of England) on enabled him to be positively identified and his parents informed. A signet ring with the initials 'WB', Wilfrid Bailey, likewise. The 3 Unknown were Disbury, Hougham and Calder. Turner was found separately a few weeks later and correctly assumed to be part of the same crew.

Fragments of olive green clothing and a Lieutenant's bar were found from Rosner's uniform. There was also a number of personal effects amongst his possessions; a large white metal knife, a British coin, a case of a rectangular shaped watch and a handkerchief with the wording 'Seylos' - which means 'loyal'. 1st Lieutenant Rosner was initially interred under the name Seylos for this reason.

The Commonwealth War Graves Commission (CWGC) suggest that the crew were buried initially in Cambrai East Military Cemetery and reburied sometime in 1947.

By December 1950 the Air Ministry reported that over half of the original airmen listed as missing had been accounted for with 23,881 in known burials. 9,281 further airmen had been confirmed as being lost at sea but 8,719 were still unaccounted for at that point.

In keeping with RAF policy, all aircrew killed abroad in WWII were buried together, as far as possible, in a convenient cemetery close to the place where they fell. Even though Jack Hougham, in his will, requested to be buried in Ash church yard, he and five other

Lancaster Bale Out

members of crew are buried in Cambrai Communal Cemetery, (Route de Solesmes), on the north eastern outskirts of Cambrai.

During the fifties the original, temporary, wooden crosses were gradually replaced with the permanent headstones that still stand today and that the CWGC continue to maintain in the cemeteries in immaculate condition. The next of kin were sent information about what the permanent headstones were to look like and give them an opportunity to have a personal inscription added.

Cambrai Cemetery, 1946 (C. Smith)

Cambrai Cemetery, 1996 (J.C. Lamant)

Plot 1 Row B (L to R):
Calder (9), Disbury (10), Hougham (11), Amor (12), Bailey (13), Turner (14)

Lancaster Bale Out

Epitaph in 60 letters or less (C. Smith)

Lancaster Bale Out

Eugene Rosner, having officially transferred to the USAAF before he was killed, was initially interred in Cambrai cemetery but was moved post-war to the American Military Cemetery at St. Laurent, next to the Normandy beaches. In keeping with his Jewish faith, the headstone marking Eugene's grave is a Star of David, located at position A-3-38.

American Military Cemetery, Normandy[93] (ABMC)

[93.] Note that the date of death is incorrectly shown as the 8th July 1943, instead of the 9th.

31.
The Ultimate Sacrifice - French Helpers

Fred learnt after the war that a number of his French helpers had been betrayed while he was in Stalag 4B. On 3rd November 1943 Maurice Thuru, his wife, daughter Josiane (now Bernard), Theophile Boyer and others were arrested. At 6:30 am on the 14th December 1943 Lucien Janssoone was also arrested. They were all taken to the infamous Gestapo headquarters at rue de Francois de Baedst. Interrogated by the Gestapo they were eventually condemned to death on the 12th May 1944 and deported. On the platform at Cologne station, Maurice Thuru saw his wife for the last time. The women were sent to a prison in Waldheim and the men to a prison at Diez sur Lahn, in Germany. On the morning of 23rd August 1944, Janssoone, Thuru and Boyer were taken from their cells, and executed.

Grave of Lucien Janssoone (S. Besin)

Lancaster Bale Out

Maurice Thuru's wife survived the war, albeit in a pitiful state. Marie Christine - Madame Bodin had been a member of Georges Broussine's, Bourgogne escape line and was condemned to death and died in Germany. Madame Bates was arrested in November 1943, but survived the war.

Jean Baptiste Baudouin survived the war and was awarded a citation on the 18th March 1949 for helping Allied Airmen by the BRAAEA (Bureau de Researche sur L'apportee Aux Evades Allie).

The sacrifice made by the gallant resistance people should not be underestimated. According to the RAF Escaping Society "2,803 members of the Royal and Commonwealth Air Forces aircrew who were shot down during WWII managed either to escape from captivity or, in the majority of cases, to evade capture." Some 14,000 French civilians are estimated to have been involved in assisting Allied airmen, and many were imprisoned or killed for their involvement. In Fred's evasion alone there were twenty five people directly involved in assisting him and at least the same again indirectly, including partners and children. All of these people were putting their lives at risk if they had been caught.

Over 55,500 RAF and Commonwealth Bomber Command aircrew lost their lives in the European theatre of operations, the USAAF losing similar numbers, but even this is only a small fraction of the estimated 55,000,000 people in total that lost their lives during WWII.

The final epitaph in remembrance of Lucien Janssoone, and one that can be applied to all the Allied airmen and *Passeurs*, reads:

'He died for his belief in freedom and love of his country'

32. Sources

AIR 27/127 - *9 Sqn Operations Record Book (1943)*
AIR 27/833 - *106 Sqn Operations Record Book (1943)* - National Archives, Kew
    Form 540 - Summary of Events
    Form 541 - Detail of Work Carried Out
WO208 3315 report #1457, *McMillan Evasion Questionnaire*

Library and Archives Canada
RG 24, Volume 24984, service file of R99456 F/Sgt James Reginald Calder
RG 24, Volume 28841, service file of R111837 F/Sgt Dalton Arnold Turner

Ordnance Survey Maps - GSGS 4040, 2nd Edition, France & Belgium 1:50,000, Solesmes (Sheet 87), Le Cateau (Sheet 101)
GSGS 4072, 2nd Edition 1943, Leipzig NE50/10

Alwyn Philips, J, *Valley of the Shadow of Death*, Air Research, 1991
Brammer, D, *Thundering Through the Clear Air*, TUCANN Books, 1997
Calder, R, *Correspondence*, Aug 1942 - July 1943
Charlwood, D, *No Moon Tonight*, Goodhall Publications Ltd, 1956
Chorley, B, *Bomber Command Losses (1943)*, Midland County Publications, 1996
Cooper, A, *The Air Battle of the Ruhr*, Airlife, 1991
Cunliffe, P, *A Shaky Do - The Skoda Works Raid*, 2007
Emerson L & Norman S, *The Evaders*, McGraw Hill, 1992
Garbett, M & Goulding, B, *The Lancaster at War*, Ian Allen, 1971
Garbett, M & Goulding, B, *The Lancaster at War 2*, Ian Allen, 1979
Garbett, M & Goulding, B, *The Lancaster at War 3*, Ian Allen, 1984
Garbett, M & Goulding, B, *The Lancaster at War 5*, Ian Allen, 1994
Gill, A, *The Great Escape*, Headline Book Publishing, 2002
Hadaway, S, *Missing Believed Killed*, Pen & Sword, 2008
Hampton, J, *Selected for Aircrew*, Air Research, 1993

Lancaster Bale Out

Lewis, B, *Aircrew*, Orion, 1991
Middlebrook, M & Everitt, C, *The Bomber Command War Diaries*, Penguin, 1985
Smooker, F, & Smith, C, *Correspondence*, 1993 - 2001
Taylor, G, *A Piece of Cake*, Peter Davies, 1956
Thompson, W, *Lancaster to Berlin*, Goodhall Publications Ltd, 1985
Thorne, A, *The Lancaster at War 4*, Ian Allen, 1988

Appendix A
Battle of the Ruhr[94] Ops

1943 March	Primary Target	Rosner Crew Serial	Code	Time	Duncan Crew Serial	Code	Time
5/6	Essen						
8/9	Nuremburg						
9/10	Munich						
11/12	Stuttgart						
12/13	Essen						
22/23	St. Nazaire						
26/27	Duisburg	R5611[95]	W	06:00			
27/28	Berlin	ED708	O	07:40			
29/30	Berlin						
April							
2/3	Lorient	R5492	S	05:45			
3/4	Essen	W4256	D	05:15			
4/5	Kiel						
8/9	Duisburg						
10/11	Frankfurt	ED649	X	06:10			
13/14	La Spezia	ED819	U	10:15			
14/15	Stuttgart	ED819	U	07:00			
16/17	Pilsen	ED649	X	03:35			
20/21	Stettin						
26/27	Duisburg						
30/1	Essen	ED819	U	05:05			

[94.] The Battle of the Ruhr opened on the 5 March - Target, the Krupps works at Essen. By the time it was over four months later, 1,045 Aircraft had been lost, 1,347 aircrew were missing and 4,171 aircrew had lost their lives.

[95.] Rosner's logbook notes that he flew as 2nd Pilot on this Op with F/O Les Brodrick, but the official Operational Record doesn't list him and Fred Smooker believed that the Berlin Op the following day was his first one.

[96.] W4964 'J' was one of a handful of Lancasters that completed over 100 ops. Nicknamed 'Johnny Walker' and emblazoned with the logo and motto, 'Still going strong', on completion of the 100th op the crew were presented with a case of Whisky, courtesy of their famous, unofficial sponsors!

Lancaster Bale Out

May								
4/5	Dortmund	ED819	U	05:55	W4964[96]	J	06:08
12/13	Duisburg	R5611	W	04:20	ED480	U	04:35
13/14	Pilsen	R5612	P	07:50	ED480	U	07:25
23/24	Dortmund	ED649	X	05:55			
25/26	Dusseldorf	ED649	X	05:00			
27/28	Essen	ED649	X	05:15			
29/30	Wuppertal	ED649[97]	X	05:20	ED480	U	06:00
June								
11/12	Dusseldorf				ED480	U	04:50
12/13	Bochum				ED480	U	05:20
14/15	Oberhausen				ED480	U	04:39
16/17	Cologne						
19/20	Le Creusot						
20/21	Friedrichshafen						
21/22	Krefeld	ED303[98]	J	04:55			
22/23	Mulheim	ED409[99]	E	04:20	W4133	S	04:45
24/25	Wuppertal	ED801	N	05:15	W4133	S	05:35
25/26	Gelsenkirchen	R5614	Z	04:35			
28/29	Cologne	ED360[100]	K	04:45	W4133	S	04:45
July								
3/4	Cologne						
8/9	Cologne	ED720[101]	R	03:50	W4133	S	05:40
9/10	Gelsenkirchen				ED480	U	04:40
12/13	Turin						
13/14	Aachen						
15/16	Bologna						

[97] *On this trip a 2nd Navigator, F/O Paddock, also flew to assist with the navigation*
[98] *On this trip a 2nd Pilot, Sgt W.R.P Perry, also flew to gain Operational experience*
[99] *On this trip a 2nd Navigator, Sgt Barker, also flew to assist with the navigation*
[100] *On this trip a 2nd Navigator, P/O Lintot, also flew to assist with the navigation*
[101] *On this trip a 2nd Pilot, Sgt G. F. Disbury, also flew to gain Operational experience*

Appendix B
Aircraft/Aircrew Losses

This section details the circumstances of the loss resulting in aircrew mentioned in the account evading, becoming POWs or being killed.

26/27 August 1941
9 Squadron　　　　　**Wellington IC W5703 WS-**　　**Op: Cologne**

The aircraft developed engine trouble after leaving the target area and crash-landed near Cambrai.

S/L	**H.E. Bufton**	RAF		Pilot	Evaded
Sgt.	J.T Stickles	RCAF		2nd Pilot	POW
Sgt.	**W.F. Crampton**	RAF	988755	Navigator	Evaded
Sgt.	S. Murray	RAF		Bomb Aimer	POW
Sgt.	R.P. Wright	RAF		W/Op	POW
Sgt.	K.B. Read	RAF		Rear Gunner	Evaded

Sqn Ldr Bufton and Sgt Crampton were harboured and aided in their evasion by Lucien Janssoone.

30/31 May 1942
115 Squadron　　　　　**Wellington III Z1614 KO-R**　　**Op: Cologne**

Aircraft lost without trace.

Sgt.	Emrys Edwards	RAF	1379351	Pilot	+
F/Sgt.	**William Francis Crampton**	RAF	988755	Navigator	+
Sgt.	Malcolm Boyle	RAF	1109750	Bomb Aimer	+
Sgt.	William Arnott McLeod	RAF	745477	W/Op	+
Sgt.	Hubert Sproston	RAF	1177725	Rear Gunner	+

Nine months after crashing and evading from an op to Cologne, Sgt Crampton (MiD) was killed on the first 1,000 bomber raid to the same city. All the crew are commemorated on the Runnymede memorial.

Lancaster Bale Out

4 December 1942
14 OTU   Wellington IC DV929   Op: Training
T/O 22:13 Cottesmore but climbed too steeply and crashed within 2 minutes of departure, the aircraft coming down near the local village.

Sgt.	**William Francis Rielly**	RAF	121797	Pilot	+
Sgt.	George Groves	RAF	1388416	Navigator	+
Sgt.	John William Hyde	RAF	334211	Bomb Aimer	+
Sgt.	Maurice Knapton	RAF	1026154	W/Op	+
Sgt.	DR Gladish	RCAF		Rear Gunner	inj

William Francis Rielly is mentioned in Jim Calder's letters home. He was actually American from Youngstown, Ohio, but was flying for the RAF. Initially interred in the American Section of Brookwood Military Cemetary he was repatriated to the US post war.

28 January 1943
14 OTU   Wellington IC Z8896   Op: Training
T/O 09:45 Cottesmore for a navigation flight. While attempting to land at RAF Waddington the crew were experiencing problems with the port engine, entered a spin in a left hand turn and crashed 12:30 near the runway.

F/Sgt.	Douglas Joseph Farrell	RCAF	R/127628	Pilot	+
Sgt.	Frank James Emberson	RAF	1254332	Navigator	+
Sgt.	Richard Badcock	RAF	1239676	Bomb Aimer	+
Sgt.	Malcolm McMillan	RAF	1187788	W/Op	+
Sgt.	Gordon Cornelius Nielson	RAF	702262	Rear Gunner	+

F/Sgt. Farrell was the Pilot that Fred Smooker first spoke to when getting crewed up.

14/15 April 1943
106 Squadron   Lancaster III ED752 ZN-H   Op: Stuttgart
Aircraft crash landed at Sauvillers-Mongival, France around 3:30 am.

F/L	**Les C.J. Brodrick**	RAF		Pilot	POW
S/L	Jerrard Latimer DFC	RAF	39286	2nd Pilot	+
Sgt.	Gordon William Hancock	RAF	576889	Flight Eng	+
P/O	J.A. Burns	RCAF		Navigator	POW
Lt (A)	Gerard Muttrie	RNVR		Bomb Aimer	+
Sgt.	Harold Buxton	RAF	1177603	W/Op	+
Sgt.	William Thomas McLean	RAF	1551176	Mid Upper	+
Sgt.	H. Jones	RAF		Rear Gunner	POW

Lancaster Bale Out

It was on the return flight from the target that the Lancaster got into trouble. The aircraft had been hit over the target which resulted in it losing considerable altitude. Flying at about 100 feet over Amiens the bomber was raked by machine gun from the ground and set on fire. With no height to bale out F/L Brodrick crash landed and five of the crew were killed and the Navigator was very badly injured. After scrambling from the wreckage F/L Brodrick and Sgt Jones, the Rear Gunner, realised that any chance of evasion was very slim as urgent medical help was required for the Navigator, P/O Burns. Both airmen went to a nearby farmhouse to ask for help and soon a party of German soldiers arrived on the scene and arrested them. On returning to the crash site, Sgt Jones was asked to identify the bodies of the other airmen that had been killed and the three survivors were taken by ambulance to the nearby aerodrome, from where P/O Burns was taken to hospital. Brodrick and Jones were taken to Dulag Luft and then onto POW camps; Jones to Stalag Luft I, Barth Vogelsang, Brodrick to Stalag Luft III, Sagan. Later on Brodrick participated in the 'Great Escape' on 29th March 1944. He escaped through tunnel 'Harry' in the north compound. He was the 52nd of the escapers to leave the tunnel, dressed in his own battle dress over which he wore an airman's great coat, the buttons of which had been covered by dark cloth. With false identity papers and some survival rations he joined up with a party of ten other airmen in a nearby wood, led by a Canadian officer, Flight Lieutenant Hank Birkland. The party walked together for about 2km before agreeing to split up into smaller groups, Brodrick, Birkland and F/O Street staying together. They continued walking in a southerly direction, resting up in the woods the next day. Before dark they set off once more but by now they were very wet from the heavy rain that had been falling steadily all the time. Just before dawn on the 27th they were soaking wet and suffering badly with the terrible cold. They realised that their chances of getting any further were practically nil and so decided to give themselves up. They approached a small cottage near Kalkbrugh and discovered that it was occupied by four German soldiers who were out on a search party looking for the escapers. They were quickly arrested and taken to the local Police station before being transferred to the civil prison at Gorlitz for interrogation. They all managed to get rid of their false papers by burning them in a fire at the Police station on the pretence of getting warm. From Gorlitz, Brodrick was taken back to Sagan to serve 21 days of solitary confinement, a small price to pay he felt for the disruption and chaos that the escapes had caused the Germans. F/Lt Birkland and F/O Street were no so fortunate and fell victim to Hitler's reprisal order for this mass break out and were murdered by the Gestapo.

Lancaster Bale Out

Lt Muttrie was a Naval Officer from HMS Daedalus on detachment to the RAF.

8/9 July 1943
106 Squadron   Lancaster III ED720 ZN-R   Op: Cologne

Aircraft crashed at Fontaine au Tertre, E of Cambrai, France, 2:30 am.

1/Lt	**Eugene Leon Rosner**	USAAF	O-885994	Pilot	+
P/O	**Geoffrey Francis Disbury**	RAF	149510	2nd Pilot	+
Sgt.	**Edward William John Amor**	RAF	752196	Flight Eng	+
Sgt.	**Wilfrid Bailey**	RAF	1440585	Navigator	+
Sgt.	**Frederick Henry Smooker**	RAF	1048639	Bomb Aimer	POW (4B)
Sgt.	**Jack Hougham**	RAF	1271588	W/Op	+
F/Sgt.	**James Reginald Calder**	RCAF	R/99456	Mid Upper	+
F/Sgt.	**Dalton Arnold Turner**	RCAF	R/11837	Rear Gunner	+

Flight Sergeant Turner managed to parachute out of the aircraft but his body was found three weeks later by farm labourers lying dead in a cornfield.

All of the crew are buried at Cambrai Route de Solesmes communal cemetery, except 1st Lieutenant Rosner, who is buried at the American Military cemetery in Normandy.

Note: Rosner's service number was previously R117639 (Sgt) and J20017 (P/O) Disbury's service number was previously 1537036

8/9 July 1943
106 Squadron   Lancaster III R5573 ZN-B   Op: Cologne

Aircraft crashed at Oupeye, near Liege, around 3:30 am.

Sgt.	Kenneth Hector Wally McLean	RCAF	R/109281	Pilot	+
Sgt.	Samuel Leigh	RAF	616090	Flight Eng	+
Sgt.	Donald Hugh McLeod	RCAF	R/128853	Navigator	+
Sgt.	Reginald William Lingfield Muir	RAF	1388470	Bomb Aimer	+
Sgt.	Ronald Charles Barrett	RAF	1164249	W/Op	+
Sgt.	Leslie Ronald Johnson	RAAF	412967	Mid Upper	+
Sgt.	Edward Hannell	RAF	1388875	Rear Gunner	+

This aircraft was one of the other 106 Squadron losses on the 8/9 July 1943.

Lancaster Bale Out

8/9 July 1943
106 Squadron   Lancaster III ED360 ZN-   Op: Cologne
Aircraft crashed on fen land, NW of Wisbech, Cambridgeshire, around 1:40 am.

F/Sgt.	Arthur George Bristow	RAF	1333752	Pilot	+
Sgt.	F. Scattergood	RAF		Flight Eng	inj
Sgt.	James Stuart Johns	RAF	1238520	Navigator	+
Sgt.	L. J. Hazell	RAF		Bomb Aimer	inj
Sgt.	Wilfred Worthington	RAF	1126476	W/Op	+
Sgt.	Kenneth William Murphy	RCAF	R/147182	Mid Upper	+
Sgt.	Clifford Simm	RAF	945654	Rear Gunner	+

This aircraft was one of the other 106 Squadron losses on the 8/9 July 1943.

9/10 July 1943
9 Squadron   Lancaster III ED480 WS-U   Op: Gelsenkirchen
Aircraft crashed at Troisvilles, SW of Le Cateau, France.

Sgt.	John Duncan	RCAF	R/119731	Pilot	Evaded
Sgt.	Stan G. Blunden	RAF	913554	Flight Eng	POW (357)
F/Sgt.	**Harry Brown**	RAF	1262465	Navigator	Evaded
Sgt.	Gerard Bartley	RAF	1499890	Bomb Aimer	Evaded
Sgt.	Sidney Hughes	RAF	1127645	W/Op	Evaded
Sgt.	L.G. Warner	RAF	1267098	Mid Upper	POW (357)
Sgt.	**David McMillan**	RCAF	R/84436	Rear Gunner	Evaded

The aircraft was abandoned over Le Cateau as it had been damaged by flak. All crew parachuted out successfully.

29/30 July 1943
76 Squadron   Halifax V ED244 MP-X 'Bar'   Op: Hamburg
Aircraft crashed at Obendorf, 27km NW of Stade, Germany.
According to Vic Daniels only he and the other gunner, Stan Bates, parachuted out. The other crew members crash landed.

Sgt.	A.R Bjercke	RNZAF		Pilot	POW
Sgt.	**Dennis M. Morrison**	RAF		Flight Eng	POW (4B)
F/O	Clifford Daniel	RAF	132713	Navigator	+
Sgt.	H. Roberts	RAF		Bomb Aimer	POW
Sgt.	O.C. Olsen	RNZAF		W/Op	POW
Sgt.	**Victor Cliff Daniels**	RAF		Mid Upper	POW (4B)
Sgt.	Stan H. Bates	RAF		Rear Gunner	POW

F/O Daniel is buried in Becklingen War Cemetery.

Lancaster Bale Out

30/31 July 1943
408 Squadron Halifax II JD365 EQ-J   Op: Remscheid
Aircraft crashed at Düren, Germany.

Sgt.	Albert Edward Chalk	RAF	1322049	Pilot	+
Sgt.	John Crammond	RAF	1675338	Flight Eng	+
Sgt.	**Reginald A. Dernam**	RAF	222447	Navigator	POW (4B)
Sgt.	R.C. Davies	RAF		Bomb Aimer	POW
Sgt.	William Lewis Reed	RAF	1330193	W/Op	+
Sgt.	Robert George Edwards	RCAF	R/125516	Mid Upper	+
Sgt.	Frank Berry	RAF	1604340	Rear Gunner	+

Sgt. Reed is buried in Rheinberg War Cemetery, the others who died have no known graves and are commemorated on the Runnymede Memorial. Sgt. Reg Dernam was repatriated to the UK in October 1944.

2/3 August 1943
158 Squadron Halifax II HR751 NP-J 'Jane' Op: Hamburg
Aircraft crashed in the eastern suburb Eidelstedt, Hamburg, Germany.

Sgt.	**Charles Kenneth Davie**	RAF	1001169	Pilot	POW (4B)
Sgt.	**Arthur Kevern Snell**	RAF	921658	Flight Eng	POW (4B)
Sgt.	Gwyn Rusbatch	RNZAF	415424	Navigator	POW
Sgt.	Henry Patrick Jarman	RAF	1338157	Bomb Aimer	POW
Sgt.	Raymond Brown Farmery	RAF	1482428	W/Op	+
Sgt.	James Mark Lally	RCAF	R/143209	Mid Upper	POW
F/S	Clement Robert Buckland	RAF	1102306	Rear Gunner	POW

In Kevern 'Lofty' Snell's words "We were flying over Hamburg during a storm and were hit by flak. The plane started to spiral downwards. It was my job to stay and help the pilot on with his parachute, which I did, and then I made my way to the hatch. This was not easy as the plane was spiraling fast and we were held to the floor by centrifugal force. When I got out of the plane I put both hands to my chest to release the parachute but found nothing there. After a moment's panic I realised that the parachute was not strapped round me but was hanging above my head. I reached up and managed to pull the cord and so the parachute opened. I landed in a cornfield in torrential rain and stayed there all the next day in the blazing heat of an August summer. The next night I began to make my way as we had been instructed, going through hedges and across fields. I went through one hedge and came face to face with a young German soldier, who looked as shocked as I was. I was taken for interrogation and ended up as a POW".

Lancaster Bale Out

Sgt. Raymond Farmery (J Farmery)

Sgt. RB Farmery Temporary Cross, Hamburg (J Farmery)

All the other crew had baled out successfully, but Sgt. Farmery's parachute failed to open and he is buried in Hamburg Cemetery, Ohlsdorf.

Lancaster Bale Out

9/10 August 1943
35 Squadron   Halifax II HR908 TL-Z   Op: Mannheim

F/S	E.G. Brown	RAAF		Pilot	POW
F/S	**James. E. Jones** DFM	RAF	610981	Flight Eng	POW (4B)
F/O	Harold Luttrell Temple	RAF	127971	Navigator	+
P/O	E.C. Dobie	RAF		Bomb Aimer	POW
Sgt.	Arthur Patrick Bowker	RAF	1194726	W/Op	+
Sgt.	Allen Sunley	RAF	1302029	Mid Upper	+
F/S	William Richard Pallister	RAF	627672	Rear Gunner	+

All those who died are buried in the Rheinberg War Cemetery. F/S James 'Taffy' Ellis Jones, from Monmouthshire, was killed on a coal stealing detail at Stalag 4B, on 2nd April 1944, while held captive as a POW. He is buried in Berlin War Cemetery.

16/17 September 1943
419 Squadron   Halifax II LW240 VR-S   Op: Modane
Aircraft crashed at Lisieux, France at 3:00 am.

F/L	A.N. Quailie	RAF	Pilot	POW
Sgt.	E.E. Bowden	RCAF	2nd Pilot	POW
Sgt.	L.F. Martin	RCAF	Flight Eng	Evaded
P/O	L.E. Aspinall	RCAF	Navigator	POW
P/O	G.T. Graham	RCAF	Bomb Aimer	Evaded
F/S	T.J. Bright	RAF	W/Op	Evaded
F/O	H.F. Smith	RCAF	Mid Upper	Evaded
F/L	**Bennet Ley Kenyon**	RAF	Rear Gunner	POW

F/L Kenyon was on his 44th operational sortie and was the Squadron's Gunnery Leader.

3/4 November 1943
76 Squadron   Halifax V LK949 MP-V   Op: Düsseldorf

Sgt.	F.S. Giortz	RNZAF	Pilot	
Sgt.	J. Picken	RAF	2nd Pilot	
Sgt.	**Stan J. Cancea**	RAF	Flight Eng	POW (4B)
F/S	A. Prenter	RAF	Navigator	
Sgt.	D.P. Roberts	RAF	Bomb Aimer	
Sgt.	W. Iverson	RAF	W/Op	
Sgt.	D.H. Stocker	RAF	Mid Upper	POW
Sgt.	G.C. Harris	RAF	Rear Gunner	Injured

The aircraft was attacked by a night fighter shortly after bombing the target. In the confusion the Flight Engineer and mid Upper Gunner baled out but the pilot managed to get the Halifax back to Holme-on-Spalding Moor.

Appendix C
Fred Smooker Escape and Evasion Diary

July 1943
Th	8	Take off Syerston 10:30 hours for Op to Cologne
Fr	9	Shot down near Cambrai 2:30 am
Sa	10	Béthencourt (Harry and Mac shot down)
Su	11	
Mo	12	
Tu	13	
We	14	
Th	15	Caudry
Fr	16	
Sa	17	
Su	18	
Mo	19	
Tu	20	
We	21	
Th	22	
Fr	23	
Sa	24	Arras (Joined Harry and Mac)
Su	25	
Mo	26	
Tu	27	
We	28	
Th	29	
Fr	30	
Sa	31	Bapaume

August 1943
Su	1	
Mo	2	
Tu	3	
We	4	
Th	5	
Fr	6	
Sa	7	
Su	8	
Mo	9	

Lancaster Bale Out

Tu	10		
We	11		
Th	12		
Fr	13		
Sa	14		
Su	15		
Mo	16		
Tu	17		
We	18		
Th	19		
Fr	20		
Sa	21	Paris 1	(Mac leaves)
Su	22	Paris 2	
Mo	23	Paris 3	
Tu	24		
We	25	Paris 4	
Th	26	Paris 5	
Fr	27	Paris College	
Sa	28		
Su	29		
Mo	30		
Tu	31		

September 1943

We	1	
Th	2	
Fr	3	
Sa	4	
Su	5	Marie Christine (Harry leaves)
Mo	6	Annette
Tu	7	
We	8	
Th	9	
Fr	10	
Sa	11	
Su	12	Marie Christine
Mo	13	
Tu	14	
We	15	
Th	16	
Fr	17	
Sa	18	

Lancaster Bale Out

Su	19	
Mo	20	
Tu	21	
We	22	
Th	23	
Fr	24	
Sa	25	
Su	26	
Mo	27	
Tu	28	
We	29	
Th	30	

October 1943

Fr	1	
Sa	2	Train to Dax
Su	3	Biarritz
Mo	4	Bayonne Prison
Tu	5	
We	6	
Th	7	Fresnes Prison
Fr	8	
Sa	9	
Su	10	
Mo	11	
Tu	12	
We	13	
Th	14	
Fr	15	
Sa	16	
Su	17	
Mo	18	
Tu	19	
We	20	
Th	21	
Fr	22	
Sa	23	
Su	24	
Mo	25	
Tu	26	
We	27	
Th	28	

Lancaster Bale Out

Fr	29
Sa	30
Su	31

November 1943

Mo	1
Tu	2
We	3
Th	4
Fr	5
Sa	6
Su	7
Mo	8
Tu	9
We	10
Th	11
Fr	12
Sa	13
Su	14
Mo	15
Tu	16
We	17
Th	18
Fr	19
Sa	20
Su	21
Mo	22
Tu	23
We	24
Th	25
Fr	26
Sa	27
Su	28
Mo	29
Tu	30	56th Day Solitary Confinement

December 1943

We	1	Frankfurt - Dulag Luft
Th	2	
Fr	3	Stalag IVB - Mühlberg
Sa	4	
Su	5	

Lancaster Bale Out

Mo	6
Tu	7
We	8
Th	9
Fr	10
Sa	11
Su	12
Mo	13
Tu	14	Lucien Jannsoone arrested by the Gestapo
We	15
Th	16
Fr	17
Sa	18
Su	19
Mo	20
Tu	21
We	22
Th	23
Fr	24
Sa	25
Su	26
Mo	27
Tu	28
We	29
Th	30
Fr	31

Appendix D
Bomber Loss Card

ED720 Bomber Loss Card (RAF Museum)

Appendix E
Gendarme Reports

GENDARMERIE NATIONALE   Cambrai, le 9 Juillet 1943

I° Légion
Compagnie du Nord   R A P P O R T
Section de Cambrai   du Capitaine WERQUIN, Commandant la Section
     N° 438/2   de Gendarmerie de Cambrai,

sur la chute d'un avion de nationalité britannique à QUIEVY (Nord).

REFERENCE : Article 53 Décret du 20 Mai 1903.

Le 9 Juillet 1943, vers 2 heures 30, un avion de nationalité britannique est tombé en flammes dans un champ de blé, au Nord-Est de la commune de QUIEVY (Nord). Il n'y a eu aucune victime parmi la population française.
L'autorité allemande avisée s'est rendue sur place et a pris les mesures qu'elle a jugé nécessaires.
Les dégâts causés aux récoltes peuvent être évalués à quelques milliers de francs.

         Pour le Capitaine WERQUIN en permission
       L'Adjudant SORRIAUX Adjoint, Cdt Pt. la Section

DESTINATAIRES

1°- Chef du Gouvernement (Direction Générale de la Gendarmerie-Section des T.O.)
     2 exp.
2°- Préfet Régional
3°- Préfet départemental
4°- Général Inspecteur Général de la Gendarmerie de la Z.O
5°- Général Inspecteur Légion
6°- Sous-Préfet
7°- Procureur de la République
8°- Commandant de Légion
9°- Commandant de Compagnie
10°- Kreiskommandantur (s/c Sous-Préfet)

Service régional de   LILLE ce 9 Juillet 1943 à 9h50
Police de Sûreté
Service Signalétique   Le Commissaire Chef du District de Cambrai
et des Diffusions   communique :

Cette nuit, vers 2heures 45, un avion en flammes, présumé de nationalité britannique, est tombé en flammes près de la gare de Quiévy. Il n'y a aucune victime et pas de dégât aux immeubles.
Les aviateurs, sauf un ou deux qui sont en fuite, ont été carbonisés. Autorités Allemandes sur les lieux.

L'Intendance de Police communique ce jour à 10 Heures

Un bombardement aérien a eu lieu ce matin à 8heures du Sud au Nord de la ville de St Omer.
       Renseignements complémentaires suivent

          L'Inspecteur de permanence.

Transmis aux Autorités Régionales

Appendix F
Luftwaffe Night Fighters

In trying to complete the whole picture as far as possible I have made attempts to find out the names and identities of the Night Fighter unit and personnel involved that shot down Lancaster ED 720 'R' for Robert at around 2:30 am on 9th July, 1943. In trying to track down information about Luftwaffe crews the sources of research are somewhat limited as there are very few official records that can be accessed, unlike the very well documented RAF records in the Public Record Office. The only information that I have been able to trace has been provided by a Luftwaffe historian; Herr Horst Diener of the Nachtjagdzentrale. He provided me with details from a book that was written by a former night fighter pilot, in which he documented over eight-thousand interceptions against bomber aircraft.

According to *Bomber Command Losses (1943)* there were nine Lancasters lost on the Cologne op on 8/9 July, 1943, of which one was abandoned over Holland, two crashed in the UK and the other six were shot down. The following information details the six Luftwaffe claims for the night, the pilot credited with the kill, the unit, the approximate time and the area of the loss, and the Lancaster serial where confirmed:

Pilot	Unit	Time	Location	Lancaster
Lt. Ehrlinghagen	II/NJG1	1:05 am	Bassenge onthe Geer, Liege	ED923 'V'
Oblt Schnaüfer[102]	II/NJG1	2:33 am	Grobbendonk, Antwerp	ED663
Uffz Kurz	I/NJG2			
Oblt Zorner	I/NJG3	2:20 am	West of Malmédy	
Hptm Wohlers	IV/NJG4			
Lt. Graeff	I/NJG4	2:50 am	North of Hirson	

Ehrlinghagen and Schnaüfer have been confirmed from other sources, and if the locations for Zorner and Graeff are accurate, it can be assumed then that either Kurz or Wohlers were responsible for shooting down ED720. As Kurz and Wohlers have both since died, from the location of the fighter bases, I/NJG2 were based at Gilze Rijen and IV/NJG4 were based at Mainz-Finthen, it is only possible to speculate that as Gilze Rijen is the closer of the two bases to Cambrai, Kurz is the more probable of the two.

---

[102] *Oblt. Heinz Wolfgang Schnaüfer, known as the 'Ghost of St. Trond' was the most successful of the Luftwaffe night fighter pilots, being credited with 121 kills to his name.*

Appendix G
Gestapo Warning to French Helpers

NOTICE
Having observed the attitude of the French population in the occupied zone, I have noticed that the majority of the population continue to work as normal. We disapprove of the acts of sabotage, etc carried out by the English and Soviets, directed towards the occupied forces, and we know it is the French civilian population who will suffer the consequences.

I am resolved to guarantee in a resolute manner, that during the course of the war, the French population shall be able to continue to work in calm and safety. I have observed that it is primarily the close family of the perpetrators of sabotage and trouble makers that have helped them before and after their acts. I have therefore decided to hit the grieved with the most severe measures, not only the saboteurs and trouble makers but also in the case of escape as soon as the name of the perpetrators is known, the family of these criminals must present themselves within 10 days after the act to the head quarters of the Police, German or French.

As a consequence I announce the following measures:

1) All the male close parents and family in direct line of ascendance and descendance as well as the brother in laws and cousins, eighteen years and over shall be shot.

2) All the females of the same parenthood shall be condemned to forced labour.

3) All the children up to the age of seventeen years old conceived from men or women will be hit by the most severe measures and placed in an education reform house.

Therefore I appeal to all, in order to stop the attempts, saboteurs and trouble-makers to inform the authorities of the slightest piece of information in order to apprehend the criminals.

Paris, 10 July 1942.
The Head of the SS and Police - France

Appendix H - Abbreviations and Terms

1st Lt.	First Lieutenant
ABMC	American Battle Monuments Commission
AFU	Advanced Flying Unit
AG	Air Gunner
AGS	Air Gunnery School
ANS	Air Navigation School
B/A	Bomb Aimer
BGS	Bombing and Gunnery School
Blockbuster	8,000 or 12,000lb Bomb
BRAAEA	Bureau de Researche sur L'apportee Aux Evades Allie
Cookie	4,000lb Bomb
CWGC	Commonwealth War Graves Commission
DFC	Distinguished Flying Cross
DFM	Distinguished Flying Medal
DH	de Havilland
DNCO	Duty Not Carried Out
F/E	Flight Engineer
F/O	Flying Officer
F/Sgt.	Flight Sergeant
Gee	Code name given to a Radio Navigation system
Geneva Convention	Treaty of 1929 laying down the rules for humane treatment of Prisoners of War
GI	General Issue
HCU	Heavy Conversion Unit
ITW	Initial Training Wing
LAC	Leading Aircraftman
Lt.	Lieutenant
Mae West	Slang name for the standard Aircrew Life Jacket
MoD	Ministry of Defence
MRES	Missing Research and Enquiry Service
MRS	Missing Research Section
NAAFI	Navy, Army and Air Force Institutes
NCO	Non-Commissioned Officer

NJG	Nachtjagdgeschwader - Luftwaffe Night Fighter Wing
OCM	L'organisation Civile et Militaire
OTU	Operational Training Unit
P/O	Pilot Officer
Paramatta	Code name used for an operation in which navigation aids were used to mark the target on the ground.
Pathfinder	The Pathfinder Force that were tasked with marking the Target.
POW	Prisoner of War
PT	Physical Training
RAAF	Royal Australian Air Force
RAF	Royal Air Force
RAFVR	Royal Air Force Volunteer Reserve
RAMC	Royal Army Medical Corps
RAOB	Royal Antediluvian Order of Buffaloes
RC	Reception Centre
RCAF	Royal Canadian Air Force
RNVR	Royal Navy Volunteer Reserve
RNZAF	Royal New Zealand Air Force
S/L, Sqn. Ldr	Squadron Leader
Sgt.	Sergeant
SOE	Special Operations Executive
SoTT	School of Technical Training
SS	Signals School / Steam Ship / Schutzstaffel
Stalag	Stammlager - German Prisoner of War Camp
USAAF	United States Army Air Force
VE	Victory in Europe
W/T	Wireless/Telegraphy
WAAF	Women's Auxiliary Air Force
Wanganui	Code name used for an operation in which navigation aids were used to mark the clouds over an obscured target.
Wg. Cdr	Wing Commander
Wilde Sau	Wild Boar - Luftwaffe fighters tasked with intercepting bombers over the Target
WO	Warrant Officer
WOp	Wireless Operator

Index of People, Aircraft and Places

Aberystwyth, Wales 23
Barrington, Winston 205, 206
Babbacombe, Devon 22, 23
Bamberger, Freddie 206
Bournemouth, Dorset 32, 33, 51, 91
Brodrick, F/O Les 63, 66, 67, 83, 275, 278, 279
Brussels 240
Calder, F/Sgt Jim 10, 16, 45, 46, 48, 49, 51, 52, 56-58, 63, 65, 86-88, 90, 93, 262, 268, 278, 280
Cancea, Sgt Stan 183, 284
Carleton Place, Canada 44, 57
Chemnitz 218
Cottesmore, Rutland 34, 35, 38, 44, 45, 47, 48
Daniels, Sgt Cliff 'Danny' 204, 276
Davie, Sgt Ken 213, 242, 254, 282
Dernam, Sgt Reg 207, 282
Donisthorpe, Leicestershire 38, 84
Dungeness, Kent 82
Goderich, Canada 27
Gournock, Scotland 25
Guilton, Kent 38
Halifax, Canada 27
Halifax, Nova Scotia 23
Halle 239
Hamilton, Ontario, Canada . 29, 30, 32
Jones, F/Sgt Taffy 201
Jurby, Isle of Man 47
Kenyon, F/L B. L. 173, 284
Lake Huron, Canada 27
Lewis, F/Sgt Bruce 40
Lowestoft, Suffolk 71
Marshall, Private Bob 217, 223
Menai Bridge, Wales 47
Moncton, Canada 27
Morrison, Sgt Dennis 197, 281
Niagara Falls, Canada 29, 30, 31
Niedewiesa 218-220
No. 10 RC, Blackpool 41
No. 14 OTU, Cottesmore 34
No. 1654 HCU, Wigsley 54
No. 3 RC, Padgate 21
No. 31 BGS, Picton, Ontario 27, 29
No. 33 ANS, Hamilton 29
No.1 SS, RAF Cranwell 23
No.31 ANS, Canada 27
No.4 SS, Madley, Herts 40
No.41 ITW, Aberystwyth 23
No.8 AGS, Evanton 43, 40
Nova Scotia, Canada 27, 32
Oakham, Rutland 45, 46, 49, 50, 51
Ontario, Canada 28, 29, 44, 56, 57
Ottawa, Canada 14, 44, 45
Picton, Ontario, Canada 29
Ridd, Sgt T.J. 78
Roddymoor colliery 64
Roddymoor, County Durham 64
Schelde Islands, Holland 76
Snell, Sgt 'Lofty' 213, 215, 282
Springhill, Canada 56
St. Bees, Cumbria 64
Syerston, Nottingham 60, 61, 63, 72, 73, 75, 80, 82, 84, 92, 97
Thompson, F/O Walter 61, 82
Torquay, Devon 22
Trenton, Ontario, Canada 28, 29
Turner, LAC Arnie 44, 45, 49, 57, 64, 65, 74, 78, 92, 97, 138
Wainfleet Sands, Lincolnshire 48
Wigsley, Lincolnshire 54, 56
Zschopau 221

(Footnotes)

[1] L to R, Victor Adams, Clive Smith, Ada Hougham, John Hougham, Minnie Adams, Doris Smith

[2] Frederick Henry Smooker was born on 29 January 1916 during the Great War into a mining family in County Durham. He was the second eldest of six having a brother and four sisters

[3] The term 'Passeurs' was applied to all the members of the civilian population that helped Allied airmen in their escape and evasion. Although often referred to as members of the 'Resistance', this term is more correctly used to describe the armed partisan groups of French fighters - FFI de l'intérieur.

[4] Someone who heaved or hacked coal from the face using a hand or pneumatic pick.

[5] Those occupations deemed by the government to be essential to the war effort. People in such industries were exempt from becoming servicemen, unless by choice. Ironically in December 1943, having lost some 36,000 miners to the services or better paid work, the government realised that it needed 40,000 miners to maintain output for the war effort and so began to compulsorily direct a percentage of conscripts into coal mining. These so called 'Bevin Boys', named after the Minster of Labour, numbered approximately 48,000 by the end of the war.

[6] The SS Orbita was built in 1914 by Harland and Wolff, Belfast, for the Pacific Steam Navigation Co of London. It was first used as an auxiliary cruiser before being refitted in 1940 as a troopship.

[7] The Royal Antediluvian Order of Buffaloes, a charitable organisation akin to the Masons and still active today.

[8] The SS Stirling Castle was built in 1935 by Harland and Wolff, Belfast, for the Union Castle Line and from 1940 served as a troopship steaming over 500,000 miles and carrying 128,000 personnel.

[9] F/O Robert Marriot (129617) was killed on 10th March 1943. Sgt. Alfred Joseph Railton (1476472) was killed on 26th May 1943 whilst flying as a Rear Gunner with 166 Sqn on a raid to Dusseldorf (Wellington HE235).

[10] A term given to those who failed to meet the standards required for an aircrew discipline.

[11] The Wellington was a twin engined bomber, but did not fly well on only one engine. Inexperienced pilots could therefore easily get into trouble if an engine failed during flight.

[12] The Commonwealth and Empire countries provided over a quarter of the airmen who flew with Bomber Command.

Lancaster Bale Out

13   Jim wrote a series of 30 letters to his parents and family over the course of his serving in the UK

14   The TR9 was a type of transmitter radio set used by the pilot.

15   61 Squadron Lancaster ED332, piloted by S/Ldr Parker. All were killed.

16   This was his younger sister Dot (Dorothy) who was 14 at the time and was in hospital for two years

17   Tom Jaye was the navigator of P/O Burpee's crew. As part of the third wave, they were tasked to attack the Sorpe dam, but were hit by flak on the way out and crashed near Gilze Rijen, Holland. They are buried in the Bergen-op-Zoom cemetery.

18   It was originally Bomber Command policy to send new pilots along with an experienced crew for their first one or two Ops to see what an Operational Mission was like. As crew losses mounted later in the war this was less likely to occur.

19   This was the list that was posted up, detailing the names of the all the aircrew that would be taking part in the nights operation.

20   Wg Cdr John Searby went on to lead 83 Sqn (Pathfinders) and was the master bomber on the successful Peenemunde raid on 17/18 Aug 43.

21   Pilot Sgt John McIntosh's crew, L to R, F/E Sgt Seeley, Rear Gunner Sgt Middleton, Nav Sgt Nicholson, Mid Upper gunner and B/A Sgt Ball

22   Wireless Operator Sgt John Hyde adjusts the tuning on the R1155 Receiver at the Lancaster's port Wireless position.

23   An example of what could happen to Syerston crews if they had problems during take off or landing. F/O Peter Todd and crew crashed their 61 Squadron Lanc, DV232 QR-K, in the River Trent, after engine problems on landing returning from Mannheim, 6 September 1943.

24   The Ruhr and Wupper valleys were the industrial heartland of Germany producing steel and munitions for war production. Essen, Dortmund, Wuppertal and Duisburg were all clustered around there because of the coking coal, iron ore and the River Ruhr, a tributary of the Rhine. It was Sir Arthur Harris who referred to this period as the 'Battle of the Ruhr'.

25   Pathfinders were special squadrons that dropped red or green flares over the target to mark it, so that the following aircraft could drop their bombs more accurately.

26   Bomber Command War Diaries details the number at 348 aircraft, 225 of which were Lancasters - this being the first time that over 200 Lancasters were used on the same op

27   The word left was always repeated twice so that there was more chance of the instructions being understood over high levels of background noise.

28   Pilot Sgt John McIntosh adjusts the seat in the Lancaster's port Pilot position.

[29] Sgt Iain H. Nicholson puts on his C-Type flying helmet in the Lancaster's port side Navigator's position.

[30] 61 Sqn Lancaster ED717 that ditched around 7:45 am off the Isles of Scilly. The crew were in their dinghy for sixty-three hours before all of them were picked up safely. See 'Thundering through the Clear Air' by Derek Brammer, Pages 95-98 for details.

[31] F/O Brodrick and and 2 other crew members spent the rest of the war as POWs, the remaining members were killed. See Appendix B.

[32] See 'A Shaky Do' by Peter Cunliffe for an in depth account of this Operation

[33] Ralph Calder was Jim's younger brother

[34] The armament factory of Alfred Krupp known as the 'Weapon Smithy of the Ruhr' produced over 2,000 heavy guns during the course of the war and was therefore a prominent target for attack by Bomber Command.

[35] This was a distance of around 6 miles so probably would have taken him a couple of hours

[36] Flight Engineer Sgt Ron Seeley of 207 Sqn adjusting the controls on the Lancaster starboard panel.

[37] It was extremely rare for the nose guns in a Lancaster to be used for defence, as attack from enemy fighters was usually from behind and below.

[38] He had left on 9th May 1943 to join 83 Squadron, Pathfinder Force.

[39] This was primarily a Lancaster only raid, with 282 aircraft detailed, according to the *Bomber Command War Diaries.*

[40] Geoffrey Francis Disbury was the son of Robert and Frances Gertrude Disbury of Whitby, Cheshire. He was born on 11th June 1922. He had studied history at Manchester University and then after volunteering for the RAF, was sent to Oklahoma, America, to carry out his initial pilot training.

[41] A photoflash picture captures another Lanc over Hamburg on 30/31 January 1943.

[42] The initial 'I' on the telegram was incorrect and should have been 'J' for Jack

[43] ED 720 'R' crashed into a field of wheat, adjacent to the Cambresis railway station at L'Epinette, north east of the village of Quiévy.

[44] Lancaster ED 781 from 57 Sqn, was shot down on night of 24/25 June 1943 returning from Wuppertal. The circumstances of the loss were very similar and as can be seen the aircraft crashed into a wheat field at Lantin, near Liége, Belgium. Only the bomb aimer, Sgt Lambdin, survived to become a POW.

[45] The Lancaster was the most difficult of the heavy bombers to get out of in an emergency because of the positioning of the escape exits, followed by

Lancaster Bale Out

the Stirling and then the Halifax.

[46] The Escape hatch above the cockpit on a Lancaster was only supposed to be used when ditching on water and therefore Rosner would have had to exit via the front hatch in the nose

[47] The cottage was at 41 rue Voltaire, Béthencourt.

[48] Jean was born on 18th December 1886 so was 57 years old

[49] One of these children would have been Genevieve, the Bauduin's only daughter who was seven at the time. Fred was not told about her though - probably because the Bauduins were afraid that she might give him away. Genevieve Pointeau died in 1999, and was still living in the same house that Fred had been sheltered in.

[50] In fact the Bauduins never forgot this "Anglais" whose memory was so dear to them.

[51] The house was at 12 rue Zola, Caudry.

[52] Gilbert subsequently married Jacqueline after the war but she was tragically killed in a road accident in 1976. Gilbert still lives in Cambrai today.

[53] Note the French-English dictionary on the table.

[54] Lucien Janssoone. Born 23 march 1898 at Ghyvelde (Nord) would have been 45 and was part of the Réseau Castille

[55] Edith Cavell was born in 1865 in Swardeston, Norwich, and in her twenties moved to Brussels and began a nursing career. After the start of the First World War, she began helping wounded British soldiers to avoid capture by the Germans, and certain death. She had aided over two hundred men, before she was caught and arrested by the Germans. Tried, and sentenced to death by a military court, she was executed by firing squad on 12 October 1915. Her death caused world-wide condemnation and turned her into a martyr.

[56] Sqn Ldr 'Hal' Bufton later became the first person to bomb a target using the Oboe electronic aid, on 20th/21st December 1942 flying a Mosquito with 109 Squadron.

[57] Sgt Crampton survived this incident only to be killed on the first 1,000 bomber raid to Cologne, on 30/31 May 1942.

[58] David Basil McMillan was born on 3rd April 1922 and came from Hamilton, Ontario, Canada.

[59] Lancaster ED480 at Waddington in February 1943. The pawnbroker's symbol was quite a popular emblem on many a 'U' Uncle.

[60] Mac actually wrote to Irvin, the company that made the parachute, after the war thanking them for their product that had saved his life.

[61] The plane crashed outside Troisvilles at a place called Borne Bleu

[62] L to R: Sgt Harry Brown (Nav), F/Sgt David McMillan (Rear gunner), unknown (Pilot), Sgt Sidney Hughes (W/Op), unknown (Bomb Aimer).

This photo was probably taken at OTU whilst training as a crew of five.

[63] Mrs Mouse was born in 1879, so would have been about sixty-four in 1943.

[64] Susan Lacombe was the code name for Simone de Cormont, an active member of the Resistance. She lived in a large apartment in Rue du Rocher, near Gare St. Lazare and helped at least eight Allied Airmen during the course of the War. She was part of the Comet Line until betrayed and arrested in February 1944. Interrogated by the Gestapo she was sent to Fresnes Prison, but was fortunate to be released two months later. She survived the rest of the War and died in the mid 1990's.

[65] See Appendix G for a translation of this notice.

[66] By a strange coincidence this was the address of Henri Paul, the driver of the car in which he and Diana, Princess of Wales were killed, in 1997.

[67] Flt Lt Geoffrey Francis Ball (89410) was flying with 182 Squadron, Fighter Command, when on 19 Aug 1943, during a fighter sweep over France, his Typhoon was damaged by flak and he force-landed at Blagny around 12:30pm.

[68] When France was invaded by the Germans during the war the new French government agreed to collaborate with the Nazis and give them control of the northern part of the country, what became known as the occupied zone, and they would control the southern, unoccupied 'Vichy' zone, under Marshal Petain.

[69] Fresnes prison was built in 1898 and was unusual at the time for its adoption of the telegraph-pole layout (in which the cell houses extended crosswise from a central corridor), designed by Francisque-Henri Poussin.

[70] A number of SOE agents were sent to Fresnes and horribly tortured by the Gestapo. Two of the most famous ones being; Violette Szabo, who was later sent to Ravensbrück concentration camp and executed in January 1945 and Odette Sansom (later Lady Churchill) who was also sent to Ravensbrück but survived until her death in 1995.

[71] See Appendix B for the circumstances leading up to becoming a POW.

[72] This was another 106 Squadron Lancaster lost on the Cologne op of 8/9 July 1943, piloted by Sgt McLean and crew. All were killed.

[73] *Window* was first used on 24 July 1943 over Hamburg and was extremely successful initially in confusing the enemy radar systems. As soon as the Germans discovered its existence however, they were forced to change night fighting tactics in favour of Wilde Sau - Wild Boar - fighters loitering over the target area.

[74] See Appendix B for the circumstances leading up to becoming a POW.

[75] In *'With a machine gun to Cambrai'*, George Coppard, HMSO, 1969, the author mentions trains with the exact same markings being used during the First World War.

76   Someone at the Red-Cross must have had a sense of humour to come up with a brand name that is a palindrome of the word 'milk'!
77   See Appendix B for the circumstances leading up to becoming a POW.
78   See Appendix B for the circumstances leading up to becoming a POW.
79   Lofty Snell is 3rd from the left and Pritchard is 3rd from the right holding the bugle.
80   See Appendix B for the circumstances leading up to becoming a POW.
81   The Marconi R1155 was the standard HF wireless receiver used in the heavy bombers.
82   See Appendix B for the circumstances leading up to becoming a POW.
83   See Appendix B for the circumstances of Snell and Davie becoming POWs.
84   Stalag 4B was luckily not too far from the American lines at liberation. A lot of the camps much deeper into Eastern Germany were not so fortunate though.
85   The repatriation of POWs, Operation 'Exodus', was well under way by VE Day and each Lanc carried twenty five passengers, dressed in whatever motley clothes they stood up in.
86   This was likely to have been Squadron Leader (now Group Captain) Bufton, one of the other airmen that the Janssoones had harboured.
87   It is difficult to believe that Mrs Mouse would have deliberately betrayed Janssoone, Thuru and Boyer as there had been numerous previous occasions when she could have done so.
88   James Reginald Calder's Great Niece
89   Note that the handwriting is different between the two parts
90   'Missing Believed Killed', Stuart Hadaway.
91   P/O Disbury was killed just 3 weeks after his 21st Birthday
92   Note that 'Hougham' has been incorrectly spelled as 'Houghman'.
93   Note that the date of death is incorrectly shown as the 8th July 1943, instead of the 9th.
94   The Battle of the Ruhr opened on the 5 March - Target, the Krupps works at Essen. By the time it was over four months later, 1,045 Aircraft had been lost, 1,347 aircrew were missing and 4,171 aircrew had lost their lives.
95   Rosner's logbook notes that he flew as 2nd Pilot on this Op with F/O Les Brodrick, but the official Operational Record doesn't list him and Fred Smooker believed that the Berlin Op the following day was his first one.
96   W4964 'J' was one of a handful of Lancasters that completed over 100 ops. Nicknamed 'Johnny Walker' and emblazoned with the logo and motto, 'Still going strong', on completion of the 100th op the crew were presented with a case of Whisky, courtesy of their famous, unofficial sponsors!
97   On this trip a 2nd Navigator, F/O Paddock, also flew to assist with the navigation

[98] On this trip a 2nd Pilot, Sgt W.R.P Perry, also flew to gain Operational experience

[99] On this trip a 2nd Navigator, Sgt Barker, also flew to assist with the navigation

[100] On this trip a 2nd Navigator, P/O Lintot, also flew to assist with the navigation

[101] On this trip a 2nd Pilot, Sgt G. F. Disbury, also flew to gain Operational experience

[102] Oblt. Heinz Wolfgang Schnaüfer, known as the 'Ghost of St. Trond' was the most successful of the Luftwaffe night fighter pilots, being credited with 121 kills to his name.